ONE PITCH AWAY

THE PLAYERS' STORIES OF
THE 1986 LEAGUE CHAMPIONSHIPS
AND WORLD SERIES

MIKE SOWELL

A Macmillan Sports Book

Macmillan   ◆   USA

To my mother, Lee Sowell

MACMILLAN
A Prentice Hall Macmillan Company
15 Columbus Circle
New York, NY 10023

Library of Congress Cataloging-in-Publication Data available
ISBN 0-02-612416-5

Macmillan books are available at special discounts for bulk purchases for sales promotions, premiums, fund-raising, or educational use.

10 9 8 7 6 5 4 3 2 1

Printed in the United States of America

CONTENTS

ACKNOWLEDGMENTS

I owe a special debt of gratitude to Rick Wolff, who conceived the idea of this book and encouraged me to carry through with it. I also want to thank Traci Cothran, my editor at Macmillan, who did an outstanding job after being called on in relief in the middle of the game.

Special thanks also go to Ted Bakamjian, loyal Red Sox fan, for the use of his video library of the 1986 postseason games; Doug Roberts for his many trips to the National Baseball Hall of Fame Library; Rob Neyer, who assisted with much of the research; John Hinds, my old army buddy from Berlin, who provided timely help in tracking down players; Ted Rodgers for the many clippings he provided; Harry Shattuck, former colleague and mentor at the *Houston Chronicle*, who was generous with his time and knowledge; Johnny McGraw for seeing the project through to its completion; and good friends Robin and Steve Schoenfeld for their hospitality on my travels through Arizona.

Also Dave Sittler, Barry Lewis, Art Richman, Zack Cooper, Dave Cataneo, Marty York, Barry Bloom, Bill Reynolds, Kathy Cooper, Andy Furman and fellow Sports AnswerMan Wayne McCombs for their assistance.

Numerous players and baseball people also were generous with their time, and I especially want to thank Alan Ashby, Wade Boggs, Bob Boone, Bill Buckner, Gary Carter, Stewart Cliburn, Doug Corbett, Glenn Davis, Doug DeCinces, Rich Gedman, Billy Hatcher, Dave Henderson, Bob Knepper, Ray Knight, Tonya Moore, Vern Ruhle, Calvin Schiraldi, Mike Scott, Bob Stanley, Dave Stapleton, Mookie Wilson and Mike Witt.

And always, to Ellen, my partner on the journey.

PART I

THE GAMES

1

WAIT 'TIL THIS YEAR

I understand. I've been there . . . lots of times . . . lots of games . . . lots of places . . .

—GENE MAUCH

The game took place in 1982, but it could have been 1962, or 1972, or any of the twenty-six seasons Gene Mauch managed a major-league baseball team.

It was the ninth inning, and things were not going well for his California Angels. There were runners on base, and his pitcher was struggling to put down this late rally by the opposition.

Reggie Jackson was stationed next to Mauch in the dugout. Jackson had seen this before, and he was worried. The powerful California hitters would build up a big lead, only to see their efforts wasted by the team's erratic relief pitching.

"Again?" Jackson whispered to Mauch.

Mauch said nothing but raised his hand in a reassuring gesture, as if to say, "Don't worry, everything will be all right."

Sure enough, the California pitcher settled down to retire the side, and the Angels escaped with another hard-earned victory.

Afterward, Jackson called out to his manager.

"Hey, Gene, how'd you know we'd get out of that?"

Mauch smiled knowingly.

"Listen," he said, "when you want something bad enough and you try hard enough, you've got a pretty good chance of getting it."

At least, that was the way it was supposed to work.

◇ Four years later, on a Friday afternoon late in the 1986 season, Gene Mauch sat in the dugout filling out a lineup card. He still hadn't gotten what he wanted, but he still was trying.

And on this day, September 26, 1986, he had a chance to get a step closer to his lifelong goal.

Mauch was sixty years old, and his well-tanned face and silver hair gave him a regal appearance. He still had the military bearing that had earned him the nickname "the Little General," and like an army commander, he spent many hours each day in preparation for the upcoming confrontation.

Even a routine task such as choosing a lineup was handled with the same care and planning as devising a battle plan. Who would bat leadoff that night against the Texas Rangers? Already that season, Mauch had used nine different players in this spot. Which of his three second basemen should he play? Who would play right field? Who would be the designated hitter? All managers faced these decisions, but no one analyzed them more closely than did Mauch.

He kept on his office desk fifty different lineup combinations for his team. Each day, he would write out several of these lineups for possible use that game.

Is there any pattern to these lineups, he once was asked.

"I sure hope so," answered Mauch. "When you spend five hours on them, I hope there's some consistency."

He played out the upcoming game in his mind, using his various lineups. He saw various scenarios unfold, anticipated his opponent's moves and planned his countermoves accordingly. This was Mauch's style—always plotting, always thinking ahead, always scheming.

The record book later would show that he managed 3,942 games in his career. In reality, Mauch managed three times that many games.

"I play four hundred eighty-six games a year," he explained. "I play one game before with myself. Then there is the actual game. And unfortunately, there is a third game I have to play again for the people that want to write about it."

That was Mauch. The adjectives that had been used to describe his managerial prowess included *brilliant, shrewd, intense, passionate* and *cunning*. He was a baseball genius, said many who had studied him. No one was better at taking an outmanned team and turning it into a winning ball club. No one was more skilled at plotting and planning ahead to put his players in the situations he wanted at the crucial stage of a game.

"He's the thinking man's manager," Pete Rose said of Mauch.

"The Little General," they called him, and Mauch looked and acted the part.

And yet, for all his brilliance, and all the accolades, there still was one thing that separated him from the really great managers the game had known. Maybe Mauch was a genius, but still . . .

He wrote the names on the final lineup card, the one he would use that night. Gary Pettis. Wally Joyner. Brian Downing. Doug DeCinces. George Hendrick. Dick Schofield. John Candelaria.

It was a mixture of aging veterans and talented but inexperienced youngsters. Back in the spring, there had been much skepticism about the team's abilities. The hitters seemed too old, and the pitchers too fragile. There was an unproven rookie, Wally Joyner, at first base. Two of the team's best hitters from the previous season, Rod Carew and Juan Beniquez, had been cut loose over the winter, and that had caused some unhappiness in the clubhouse. Nine of the Angels were in the final year of their contracts, and that created a distraction among the players as they approached free-agent status.

Few people gave the Angels a chance. But Mauch knew better. During spring training, he wrote the number "90" on a piece of paper and held it up for his players to see.

"Give me ninety victories," he said. "Ninety will get the job done."

The season started, and the pitching staff was depleted by injuries. Donnie Moore, the star reliever, battled a sore shoulder and bad back all year. But other pitchers stepped forward to bridge the gap, and Mike Witt, the ace of the staff, turned in a brilliant season. The offense got an early boost from Joyner, who was sensational the first half of the season. When he cooled off in the second half, Doug DeCinces, the veteran at third base, picked up the slack in August and September.

To the surprise of many, the Angels took over first place on their eighty-first game—the halfway point of the season—and held their position the rest of the way.

And now, with just over a week remaining in the season, they had eighty-nine victories and a ten-game lead in the American League West Division. All they had to do to clinch the division title was beat Texas that night. As Mauch had predicted, ninety victories would get the job done.

The game started slowly for the Angels. They trailed 2–0 as they came to the plate in the sixth. Wally Joyner went to pick out a bat when he heard the voice of his manager.

"When are we going to get them?" asked Mauch.

Joyner looked up at the scoreboard clock. It was 8:58.

"Nine o'clock," he answered.

Five minutes later, Gary Pettis, a slender left-handed hitter known for his speed and not his power, lined the ball over the left-field fence for a home run. Joyner followed with a hard grounder to second base. Toby Harrah bobbled the ball for an error. The next batter, Brian Downing, hit a drive into the left-field seats for another homer.

Suddenly, the Angels led 3–2, and the crowd of 46,000 was on its feet cheering. It was a few minutes past schedule, but the Angels were getting them.

Later in the inning, George Hendrick, thirty-six years old and one of the many old-timers on the team, connected for yet another home run. The Angels scored four more in the seventh. The excitement and anticipation in the stadium began to build.

Just past ten o'clock, Donnie Moore, ignoring the pain in his right shoulder, threw a third strike past Geno Petralli for the last out of the game. The Angels won 8–3 for their ninetieth victory of the season and the division title.

Afterward, Gene Autry, two days shy of his seventy-ninth birthday, entered the clubhouse smiling. He found his manager and put his arm around him in congratulation.

"He said if we could win ninety games, we would win the West," Autry boasted to a group of bystanders. "And he had it right on the nose!"

Autry, the "Singing Cowboy" in the old Hollywood westerns, had owned the Angels since their inception in 1961, and he was still looking for his first league championship. He had spent millions of his fortune trying to bring a World Series to Anaheim, only to keep coming up short. The Angels had won two other division titles, in 1979 and 1982, but both times had been beaten in the league playoffs. Maybe the third time would be the charm. Maybe this year, the dream would come true.

Everywhere around them, players were celebrating, alternately taking swigs of champagne or beer and spraying the contents of their bottles on their teammates.

But Mauch was restrained in his reaction. He still hadn't achieved the main prize, the one that had eluded him for a quarter of a century as a baseball manager. Only three men in baseball history had managed more seasons than he had. They were Connie Mack, John McGraw and Bucky Harris. That was pretty heady company. But those men all had won league pennants. They had taken teams to the World Series. Gene Mauch hadn't. That was the knock. That was what made Mauch such an enigma. He was baseball's greatest manager never to win a pennant. That was the tag that followed him around.

Mauch took only a single drink of champagne to toast the triumph of a division title.

"I hope to drink a whole bunch more," he said, looking ahead to the playoffs and, beyond that, the World Series.

◇ It was still dark when Gene Mauch awoke on Tuesday, October 7. He looked at his watch. Two-thirty in the morning. Another sleepless night in another dark hotel room.

Mauch was used to it. He figured he had averaged only four, maybe four-and-a-half, hours of sleep a night during his years as a manager. He barely would get one day's game played and out of his mind before he was thinking about the following one. He would lie there, still in bed, but already playing out that next game.

The one coming up was the most important of the season. The playoffs were opening in Boston that night. It was the crucial first game of the best-of-seven American League Championship Series. Four more victories, and the Angels would be in the World Series.

Mauch woke up thinking about Bill Buckner, the Boston first baseman. He remembered two hits Buckner got on low curveballs he scraped off the ground.

Mauch had an amazing memory. He could recall which hitters did what against which pitchers and in which ballparks at which stage of a ball game. He planned ahead to avoid or set up those situations, as it fit his team's needs.

He also thought about Rich Gedman, the Boston catcher. Mauch recalled a hit Gedman got after taking six or seven curves in a row. He remembered another time Gedman hit a home run in Anaheim. You had to be careful with Gedman. He could break your heart if you weren't careful.

Rich Gedman. He would be on Mauch's mind a lot in the coming days.

That evening was chilly and overcast in Boston, with a hint of rain and temperatures dropping into the upper forties. The opening game would be a battle of the two teams' ace pitchers, Mike Witt for California and Roger Clemens for Boston.

Earlier that day, Witt had spread the daily newspapers out in front of him and seen his picture next to that of Clemens. It gave him a good feeling. Witt was traveling in fast company.

Everyone knew about Roger "the Rocket" Clemens. He had won twenty-four games against only four losses and led the league with a 2.48 ERA that season. He also broke a long-standing major-league record by fanning twenty Seattle batters in a single game. Witt, who two years earlier had pitched only the thirteenth perfect game in major-league history, was not so well known. His 18–10 record and 2.84 earned-run average had mostly been overlooked. That didn't bother Witt. Tonight, people would find out about him.

He said little when he arrived at Fenway Park to begin his preparations for the game. That wasn't unusual. Witt was a quiet, introspective man who kept his thoughts and his feelings to himself.

"'Hello' is a speech for him," his manager, Gene Mauch, once said.

The Angels failed to score in the first against Clemens, and Witt set down the Red Sox without a hit.

Instead of returning to the dugout, Witt withdrew to the clubhouse while the Angels batted. It wasn't the evening chill that bothered him. He thrived on cool weather, thanks to a metabolism that was such that he could work up a sweat whether the temperature outside was fifty degrees or seventy degrees. It was solitude he sought.

There was a television monitor showing the game, and Witt sat to watch the telecast. On the screen, Clemens was struggling. With two outs in the second, he walked two batters and then allowed three hits in a row. Four runs crossed the plate for the Angels.

But Witt was barely aware of the hits by his teammates. His attention was focused on the catcher's mitt on the screen. Concentrate on the mitt, he reminded himself. By zoning in in this way, when he resumed his pitching duties he saw only the glove catcher Bob Boone presented as a target.

Witt followed the same routine throughout the evening, pitching half an inning, watching the TV monitor half an inning.

His concentration, like his pitching, was incredible. The day before, his wife, Lisa, had given birth to the couple's first son, Justin Michael.

Witt was a proud father, but once he stepped between the lines, he put everything out of his mind but the Red Sox.

Witt was an awesome sight on the mound. At six feet, seven inches, he looked more like a basketball player than a baseball pitcher. But he could throw the ball ninety-three miles an hour, and he had a wicked curveball that Reggie Jackson called the "Mercedes bends."

"It's the top of the line," said Reggie.

The Red Sox didn't get their first hit until there were two outs in the sixth. Spike Owen walked, and Wade Boggs and Marty Barrett followed with singles to score Boston's first run. But Witt retired Bill Buckner on a fly ball to end the threat.

He set down the Red Sox again in the seventh and pitched out of trouble in the eighth without giving up a run. He never lost his focus. He methodically dispatched of the Red Sox again in the ninth inning to complete the 5–1 victory.

It was an overpowering performance, Witt's best since his perfect game. He gave up only five hits, two walks and one run, never losing his concentration or his strength.

Witt had pitched fourteen complete games in the regular season. Now, he had another to start the playoffs. This was a man who got the job done.

◊ One down, three to go. The Angels arrived at Fenway Park on Wednesday with the confident air of a winner.

Game time had been moved to 3:07 in the afternoon to accommodate television, and that meant that when the first pitch was thrown, the sun would hang over home plate directly in the eyes of the fielders.

The game began, and a stiff breeze whipped around the ballpark. The afternoon sun cast a shadow across the infield, while the fans in the outfield bleachers were in bright sunlight. It was going to be a perilous day on the field.

In the bottom of the first, Boston's Wade Boggs hit a windblown triple off the wall in left field, leading to a run. In the second, a ground ball took a crazy hop over the head of California shortstop Dick Schofield, who was noted for his glove work. With two men on base, Kirk McCaskill, the Angels pitcher, tried to field a high-bouncing ground ball but lost it in the glare of the sun, leading to another run.

The score was tied 2–2 in the fifth when a windblown pop-up eluded California second baseman Bobby Grich, allowing the go-ahead run to score for Boston.

In the sixth, a California rally was killed when third-base coach Moose Stubing failed to give Bobby Grich the proper signal and Grich was thrown out rounding the bag.

The Red Sox, aided by the numerous Angels misplays and dropped balls, won handily, 9–2.

Afterward, Gene Mauch went to the interview room to give his assessment of the ball game.

What about the sun, someone asked.

"Bad. Terrible on ground balls."

Someone else wanted to know about Stubing's base-coaching blunder. It was the wrong question.

Mauch stood up to leave.

"Bye," he said. "See you later."

Mauch's temper was legendary. He had thrown food in clubhouses, broken windows and punched his fist through a locker. But he had mellowed in recent years. After one game, he chewed out a writer over a question he didn't like. When he calmed down, Mauch offered the man part of his sandwich.

But how could you intelligently discuss a game like this one? Ground balls that jumped over the shortstop's head. Windblown pop flies that no one could see! A pitcher losing a ground ball in the sun.

Mauch returned to the clubhouse to change out of his uniform.

John McNamara, the Boston manager, must have been enjoying himself across the way. The Angels had handed him the game on a platter.

Mauch knew McNamara well. Their careers had been closely tied these past few years. In 1982, Mauch resigned as manager of the Angels after the team blew a two-game lead to lose a playoff series to Milwaukee. He stayed out of baseball two years, a painful pe-riod during which his wife, Nina Lee, died of cancer. In the interim, McNamara took over as manager of the Angels, with disappointing results. The team posted a losing record one year and broke even the next.

In a strange twist, McNamara left California to take the Boston job in 1985, and Mauch came out of retirement to replace him. The Angels made a turnaround, winning nineteen more games than they had the year before and finishing just one game back of Kansas City. Then came the division title.

If anyone doubted Mauch's skills as a manager, he needed only to look at that five-year period. The three years Mauch managed the Angels, they won ninety-three, ninety and ninety-two games, respectively, and finished first twice and second once. The two years he was away from the ball club, it won seventy and eighty-one games.

Mauch dressed and went outside, where the bags and equipment were being loaded for the return trip to California. Before boarding the bus, he turned to joke with a reporter he knew.

"If you see McNamara," said Mauch, "tell him that if there's anything else I can do for him, let me know."

◇ It felt good to be home. Donnie Moore walked to the bullpen at Anaheim Stadium and slowly began to throw a baseball, easily at first and then harder as his arm loosened up.

He looked around the stands at the Big A, as the ballpark was known. It was a typically beautiful California day. Moore threw another pitch, this one harder than the last.

The two teams, tied at one game apiece, had taken a day off for travel in preparation for Friday's Game 3 of the American League playoffs. Moore was glad for the extra day of rest. That was one more day for his arm to get better—twenty-four more hours of recuperation for his many ailments.

He felt the soreness in his right shoulder, but he blocked it out of his mind as he continued throwing. Pain was a constant in Donnie Moore's life. He had learned to endure it.

It had started in the spring of 1986. At first, it was no more than a soreness in his rib cage. Moore ignored it and kept pitching. He didn't have to. For the first time in his baseball career, he had job security that spring.

He had spent twelve years bouncing around among ten major- and minor-league teams before coming to California in 1985, where he was an immediate sensation. He saved thirty-one games for the Angels that season and was named the team's Most Valuable Player. His reward was a three-year, $3 million contract, which he signed in January 1986. At the age of thirty-two, Moore had hit it big in baseball.

But despite the big contract, or perhaps because of it, Donnie Moore felt obligated to keep pitching. He spent one month on the disabled list with the rib-cage injury but continued to experience discomfort when he returned to action. This led to problems with his elbow and then his shoulder.

It was thought Moore had strained a muscle in his rib cage, but in fact he was suffering from an undetected bone spur near his spinal column. In an effort to combat the pain, he took a series of nerve-block shots in his rib cage, cortisone shots in his sore right shoulder, anesthetic and more cortisone. In desperation, he even experimented with acupuncture. Nothing got rid of the pain.

Late in the season, Moore began to experience frequent migraine headaches. A CAT scan was performed on his skull and medication was prescribed, and afterward the headaches did not come as often, but they never completely went away.

All the while, Donnie Moore continued to pitch, despite his ailing shoulder, his intense headaches and his sore ribs. He was a competitor. He was taught to play with pain, and that is what he did.

Rest was what Moore needed, but there was precious little time for that during the season. The team had not needed him to pitch in the first two playoff games in Boston, however, and now Moore's arm felt better.

He threw a final pitch and signaled an end to the warm-up session. Donnie Moore was ready to pitch that night, if needed.

Gene Mauch smoked a cigarette and paced up and down the runway leading from the home-team dugout to the clubhouse. Occasionally, he stopped to peek out at the action on the field.

It was the seventh inning, and the game was tied 1–1. Mauch, however, had been ejected by the umpires after going onto the field to argue a call three innings earlier. Banished from the dugout, he could only watch on the sly while his two lieutenants, Marcel Lachemann and Moose Stubing, directed the ball club. Lachemann handled the defense, and Stubing the offense.

Mauch puffed on his cigarette without really noticing
He was such a habitual smoker that he once put a cigar
and lit it with his right hand, realized he already was hold
left hand and then looked down to see another burning in the ashtray.

Smoking and managing. For Mauch, the two activities seemed to go
together. His first big-league managing job in Philadelphia, the writers
would come at him after games with questions from all different
angles. He quickly learned that in the ten seconds it took him to light
a cigarette, he could compose an answer, or decide if he even wanted
to give an answer.

Out on the field, Ruppert Jones hit a routine ground ball and was
thrown out at first. Boston pitcher Dennis "Oil Can" Boyd fidgeted and
tugged at his uniform. Mauch went back to work on his cigarette.

He quit smoking once, in 1961, just before his second season as a
manager of the Phillies. Then he got on one of the old DC-6s to fly to
spring training in Florida, and the stewardess passed out a miniature
pack of Pall Malls. Mauch smoked his four cigarettes before the plane
even reached cruising altitude. He would smoke a lot more before the
season was over. The Phillies lost a record twenty-three games in a row
that year.

Bobby Grich swung and missed for a third strike, and the high-
strung Boyd strutted around the mound in that excitable manner of
his. Mauch paced down the runway some more.

A moment later, there was a loud cheer outside, and the stadium
above Mauch shook with excitement. The Oil Can had hung a slider to
Dick Schofield, and the light-hitting shortstop had sent the ball flying
into the outfield seats. Just like that, the Angels led 2–1.

Bob Boone followed with a single. That brought up Gary Pettis, who
had hit only eight home runs in three seasons. But one of them had
come off Boyd, and that was why Mauch had elevated him to the leadoff position this game. His lineup change paid off.

Boyd tried to throw a screwball past him, and Pettis drove the ball
into the seats in right-center field. Another home run. Two more runs
scored. The Angels led 4–1.

Mauch checked his supply of cigarettes. He put aside two of them to save for after the game. He would smoke the rest in the runway, while he was pacing.

Donnie Moore heard the crowd noise and turned to see the drive by Pettis sail into the stands. He paused for a moment, then resumed throwing.

The call had come to the bullpen earlier in the inning for him to warm up. John Candelaria, the tall left-hander, had pitched seven strong innings, then retired to the clubhouse to ice down his elbow. It would be up to Moore to hold the lead.

He grabbed his warm-up jacket and began the long walk to the pitching mound for the eighth inning. He hadn't pitched since the previous Sunday. The extended rest had been a calculated gamble. It helped Moore regain some of his arm strength, but it also robbed him of his sharpness. That was the trade-off.

Boston's first batter in the eighth inning was Marty Barrett. He hit one of Moore's pitches into the outfield for a single. Bill Buckner drove a ball into center field, where Pettis caught it for an out.

Gene Mauch continued smoking. He once said he smoked seventy cigarettes a day. Seventy a day—that was a lot. If you allow for six hours of sleep, that averaged out to about four cigarettes an hour for eighteen waking hours. That was one every fifteen minutes. Then again, who was counting?

Jim Rice drilled a double into right field. There were runners on second and third, and only one out. Moore appeared rattled. He committed a balk, scoring Barrett and advancing Rice to third. It was 4–2.

Mauch continued to pace. He wore out two pairs of shoes while pacing that night, he would joke later.

Don Baylor, another power hitter, was up. He lifted a high pop foul down the third-base line. Schofield raced over from his shortstop position to make the catch. Two down.

Moore still couldn't find his rhythm. He walked Dwight "Dewey" Evans.

More smoke drifted out of the tunnel. There was a coughing sound. Mauch once said he smoked two brands of cigarettes a day. "Changing brands makes you cough in a different key," he had explained.

Rich Gedman followed with a base hit to left. Now it was 4–3, and there were runners on first and third.

Mauch stuck with his pitcher. He had managed some great relievers in his time—among them Mike Marshall, the bionic man who pitched 106 games one season, winning 15 and saving 21 others—but Mauch said Donnie Moore was the best he had ever had. Of course, that was last year, when Moore had been healthy.

Tony Armas, the center fielder, stepped in. He hit the ball hard into center field. The crowd groaned. But there was Pettis racing over to make the catch, ending the inning at last.

The Angels added a run in their half of the eighth, and Moore went back out to pitch the ninth. He got the first two batters out. He seemed to be settling down. Then Marty Barrett knocked out a base hit. The fans held their breath. Gene Mauch paced some more. Bill Buckner stepped to the plate. He hit a fly ball into left field. Brian Downing drifted over and made the catch. Finally, the game was over. The Angels won 5–3. They had a two-game-to-one lead in the series.

Moore got the save, his first in postseason play. But his performance did nothing to instill any confidence in his effectiveness. He had faced eleven batters, and all of them either got a base hit or hit the ball into the outfield.

No wonder managers smoked.

◇ Two down, two to go for the Angels. The fans at the Big A greeted their Angels with a loud round of applause during the pregame introductions on Saturday.

Gene Mauch grabbed a catcher's mitt and went out to catch the ceremonial first pitch. The crowd cheered. His mother, Mamie Mauch, would do the honors.

Mrs. Mauch had been quite an athlete in her own right. When she was thirty-five and Gene was twelve, they would run footraces, and most ended in dead heats. Mamie Mauch was quite a woman. Her husband, George Mauch, had lost his bakery business in the Great Depression and been forced to go to work as a roughneck in the oil fields of Kansas. While George moved around from one dusty Kansas town to another, Mamie raised her two kids, Gene and his sister, Jolene. When George moved to California to find work, the rest of the family stayed back in Kansas. It wasn't until George found steady employment a few months later that Mamie and the children joined him out West.

Her throw came straight and true, and Gene let it hit him in the chest before coming to rest in his mitt. He went over and gave his mother a hug and a kiss as the crowd roared its approval.

"My mother is a lot like her son," he said. "She's unpredictable."

The Angels entered the game shorthanded. Wally Joyner, their rookie sensation at first base, had been hospitalized with an inflamed right leg, resulting from a leg abrasion that got infected from the foul balls he kept hitting off his shin and from the sweat in the socks he wore. It was hoped he would return to the lineup the next day. Roger Clemens recovered from his shaky performance four days earlier and shut out California for eight innings, taking a 3–0 lead into the bottom of the ninth. Then, Doug DeCinces hit a lead-off homer, and one out later, Dick Schofield and Bob Boone singled on two-strike pitches.

Suddenly, Clemens was gone and the young Boston reliever Calvin Schiraldi was in the game with two men on base. The first batter he faced, Gary Pettis, hit a ball into left field and Jim Rice lost it in the lights for a double, scoring another run to make it 3–2. An intentional walk loaded the bases, setting up a potential double play.

Schiraldi almost got out of the jam. He struck out Bobby Grich for the second out and got ahead of Brian Downing one ball and two strikes by throwing fastballs.

Everyone in the ballpark figured another fastball was coming. But Schiraldi tried to outguess Downing with a breaking ball. The pitch sailed inside and hit Downing on the thigh. A hit batsman. Downing got a free trip to first, and the tying run came home, sending the game into extra innings.

Schiraldi was still on the mound in the bottom of the eleventh, when a single, sacrifice bunt and intentional walk put two men on base.

Bobby Grich was the next batter. He was having a rough night. Two costly misplays in the field. Three strikeouts. Hitless in his past ten at-bats. Mauch called him back before he went to the plate, and Grich wondered if he was being pulled for a pinch hitter.

Instead, Mauch told him: "Don't go up there looking for a base on balls. Hit this guy!"

That was typical Mauch. When he brought in a pitcher, he never asked, "How are you feeling?" Mauch didn't want his players thinking about how tired or sore they might be. Instead, he would say to them, "Get this guy." The same with a batter. "Hit this guy," Mauch would tell him. Only positive thoughts. Mauch believed in his players and he wanted players who believed in themselves.

Schiraldi's first pitch to Grich was a fastball. Two innings earlier, Grich had struck out on just such a pitch. This time, he lined the ball into the left-field corner, driving home the winning run.

While the Angels exchanged high fives at home plate, Schiraldi walked to the Boston dugout, sat down and cried as his teammates tried to shield him from the television cameras.

The Angels won 4–3. It was an unbelievable comeback.

Three down, one to go. Ice down the champagne. It was almost time to celebrate.

◇ Gene Mauch had heard the question before. His team had a three-game-to-one lead, the World Series at its fingertips, had just pulled off a stunning comeback to pull out a victory, and yet . . .

"Can something still go wrong?" he was asked.

The meaning hung in the air, unspoken. Like Philadelphia in 1964? Like Milwaukee in 1982? Back then, his teams had been so close to winning, had overcome so much, and then at the last moment . . .

"You don't have that attitude that anything bad is going to happen until it happens," answered Mauch.

But what was he thinking at this moment? After all those years of guiding outmanned teams, those two stunning reversals when victory seemed at hand, and now to be on the threshold again . . .

Another questioner raised the subject, mentioning the possibility of Mauch winning his first pennant.

"I'm not going to say a word on that," he snapped.

That night, Mauch made the one-hour, fifteen-minute drive along the darkened freeways to his home in Rancho Mirage, near Palm Springs. He passed the nearby golf course where in the off-season he played as many as fifty-four holes a day in his personalized golf cart.

Inside his condominium, Mauch had a videocassette recorder set up to tape the California ball games. He routinely recorded the games and viewed them again when he returned from the ballpark, sitting up into the early hours of morning studying the action and fast-forwarding through the advertisements.

"As near as I could figure it," he said after reviewing one playoff game in this manner, "I missed twelve million dollars' worth of commercials."

But Mauch did not need videotapes and modern electronic gadgets to replay the ball games. He had volumes of notebooks containing box scores and detailed notes of every game he had managed, dating all the way back to 1961, his second year as a big-league manager.

"Oh, I look back at those notebooks all the time, especially in the winter," he told an interviewer. "You wake up at four A.M. and can't sleep. It's fun remembering and reliving."

Remembering and reliving. All the games. All those years. Even the two seasons that people would not let him forget . . .

◇ . . . Nineteen sixty-four. Every baseball fan knows what it means. The year of the great collapse by the Philadelphia Phillies. They had a

Gene Mauch guided the Angels to within one out of their first league pennant before disaster struck: "We won it once. We just couldn't win it twice." *Photo courtesy California Angels.*

six-and-one-half-game lead with twelve games to play, and they blew the pennant. No other first-place team in baseball history ever fell apart so quickly so close to the finish line.

Gene Mauch was the manager of that team. He was the boy wonder of baseball managers. Thirty-eight years old, and he had the hottest ball club around. Five years on the job, and he had turned a bunch of losers into winners.

To appreciate the magnitude of what Mauch had achieved in Philadelphia, one had to go back to April 1960, when kindly old Eddie Sawyer abruptly quit as manager of the Phillies one game into the season.

"I'm forty-nine, and I'd like to see fifty," said the exasperated Sawyer, who had grown weary of his players' drinking and carousing.

That night, the phone rang in Mauch's hotel room in Pompano Beach, Florida, where his minor-league Minneapolis team was training. It was Philadelphia general manager John Quinn, who had first gotten to know Mauch ten years earlier when Quinn worked for the Boston Braves and Mauch was a sharp young infielder on the team.

"A friend of mine wants to know if you're interested in managing a major-league club," said Quinn.

"Who is it?" Mauch asked skeptically. "The Phillies?"

The Phillies—everyone in baseball knew about them. In the words of Philadelphia columnist Sandy Grady, "The team's feature was the 'Dalton Gang,' boozy nightriders who set records for demolishing saloons."

The Phillies also were adept at losing games. Two last-place finishes in a row. Eight years since their last winning season.

Ten years earlier, when they won their last pennant, the youthful Phillies had been known as the "Whiz Kids." These aging and inept Phillies were the "Whiff Kids."

Mauch jumped at the offer.

It didn't take him long to start cleaning up the ball club. He weeded out the troublemakers. He laid down his set of rules and enforced them with tough words and tough actions.

"Managing that team wasn't the hardest part," Mauch later told Grady. "First, you had to go into bars or bust down hotel doors to find them. It's a good thing I was a young man. An old one would never have survived."

But Mauch survived. And he taught his Phillies to play winning ball. Success did not come overnight, and in 1961 Philadelphia set a major-league record by losing twenty-three games in a row. But even in those losing years, the Phillies were coming together as a ball club.

Slowly, Mauch began to piece together the kind of team he wanted. It was a team of scrappers and hustlers and hard-nosed ballplayers. They moved up to seventh in 1962, fourth in 1963.

They would go on the field to warm up before a game, and with every throw by a Philadelphia outfielder, the bench players would shout at the opposition: "You ain't go no arms like those!" The Philadelphia hitters would take batting practice, and those waiting their turn at the plate would yell toward the enemy dugout: "You ain't got guys who can hit like they can!"

And Mauch, the team's ringleader, never missed a trick. In right field was a corrugated iron fence which balls bounced off at crazy angles. So, Mauch moved his bullpen from left field to right and had his spare pitchers use towels to signal the Philadelphia base coaches how balls were going to strike the fence. This enabled the Philadelphia base runners to know when to take an extra base and when to stay put.

Mauch shaved down the pitcher's mound to help his pitchers. He schemed and plotted from the dugout, once sending up seven pinch hitters in a row, another time putting three pitchers in his starting line-up. He changed pitchers while the same batter was at the plate to get the results he wanted.

No one knew the rules better than Mauch did. When an opposing catcher reached into the Philadelphia dugout to catch a pop foul, Mauch karate-chopped his arm to knock the ball loose. An argument ensued, but Mauch prevailed. The rule book stated that a player enters the other dugout at his own risk.

Mauch also used his fierce temper to motivate his players. In a celebrated incident in Houston late in the 1963 season, he reacted to a ninth-inning loss by knocking over the postgame buffet and throwing a pan of spare ribs across the locker room. What people overlooked was that after that outburst, the Phillies won five of their final six games to squeeze into fourth place, earning each player on the squad an additional seven hundred dollars.

Later, in an interview with Myron Cope of the *Saturday Evening Post,* Mauch pointed to the name "Phillies" on the front of his jersey.

"I've appeared as an ogre many a time for the purpose of getting this thing imprinted on our players' minds," he said.

Then came 1964. The Phillies won ten of their first twelve games to move into first place and then held their position throughout the summer. They were a model of consistency, never losing more than four games in a row.

"The most unselfish bunch of ballplayers I've ever seen," Mauch called them.

Late in the season, the Phillies departed on a ten-day, ten-game road trip that would have them log more than eight thousand miles of travel. On the second leg of the trip, in Houston, Mauch went for a sweep of the three-game series by starting his ace, Jim Bunning, who had gone ten innings just two days earlier. Bunning was knocked out of the box in the fifth inning, and the Phillies lost.

No matter. They still had a six-game lead. The Phillies went to Los Angeles, and their other top pitcher, Chris Short, also pitching out of turn, was rocked for six runs in the first inning. When Mauch pulled him from the game, Short angrily threw the ball to the relief pitcher. Were the players beginning to feel the pressure?

Two nights later, in the sixteenth inning of a tie game, Willie Davis of the Dodgers was on third base with two outs and two strikes on a left-handed batter. He tried to steal home. Los Angeles manager Walter Alston jumped off the bench in surprise. You don't try to steal home with a left-handed batter at the plate! But Davis did, and he slid in safely, handing the Phillies another loss.

Not to worry. The Phillies returned home leading by six-and-one-half games, with only twelve more to go. Again, they went into the sixteenth inning, this time against the Reds. Cincinnati's Chico Ruiz got to third base with two outs. Frank Robinson, the Reds's best hitter, was up. Incredibly, Ruiz broke for the plate.

"No! No!" Reds manager Dick Sisler yelled from the dugout. You don't try to steal home with your best hitter up!

But Ruiz, like Davis, was safe. The Phils lost once more.

They lost again the next day. And again. And again. They blew a 4–3 lead in the ninth to lose to the Braves.

"Don't worry," the players said, pointing toward Mauch. "Number 4 will think of something."

But there was nothing Gene Mauch, jersey number 4, could do for them.

The losing streak reached seven games, and the Phillies fell out of first place.

They traveled to St. Louis and lost 5–1. Eight in a row. The next day, their best player, outfielder Johnny Callison, was so weakened by the flu he collapsed in the clubhouse. Still, he dragged himself to the plate to pinch-hit and delivered a single. It didn't matter. The Phillies lost 4–2. Nine in a row.

That night, Mauch walked into the bar at the Chase Hotel.

"Want a drink?" someone asked.

"I'd like a million," answered Mauch.

The Phillies lost again the next day. Ten in a row.

They traveled to Cincinnati for the final two games of the season.

"We've blown the whole thing," pitcher Dennis Bennett said dejectedly. "We had it, and it's gone."

Finally, the Phillies won a game, beating the Reds 4–3. They also took the next day's game, by a score of 10–0, but it was too late. The Cardinals won the pennant.

The team flew home to Philadelphia, and Mauch sat in the front seat of the plane, his fists clenched as he anticipated the criticism that was to come—all the second-guessing and censure that would follow him throughout the remainder of his career.

"To hell with 'em!" raged Mauch. "I'm not going to defend myself to anybody. Inside, I know I did everything I could to win it."

A few days later, he was at the opening game of the World Series with his friend and general manager, John Quinn. The starting lineups were introduced, and the St. Louis ballplayers trotted out of the dugout, one by one, to line up along the foul line.

Mauch could watch only so much before getting up to leave. Quinn went after him, and found him standing in a nearby runway, trying not to throw up.

"Goddamn it," said Mauch, "that should be my team down there."

◇ . . . Nineteen eighty-two. Milwaukee. Gene Mauch's second heartbreak.

He was an older, wiser, more serene Gene Mauch. The dark hair had turned silver. The face was lined. He could still strike fear in a ballplayer with his icy, penetrating glare, but the eyes, in the words of Philadelphia writer Sandy Grady, "seem bruised from watching too many bad teams crash in flames."

But Gene Mauch still had the same passion for the game, the same intensity and the same insight.

He stood behind the batting cage during pregame practice one day in 1982, watching his California Angels hit one mammoth shot after another into the faraway stands.

"Awesome, huh?" Mauch said to the man next to him. "Aren't they a joy to watch?"

A joy, indeed. Reggie Jackson. Doug DeCinces. Bobby Grich. Don Baylor. Rod Carew. Fred Lynn.

"The Cowboy," as the players affectionately referred to owner Gene Autry, had opened up the saddlebags and paid out millions to assemble this lineup of All-Stars and MVPs. Mauch had a powerhouse on his hands.

It was about time. In the eighteen seasons since 1964, he had guided an assortment of expansion teams and cut-rate ball clubs. Mauch was always short of players, always battling the odds.

The winter after the Phillies' collapse, Mauch had spent many sleepless nights reliving the ordeal, and he could remember almost every pitch of every game in those final weeks. He drew up a list of the mistakes he had made, and he swore he would not repeat them. He kept a notepad and pencil by his bed, so that when he woke at night with an idea to remember or a new solution to a problem he could write it down.

"Wait 'til this year," he vowed in the spring of 1965. But "this year" never came, not in Philadelphia, nor his next stop, an expansion club in Montreal, nor in Minnesota, where owner Calvin Griffith kept letting his best players go in order to save on the payroll.

Mauch left Minnesota in 1980 and returned to his home on the ninth hole of the Sunrise Country Club in Rancho Mirage to play more golf. He had managed for twenty-one years, and he had lived through more losing seasons than winning ones. It was time for a break.

Later, his friend Autry persuaded him to take a front-office job with the Angels, and one day in May 1981 the two were watching a ball game when the Cowboy turned to his companion.

"Will you manage this team?" he asked.

"You don't need a manager," Mauch answered.

Autry assured him the decision to replace Jim Fregosi as manager had already been made, so Mauch took the job. It was the only way he would return to the dugout—if he had a team that could contend. And this one was a contender.

He played his hand brilliantly in 1982, guiding the Angels to the American League West Division title. He adapted his methods to fit his ball club. His fondness for "Little Ball"—using the bunt and the hit-and-run to push across one run at a time—gave way to "Big Ball," where the California sluggers used power to outmuscle opponents.

The Angels just about had it all that year—hitting, defense, starting pitching. There was just one weakness: The bullpen was shaky and often ineffective. But Mauch made do, juggling his relief pitchers to fit the situation. He got by—until the playoffs.

Things started out great. The powerful Angels pounded the Brewers twice at Anaheim Stadium, and the best-of-five series moved to Milwaukee for its conclusion. The Brewers staved off elimination with a victory in the third game. Still, the Angels had two more chances to put them away.

Then, Mauch decided to gamble. He brought back his ace, left-hander Tommy John, to pitch on only three days' rest. It was no problem for John. He had done it throughout his career with great results. But this time, he got knocked out of the box, and the Brewers evened the series with a 9–5 victory. Shades of 1964, with Jim Bunning and Chris Short pitching out of turn and the Phillies blowing a pennant.

Bruce Kison started the decisive fifth game, also on three days' rest. He lasted only five innings before being forced to the sidelines with a blister on his finger. He left with a 3–2 lead. The California advantage held up into the seventh, when the Brewers loaded the bases with two outs. Cecil Cooper, a tough left-handed hitter, was the batter. Luis Sanchez, a right-hander, was on the mound. Andy Hassler, a left-hander, was warming up in the bullpen.

Mauch had a decision to make. Stay with Sanchez, his best reliever, or play the percentages and bring in the left-hander to pitch to the left-handed Cooper. Sanchez had been awesome the last part of the season, but he normally pitched only an inning at a time. Hassler was good at making hitters bite on pitches out of the strike zone, but Cooper didn't swing at bad pitches. And a walk would force in a run.

Sanchez or Hassler? The pennant, the entire season, hung on that one decision. Which way to go?

Mauch stuck with Sanchez. Cooper lined the ball into left field for a single. Two runs scored. That was the ball game. Milwaukee won 4–3.

Another pennant lost Another stumble at the finish line. Another loss for Gene Mauch to explain.

Mauch tells an apocryphal story about the aftermath of that setback. The California players and coaches, and even many of the front-office people, gathered in the clubhouse for a final meeting. Mauch stood up to address his team.

"I can't do anything right," he said. "You guys got me a two-game lead and I blew it. I can't manage, can't handle a pitching staff and I'm too short."

From the back of the room came the voice of Gene Autry.

"I don't think you're too short."

◇ There was nervous chatter in the clubhouse before the game. This was the day. Sunday, October 12, 1986, the day the California Angels could win their first pennant. There was added excitement as the Angels gathered around the batting cage and watched the big hitters ripping line drives into the outfield.

Doug DeCinces stepped into the cage and drilled a ball off the left-field fence. Early in the season, when his bad back was acting up and he wasn't hitting, there were those who wrote off DeCinces as too old. Washed up, they said. A rookie named Jack Howell was called up to split time with him at third base. DeCinces was furious. He was no part-time ballplayer!

He got well, reclaimed the position full-time and began tearing up the league in late summer. He hit nine home runs and drove in twenty-five runs in August alone. He carried the California offense the last few weeks of the season. DeCinces had the capability to do that.

He hit another shot to deep center. He had his swing working today. The Red Sox had better watch out.

Donnie Moore arrived at the ballpark with his beautiful wife, Tonya. Donnie and Tonya made a great-looking couple. Donnie had smooth features and a well-trimmed mustache on his handsome face. Tonya was slender and pretty, like a model. She was a true baseball wife, accompanying Donnie every step of the way in his long climb to the major leagues. For more than a decade, they had been baseball gypsies, bouncing around from town to town, team to team, until Donnie finally hit the jackpot in California.

After signing his $3 million deal following the 1985 season, Donnie bought an $850,000 house in the exclusive Peralta Hills section of Anaheim. It was Donnie's dream house. It had a pool and a private lake, which he stocked with catfish. There was a trampoline out back for the three kids. It was paradise, except for those times when one of Donnie's dark moods descended on him and the sounds of angry shouts and screams could be heard from the dream house. But that was something neither Donnie nor Tonya talked about.

The house was full that week. Donnie's parents had come up from Lubbock, Texas, for the playoffs. His father, Conaway Moore, was a truck driver; his mother, Willie, was a housekeeper. They were there to see their son pitch. Everyone was excited about the ball game that Sunday afternoon.

Donnie said little as he dressed. He was sore and run-down that day, but he did not complain. Donnie Moore wasn't a complainer. Everyone could see he wasn't up to par, but that was all right. Donnie had been told he probably wouldn't have to pitch on this day. With a three-game-to-one lead, the Angels could afford to rest him for the World Series.

Mike Witt sat off by himself, glowering. There was no doubt about Witt's availability. Four full days of rest since his dominating performance in the playoff opener had left him at maximum efficiency. No one could accuse Gene Mauch of rushing his ace pitcher back into action this time. Mike Witt was strong and rested.

Gene Mauch was in his office, on the phone. On the other end of the line was Wally Joyner. The first baseman was still in the hospital with his ailing leg. The swelling had gone down, but not enough for him to get out of bed.

"Skip, if it was a night game, I could play," Joyner was saying.

The good news was, he should be back on his feet in time for the World Series. Of course, the Angels had to get there first.

One more victory. The Angels were ready for the kill.

Outside, Reggie Jackson was being interviewed by ABC-TV.

"We need to prove to people—the fans, the media—all over baseball," he was saying, "that we can close the deal."

The atmosphere in the visitors' clubhouse was quieter, more subdued. There was brave talk about duplicating the Kansas City Royals' feat of coming back from a 3–1 deficit to win the 1985 league playoffs.

"Kansas City did it; so can we," the Boston players told each other.

But deep down everyone knew it was a long shot.

Dave Henderson, the reserve center fielder, limped into the room. He had fouled a ball off his leg the night before, and it was so sore when he woke up Sunday morning he barely made it out of bed.

Henderson took a couple of aspirin for the pain and got ready to put on his uniform. He would suit up, sore leg or not.

"This is no time to take yourself out of anything," he said out loud.

Don Baylor, one of the many sluggers in the Boston lineup, sat eating some food and wondering what Gene Mauch must be feeling. Baylor had played for the Angels in 1982. When he left after the season to sign on with the New York Yankees, Mauch had taken the time to write him a letter telling him how much he had meant to the team. No other manager Baylor played for in seventeen years in the league had cared enough to do that. Only Mauch.

Walter Hriniak, the hitting coach, came over to talk to Baylor.

"You know Gene's over there just kind of loving it," said Hriniak. "Like, 'We've got you guys now, so do something—you have to beat me.'"

Mike Witt started out where he left off five days earlier. After a scoreless first inning, he gave up a leadoff single in the second, then struck out the next two batters.

But Rich Gedman, the Boston catcher whose intensity was so great he chipped three teeth grinding his jaws during the playoffs, lined a fastball over the right-field fence for a home run to give the Red Sox a 2–0 lead. That was why Gedman had kept Mauch awake nights.

In the bottom of the inning, Doug DeCinces hit a shot to deep center. Tony Armas gave chase and crashed off the wall in a futile attempt to catch the ball. DeCinces pulled into second with a double, and Armas limped back to his position with a sore ankle. The Angels failed to score, but the Red Sox were on the verge of losing a key player.

In the third, California catcher Bob Boone connected for a solo home run, making the score 2–1.

The game went to the fourth, and Tony Armas limped to the plate for the Red Sox. He popped up. When he got back to the dugout, his ankle was swollen and discolored.

"I better come out," he told Boston manager John McNamara. Armas didn't want to leave, but he had to think of the team first. It would be crazy to keep playing with a bad ankle.

Dave Henderson, whose leg also was sore, got up to do his stretching exercises prior to taking the field.

The Red Sox clung to their slim advantage into the sixth. The first two California batters went out, bringing up DeCinces. He hit another fly ball to center field. This one looked to be a routine out, but Henderson lost the ball in the sun and pulled up short, letting it drop between him and right fielder Dwight Evans for another two-base hit by DeCinces. Tony Armas, the regular center fielder, watched from the dugout. Red Sox fans had to think he would have caught that ball, if only he hadn't gotten hurt.

Bobby Grich followed with a long drive to center. Henderson raced back, leaped against the fence and for a brief moment felt the ball hit in his glove. A split second later, his wrist came down against the top of the wall, jarring the ball loose and tipping it over the fence.

Grich was between first and second when he saw the ball pop loose. He thrust his fist in the air in triumph. Home run! Two runs scored. Suddenly, the Angels led 3–2.

The fans cheered so long and loud that Grich was called back out of the dugout for a curtain call. In his excitement, he raised one leg and pumped his fist like a locomotive engine. Henderson stood in center field fuming. Nothing was going right for him.

The Angels were nine outs from the World Series. The fans started the countdown.

In the seventh, the Red Sox had the tying run at first with two outs. Henderson was the next batter. Mike Witt struck him out. Six more outs to go.

The Angels drove Red Sox starter Bruce Hurst from the mound in the bottom of the inning, scoring two more runs on Rob Wilfong's RBI double and Brian Downing's sacrifice fly. Now, it was 5–2.

Witt set down the Red Sox in the eighth. The Angels had a three-run lead with only three outs to go. The excitement was growing.

Gene Mauch stood at the end of the dugout, his arms folded in front of him. It was about to happen. He was going to win a pennant. Reggie Jackson put his arm around the manager and smiled. The Angels were closing the deal.

Mike Witt went out to pitch the ninth. The players in the California dugout were on their feet, ready for the bedlam that was sure to follow. In the Angels bullpen, the pitchers looked at each other in wild-eyed excitement. Around them, they could see fans pushing up against the fence, ready to rush onto the field for the final celebration. The noise in the stadium was incredible as the fans cheered and clapped.

Rich Gedman took off his catching gear in the Boston dugout, probably for the last time this season. He tried not to think about that. He was scheduled to bat fifth—if the inning lasted that long.

"This is it, fellows," he yelled. "We either do it or we don't."

Bill Buckner dragged himself to the plate, walking gingerly on his injured ankle. He slapped a grounder up the middle, just out of the reach of shortstop Dick Schofield. A timeout was called, and Dave Stapleton jogged out to first base to run for Buckner.

Next up was Jim Rice. He fouled off two pitches, then watched as one of Witt's curves shot past the plate for strike three. The crowd roared in excitement. Two more outs to go.

Don Baylor stepped in. The count went to three balls, two strikes, and Witt threw another curveball, down and away, an almost unhittable pitch. Baylor reached out and drove the ball deep to left-center field. Gary Pettis ran back and leaped against the fence, but it was to no avail. The ball sailed over his outstretched glove for a home run. That made it a one-run game at 5–4, but the Angels still had the lead.

Down at third base, Doug DeCinces watched as Dwight Evans walked to the plate. The two had played together on a youth league team coached by DeCinces's father. Now they were on opposite sides competing for a chance at baseball's ultimate prize, the World Series.

Witt threw two strikes past Evans. The home run hadn't broken his concentration. Evans swung on the next pitch, and popped the ball high in the air to the left side of the infield. DeCinces circled under it and made the catch, shaking his glove for emphasis. His boyhood teammate turned back to the dugout in disgust. Two outs. Only one more to go.

The security guards streamed out of the dugouts, and took their positions along the edges of the playing field. There was near pandemonium in the stands. People bounced up and down and waved their arms in the air and yelled. Brian Downing stood in left field and watched the security forces moving into place. He was in no mood to start celebrating yet. He remembered 1982 and Milwaukee. "Play it 'till it's over," that was Downing's philosophy.

Witt came off the pitcher's mound toward third, and DeCinces flipped the ball to him.

"This is the one we want," DeCinces yelled.

Witt took the ball and headed back to the mound. There was no need for words of encouragement. He was ready to finish the job. You could see it in his face.

And suddenly, there was Angels pitching coach Marcel Lachemann walking to the mound, where he signaled to the bullpen with his left arm. Gene Mauch had decided to make a pitching change.

Witt turned and stared out toward center field. Bob Boone came from behind the plate and Doug DeCinces from third base, yelling at Lachemann in protest.

Witt handed over the ball and walked off the field to a standing ovation. He walked through the runway and into the locker room, past the waiting reporters and cameramen, his cap off and his head down. He walked past the plastic sheets which had been hung to keep the lockers dry in the celebration that would follow. He walked past the champagne bottles, some of which had been opened to have them ready to pass out to the players. He said nothing, he just keep walking, all the way to the training room, where he stripped off his jersey to begin icing down his right elbow.

Mike Witt had pitched the Angels to within one out of the World Series. But now it would be up to someone else to finish the job.

Gene Mauch never batted an eye. He watched from the dugout, expressionless, arms still folded, as Gary Lucas, a tall and lean left-hander, arrived at the mound to take his warm-up throws. Mauch had his reasons for the pitching change, which he had decided upon one batter earlier.

The batter was Rich Gedman, the left-handed hitting Boston catcher. He had hit the ball hard off Witt that day. A home run in the second for Boston's first two runs. A double in the fifth. A single in the seventh. Gedman was hot.

But Mauch had a secret weapon in the bullpen. Gary Lucas was murder on Gedman. The night before, Lucas had come out of the bullpen to fan the Boston catcher. He had done the same thing during the regular season, striking out Gedman in a tight situation. Mauch kept track of stuff like that. He knew what pitchers got what hitters out, and he maneuvered his players to set up these situations.

It wasn't the popular move, but Mauch was convinced it was the right move. Lucas against Gedman. Left-hander against left-hander. This was the scenario Mauch wanted.

It was just like 1982 in Milwaukee. Only that time, Mauch had left the right-hander, Luis Sanchez, in the game to pitch to the left-handed hitter, Cecil Cooper. This time, Mauch played the percentages.

Security personnel began moving into the Red Sox dugout to protect the players from the California fans who were straining to charge onto the field in celebration.

"Come on, boys," said one cop. "There's going to be a party here."

Lucas toed the rubber. Gedman dug in at the plate, Boston's last hope. The crowd was back on its feet shouting. Lucas threw his split-finger change-up, the off-speed pitch that gave American League batters so much trouble. The ball sailed inside and struck Gedman on the forearm.

A hit batsman. The crowd was stunned. So was Lucas. He hadn't hit a batter all year. And now, at a time like this, the ball had slipped out of his hand. He watched in disbelief as Gedman picked himself up out of the dirt and trotted down to first base.

Donnie Moore threw another warm-up pitch in the California bullpen.

"Donnie, you're up!" someone shouted. "You're in there!"

Moore stopped throwing to see if pitching coach Marcel Lachemann had gone to the mound to remove Gary Lucas. "Is he coming to get him?" Moore asked.

"Yeah, he's coming to get him," came the reply.

Moore threw four more warm-up pitches, just to make sure he was ready. He took his jacket and stepped through the gate to begin the long trek to the mound. His adrenaline was pumping, masking the pain in his shoulder and his rib cage.

Gene Mauch watched from the dugout.

"I wonder what kind of out Donnie Moore will get," he was thinking. There was no doubt in the manager's mind Moore would nail down this victory.

Dave Henderson gamely hobbled to the plate on his sore leg. It had been a rough day so far. He had let a fly ball drop in for a hit, tipped another over the fence for a home run and struck out with a runner on base. Henderson was having his problems.

Moore delivered his first pitch low for ball one. He threw a fastball past Henderson for a strike. The stadium was rocking with noise.

The policemen in the Boston bullpen got ready to escort the players to the clubhouse to protect them from the soon-to-be deliriously happy California fans.

"Get your equipment!" yelled one of the policemen. "We'll take you out the back way, through the corridor."

Moore threw again, and Henderson swung and missed for another strike. One more strike and it would be all over.

The California players leaned forward on the top step of the dugout, like runners on the starting blocks, ready to charge onto the field. Reggie Jackson took off his cap and his sunglasses in preparation for the celebration.

Moore threw a fastball low. Ball two.

In the stands, Tonya Moore clapped her hands and shouted encouragement to her husband. "Come on, Donnie! One more strike!" All around her, fans were yelling the same thing.

Moore threw his split-finger pitch, and Henderson barely tapped it foul down the third-base line. The count remained two balls, two strikes.

Bob Boone, the catcher, walked toward the mound and yelled something to his pitcher. It was hard to hear in all the noise, but Moore nodded and stepped back on the rubber.

Moore delivered his next pitch, and Henderson fouled the ball straight back. Henderson stepped out of the batter's box and looked up at the sky. He took a deep breath and stepped back in.

Policemen walked along the California bench collecting the caps of the players so they wouldn't be swiped by fans. The din in the stadium increased.

Mauch was poised on the dugout steps, next to Reggie Jackson. Throw the fastball, he thought. Get this guy out with the fastball.

Boone returned to his position behind the plate and flashed the signal to his pitcher. He held out four fingers, the sign for the split-finger fastball. Henderson had the fastball timed, reasoned Boone. So, he called for the off-speed pitch.

Moore fired the ball to the plate, but his shoulder was weak and he could not snap off the pitch as he normally did. When he was healthy, his split-finger seemed to explode downward. But Donnie Moore wasn't healthy. This pitch didn't explode.

Henderson swung, and the ball shot off his bat, high and deep into left field. Henderson let out a yell, took a few steps toward first base, then turned to watch the flight of the ball. More than three hundred feet away, Brian Downing ran back to the left-field fence and looked up. Downing was the kind of player who would crash headfirst into a wall or slide belly-first across the ground to make a catch. But this time, there was nowhere to hurl his body. He watched helplessly as the ball sailed over his head and landed eight rows deep in the stands.

Henderson jumped for joy, laughing and skipping around the bases. The Boston players pushed past the security guards and streamed out of the dugout to greet him at home plate, shouting and pointing at him in excitement. Donnie Moore stomped around the mound screaming in frustration. Gene Mauch remained impassive. The California players pulled back from the edge of the dugout steps. The caps were passed back out. The celebration would have to wait. Boston led 6–5.

Doug DeCinces had never seen a game like it. Up and down, an incredible high one moment, a devastating low the next.

When Dave Henderson had hit his home run, DeCinces had sunk to a crouching position at third base, as if he had been punched in the stomach. One moment, the Angels had been going to the World Series. The next moment, they had found themselves on the short end of the score.

Now, DeCinces stood in the on-deck circle, gripping his bat. The game had taken another crazy turn.

Incredibly, the Angels had battled back in the bottom of the ninth. Bob Boone had started the inning with a single. Ruppert Jones went in to run for him and advanced to second on a sacrifice bunt by Gary Pettis. Gene Mauch was playing Little Ball again.

A single by Rob Wilfong scored Jones, tying the game. Another single by Dick Schofield sent Wilfong to third. The winning run—the pennant—was ninety feet from home plate. The Red Sox were on the ropes again. In desperation, John McNamara ordered his pitcher to intentionally walk Brian Downing to load the bases. With only one out, the Red Sox had to set up the force play at home. But it was a strategy that easily could backfire. Doug DeCinces, California's best run-producer, would be the next batter.

DeCinces walked back to the dugout while Steve Crawford, the third Boston pitcher of the inning, threw four pitches to Downing wide of the plate.

"Just nice and easy," Reggie Jackson said to DeCinces. "Hit the fly ball."

"You can do this," added Mauch. "You know how to do this."

DeCinces had driven in ninety-six runs during the season. He was the guy California wanted with the bat in his hands in this spot.

He walked back to the plate reminding himself, "Nice and easy. Just a fly ball."

Crawford threw him a fastball. DeCinces swung, nice and easy. He hit a weak pop fly into shallow right field. His old youth league teammate, Dwight Evans, was there to catch it. If it had been anyone but Evans, maybe Wilfong could have tagged up and scored from third. But Evans had the best arm in the league. Wilfong stayed at third.

Nice and easy hadn't done it. DeCinces returned to the dugout, wishing more than anything that he could have that one swing back.

The next batter, Bobby Grich, hit a soft liner to Crawford for the third out. There still was no celebration in Anaheim. Instead, the game went into extra innings.

The two teams battled into the eleventh inning, when Donnie Moore threw an inside pitch that hit leadoff batter Don Baylor. A ground ball single by Dwight Evans and a bunt hit by Rich Gedman loaded the bases with nobody out.

Dave Henderson was back up. He hit Moore's first pitch into center field, just deep enough to score Baylor from third base.

That was the ball game. The Red Sox won 7–6. Donnie Moore walked off the field where he had been cheered so many times, and this time the fans stood and booed him.

Later, he sat in the clubhouse, where the plastic liners had been taken down from the lockers, and thought about the split-finger fastball that Henderson had hit for his home run.

"Maybe if I had tried to blow it past him, we'd be drinking champagne right now," Moore said softly.

There were so many "maybes." Maybe Mike Witt should have stayed in the game. Maybe Moore should have rested another day. Maybe Doug DeCinces shouldn't have swung at the first pitch. Maybe this, maybe that.

In an adjoining room, Gene Mauch slowly packed a travel bag.

"We had it all done," he kept saying in a hoarse whisper.

Mauch removed a gray travel uniform from the closet and looked at it before stuffing it into the bag, next to his windbreaker and his baseball spikes.

"The last thing in the world I needed was to pack this sucker one extra time," he said.

The champagne also was boxed up and put away.

The flight back to Boston was quiet and subdued. Doug DeCinces looked around the airplane cabin and shook his head in disgust. The front-office people who were making the trip with the Angels seemed particularly downcast. They wouldn't talk, except maybe to criticize what had happened on the field in Game 5. To DeCinces, their attitude seemed to be that it was an exercise in futility for the Angels to even play out the remainder of the series. It was ridiculous, he thought. The Angels were the ones who led in the series. They were the ones who had two chances to win one more game.

"My God," he muttered, "we've got eighteen innings to play. Are you kidding me?"

The team checked into the hotel in Boston, and Reggie Jackson called a meeting of the players. They aired out their frustrations, and they tried to revive their sagging spirits.

"Let's go," someone said. "In the sixth game, let's forget all this stuff. We've got to go out and play."

The telephone rang in Gene Mauch's hotel room at 3:00 A.M. Tuesday. It was Wally Joyner, calling from his hospital bed in California, where his infected right leg had been lanced twice on Monday.

He had planned to take a late-night flight east, Joyner explained in a distraught voice, but when he got out of his bed he still could not walk on the leg. He sat down, tried it again and still couldn't.

"Get well, and stay there until you do get well," Mauch told him.

If the Angels were going to win the pennant, they would have to do so without their first baseman and leading hitter.

Mauch went to the ballpark later that day, and there he was surrounded by writers wanting to know his mood after the Game 5 loss. What was he thinking? How did he deal with another crushing setback? Was it like 1964, and 1982?

Mauch tapped a finger against his forehead.

"So many guys have tried to get in here," he said. "If they got in there, they wouldn't know what they were dealing with."

The questions continued. Twenty-five years without a pennant. When was he going to get that monkey off his back?

Mauch pretended to glance over his shoulder.

"Monkey, are you on my back again?"

It was cold and overcast in Boston that Tuesday evening, matching the gloomy mood gripping the Angels. Kirk McCaskill, a seventeen-game winner during the season, completed his warm-up throws in the bullpen and made the long trek to the dugout for the start of the game.

There, he watched while the Angels batted in the first inning. Reggie Jackson hit a double to drive in a run. Doug DeCinces followed with another two-base hit to score Jackson. The Angels loaded the bases. Boston starter Oil Can Boyd was on the ropes, perhaps one pitch from being driven from the game.

Bill Buckner, the first baseman, waved for a time-out and hobbled to the mound.

"No matter what you do," he yelled at Boyd, his voice rising above the crowd noise, "we're behind you. You give up four, we'll score five. You give up five, we'll score six."

Boyd nodded and went back to work. He got Rob Wilfong to pop up, ending the inning. The Angels led 2–0, but they had missed an opportunity to break open the game.

McCaskill went to the mound and tried to get loose again. The Angels had batted for twenty-four minutes, and McCaskill had lost his sharpness sitting around. He walked the first two batters, then threw a pitch in the dirt. The Red Sox tied the score without even getting a hit. After such a promising beginning, the Angels were back where they had started.

McCaskill continued to struggle in the third inning. The Red Sox knocked out six hits, and Bobby Grich, filling in for Joyner at first base, made a costly throwing error. McCaskill finally was lifted for a reliever, but not before five runs had crossed the plate.

The next batter was Rich Gedman. Mauch brought in Gary Lucas to pitch to him. Lucas struck him out, for the third time in four meetings between the two that year. Two days too late, Lucas finally did what his manager figured he would against Gedman.

"I don't know how many years I have left," Mauch would say later, "but I would gladly give up the last two to get back Lucas's pitch Sunday."

The final score was 10–4, Boston, and now the series was tied at three games each.

Afterward, Mauch called a meeting of his players behind closed clubhouse doors.

"Who's going to win tomorrow?" he asked them in an effort to boost their confidence.

The California players responded that they were. But there was a hollow ring to their words.

The Angels had one more chance on Wednesday. John Candelaria, the veteran left-hander, would pitch for California. He had the credentials for the assignment. Candelaria had struck out fourteen members of Cincinnati's famous Big Red Machine in a 1975 National League Championship Series game. He had beaten the Baltimore

Orioles on a shutout in the 1979 World Series. The "Candy Man" wouldn't crack under the pressure of a seventh game.

Roger Clemens, still weakened by an allergic reaction to cigarette smoke on the flight back from California, was the Boston pitcher.

It turned out to be a mismatch.

The Red Sox pushed across three unearned runs in the second inning following an error by the usually dependable Dick Schofield. The California defense crumbled again in the fourth. Gary Pettis muffed a Dave Henderson fly ball for a three-run error. Spike Owen singled in one run. Candelaria was having trouble getting anyone out, but Mauch left him out there. The California players on the field were asking one another, "What is going on here?" Jim Rice blasted a three-run homer. The Red Sox led by seven runs, all of them unearned. Finally, the Candy Man was taken out of the game.

When it was all over, and the Red Sox had won 8–1 to claim the American League pennant, Gene Mauch, still in uniform, stood behind a desk in the manager's office of the visitors' clubhouse at Fenway Park. His eyes were red and swollen.

"We won it once," he said softly. "We just couldn't win it twice."

An hour later, dressed in a sport coat, red sweater and tie, he got ready to leave the ballpark. Another season had ended just short of a World Series.

Mauch glanced at the reporters still in the room.

"That's it, boys. That's it. Nothing else left to say."

It turned out he had been wrong. You don't always get what you want, no matter how hard you try.

All the lost games and losing seasons, all the disappointments and all the stress and cigarettes caught up with Gene Mauch in the spring of 1988.

He showed up for training camp that year worn and haggard. He was having trouble breathing, and had not felt well since a chest cold had gripped him the summer before. He was easily fatigued, and he often sneaked in pregame naps in his office.

Mauch hated doctors, but that spring he checked himself into a hospital for a series of medical tests. He feared he might have cancer, and when he found out he didn't, he left the hospital "feeling like I'm one lucky fellow."

Medically, his illness was nothing more serious than bronchial problems. But there was something else bothering him that could not be measured by electrocardiograms or detected by X-ray machines.

Mauch returned to the dugout and managed two more ball games, which his Angels lost by the combined score of 24–1. They were just spring-training games, and did not count in the standings, but still they disturbed him deeply.

He returned home and spent a sleepless night wrestling with his discomfort. The next day, he knew the cause of his problem and what he must do about it. It was time to give up managing.

The announcement was made the following day, a Saturday. At the news conference, Mauch cited the outstanding job interim manager Cookie Rojas had done with the team in his absence. He talked about the effect "agents and certain union heads" were having on baseball.

And finally, he explained the decision by pointing to his stomach and telling his listeners, "This thing hurting too much when you've planned well and worked hard and still didn't win."

Mauch retired to Rancho Mirage, where his new condominium backed up to the adjacent golf course.

Most days, he was on the course by seven-thirty in the morning. He would play eighteen holes, then eat a sandwich for lunch and, during baseball season, perhaps watch a ball game on the satellite dish at the country-club lounge across the street. Afterward, he would play another round of golf.

He would get home by four-thirty in the afternoon, and when possible watch the Angels game on television. Two rounds of golf, two baseball games. That was Gene Mauch's day.

"It's about the only thing I know anything about, anyway," he said.

He continued to follow baseball closely, studying the box scores for about an hour every morning. He could tell a lot from a box score— the hot hitters, the hot pitchers and the tendencies of managers. He could add the number of outs and the men left on base and tell which pitchers pitched to which batters, and which were the most effective.

Mauch cut back on his smoking, but he still had a cigarette when he wanted one. Only now, he might go an hour or two after a meal before thinking about it.

What he missed more than cigarettes was baseball, and the men who played for him.

A writer from the *Los Angeles Times* came to interview him one spring, and Mauch said to him, "I miss ninety-five percent of the players so bad I can't tell you."

He was selective in the interviews he granted. He might speak to a writer from Los Angeles, or perhaps an old friend from Philadelphia. But repeated requests for an interview on the 1986 playoffs and its aftermath went unanswered.

His friends also were protective of his privacy.

"Leave Gene alone," said one of his former coaches. "He deserves a rest."

"That's all in the past," said another. "That stuff has been beat to death."

Mauch had been analyzed enough. He had heard all the questions about the losing seasons, the twenty-six years without a pennant, the last-minute collapses.

"Go look up the clips," he once told a writer who began asking questions of him for yet another Gene Mauch story. "Write what you want, and I'll sanction it."

He was the greatest manager never to win a pennant. He also might have been the unluckiest. He came so close in 1964, again in 1982 and once more in 1986. Lightning struck not twice, but three times. And in baseball, three strikes and you're out.

2

DREAD SCOTT

If you never struggle, you think it's too easy. I know what it's
like to be down at the bottom.

—MIKE SCOTT

Twenty-nine years old and washed up. The thought of it frightened
Mike Scott.

He was at home in Chandler, Arizona. It was a nice house in a nice
community, but it wasn't what he wanted. He was a southern California
native. That was where he really wanted to live. Maybe someday, if he
ever could afford the down payment on a house, he would move there.

He made a good living playing baseball, pulling down about
$350,000 a year. But he wasn't rich. The stars made the big money in
baseball. They were the ones who were independently wealthy. Mike
Scott made just enough to be an expensive liability when he wasn't producing on the field. If the ball club wanted to cut costs, it could bring
in a rookie at about one-third of what Scott was making.

He lived with uncertainty. The fringe players and the hangers-on,
like Scott, never knew from one year to the next when the paychecks
were going to end. So, they socked away what they could, sweated out
each contract, dreamed of hitting it big someday and made contin-
gency plans for a future away from baseball.

Outside, the sun was shining. The sun was always shining in Arizona.
Inside, Scott's mood was gloomy.

He took stock of his life, and his career. It was December 1984. Scott
had just completed his sixth season as a big-league pitcher. The way he
was going, it might be his last. Five wins, eleven losses, an earned-run

average of 4.68. That was the record he had posted for the Houston Astros.

He had a good arm and a ninety-plus-mile-an-hour fastball, but he lacked consistency and a good breaking pitch. His career won-lost record was 29–44. He knew time was running out on him. He couldn't last forever on his potential. He wasn't going to get many more chances.

He had a wife and two young girls to support. He had to start thinking of other ways to make a living. That was why he had gotten his real-estate license that fall. Maybe he could sell houses for a living. He also thought about selling insurance, or going back to school to complete his degree. None of his options sounded very appealing.

The phone rang. Scott answered, and on the other end of the line he recognized the voice of Al Rosen, the Houston general manager.

"I know you had a bad year, Mike," he began, "but I want you to know you're still our fifth starter next year. It's your job to lose. I'm not saying you can go to spring training and get beat up and not lose the job. But don't worry about last year."

The words of encouragement helped. Scott had been really down, and his confidence needed a boost.

But that wasn't the main reason Rosen called. He had something else in mind. Rosen's friend Roger Craig, the pitching coach for the Detroit Tigers, had taught several of his pitchers a new pitch, a version of the forkball called the split-finger fastball. It had worked so well the Tigers had won a world championship. Rosen thought the pitch might work for Scott, so he had persuaded Craig to teach it to the Houston pitcher.

"What do you think?" asked Rosen. "Do you want to go out and talk to Roger?"

"Sure," said Scott. "I'll go out there."

What else could he say to his boss after the kind of season he had just had? All he needed to be told was what to do, where to go and when to be there. He didn't know anything about this new superpitch everyone in baseball was talking about, but he was ready to learn.

At this point, Scott was willing to try just about anything to save his career.

Roger Craig met him on a baseball field at a junior college near his ranch outside San Diego. Craig made a good first impression. He was a big man at six feet, four inches, and he had a commanding presence. He also had an uncanny resemblance to Lyndon Johnson, the former president from Texas.

Craig had been good enough to pitch twelve years in the big leagues, but his main claim to fame, if it could be called that, was losing twenty-four games for the New York Mets in their first season in 1962 and twenty-two games the next year. Now, Craig was the most respected pitching coach in the game.

Scott didn't know what to expect from the teaching session. He hadn't picked up a baseball all winter. But he was eager to learn.

"I'll stay here as long as it takes," he told Craig.

They had the field to themselves, just Scott, Craig and a catcher. They met there for eight days, for about an hour and a half each afternoon.

At first, Scott just threw so Craig could see his mechanics. He had a good motion, and a good delivery. Scott was a pleasant, unassuming-looking man of six feet, three inches, with glasses and thinning blond hair. He looked more like an insurance salesman than a baseball player. He had kind of a rolling gait, and his teammates used to kid him about his unathletic body. But in Craig's eyes, Scott had a good body for a pitcher. He also threw the ball in a nice, fluid motion.

Craig changed a few things about Scott's delivery, and then got around to the main order of business. He showed him the secrets of the split-finger fastball.

In many ways, it was a simple pitch. The pitcher split his index and middle fingers when gripping the baseball, with his thumb placed underneath. He threw the ball like a standard fastball, only he pushed off on the release with his middle finger. The result was a pitch that approached the plate like a fastball, but at the last second broke sharply downward.

Scott tried the pitch, and it did nothing. He worked with it some more, with little success. But he refused to give up on it. He kept throwing and throwing, and finally his pitches began dropping down.

"Don't let up," Craig kept repeating. "Don't push the ball. Just throw it like a fastball."

The more Scott threw the pitch, the more the ball broke. And it never went the same way twice. That was one of the beauties of the pitch. It was as unpredictable as it was explosive.

"This is going to be a good pitch for you," Craig told his pupil.

Scott hoped so. His career was riding on it. He would take it to spring training and see how it worked out.

But before Scott left San Diego, Craig had one final word of advice for him.

When you start throwing this pitch, he warned, people are going to accuse you of doctoring the baseball. That was one of the hazards of the split-finger, which also was known as the "dry spitball" because of its resemblance to that outlawed pitch.

But that was to be expected. It was all part of the game, as pitchers and hitters schemed to gain an edge over one another, sometimes straying outside the rules to do so. Some hitters illegally stuffed cork in their bats, and some pitchers cheated by scuffing baseballs or adding foreign substances to them. It had been going on from the early days of the game.

When a pitcher shows up one year with a tough new pitch, naturally there are going to be raised eyebrows. Scott figured he could handle that. You do what you have to do to survive in this game.

◇ A year and a half later, on September 25, 1986, the paths of Mike Scott and Roger Craig crossed once again. Scott, who long ago had given up any notion of utilizing his real-estate license, was on the pitching mound at the Houston Astrodome. Craig, by now the manager of the San Francisco Giants, was in the visitors' dugout.

Craig watched his onetime pupil mow down the Giants in the fifth inning—three up, three down. That made twelve batters in a row retired by Scott, who was throwing his split-finger with awesome effectiveness.

"We'll never get a hit off this guy," Craig muttered to Bob Lillis, one of his coaches.

The irony of the situation was not lost on Lillis. He had been the manager of the Astros two years ago, and it was he and Al Rosen who had persuaded Craig to work with Scott. Now, Craig, Rosen and Lillis all were with the Giants, who had been held hitless through five innings by Scott.

Across the way, Scott sat in the Houston dugout and for the first time thought about the possibility of pitching a no-hitter. Only four more innings. He had a chance, he figured.

Scott wanted to mention it to someone, but he didn't. An old baseball superstition dictates that you never talk about a no-hitter in progress, for fear of jinxing it. Scott didn't believe in superstitions, but all around him his teammates made a point of checking their gloves or staring at their shoes, anything to avoid the subject. He kept his thoughts to himself. The tension was temporarily broken when Denny Walling blasted a home run to give the Astros a 1–0 lead.

Scott went back out to pitch the sixth, and once again he set down the Giants in order. Walking back to the dugout, he got a standing ovation.

Two years ago, the notion of Mike Scott pitching a no-hitter would have been preposterous. Now, his teammates waited for it to happen. The way he had been pitching, they expected it. They even talked about it among themselves. "When's Scotty going to throw a no-hitter?" they asked his catcher, Alan Ashby. Soon, Ashby figured. That was how good Scott was late that season.

The split-finger fastball had transformed his career. He had won eighteen games in 1985 and again in 1986. But that summer, his 18–10 record did not do justice to his major-league-leading 2.22 earned-run average or his 306 strikeouts. He was striking out ten batters for every nine innings pitched and getting better and stronger as the season progressed. Almost overnight, he had become the best pitcher in the league.

In the seventh inning, Ashby went to the mound to talk to his pitcher. Ashby knew how to handle these situations. He had already caught two no-hitters, one by Houston's Ken Forsch in 1979 and one by Nolan Ryan in 1981. As a kid growing up in the Los Angeles area, Ashby had witnessed two others, both by Sandy Koufax. But Ashby had never seen a pitcher dominate a game the way Mike Scott did that day.

"We're going to win this thing sooner or later," said Ashby. "It's a matter of time."

Scott nodded his head. The game had started out as an opportunity for the Astros to clinch the National League West Division championship. But the division title was inevitable. With ten games remaining in the season, Houston needed only a single victory. This game had turned into something more important.

"You're not going to get many chances to pitch a no-hitter," continued Ashby. "So, don't just lay anything in there. If you're behind somebody three-and-oh, go after him. No matter what situation you come up against, don't give in an inch."

Scott went back to work. He retired all three batters he faced in the seventh. He began the eighth by fanning Bob Brenly for the third time. That made nineteen outs in a row. The streak ended when Scott walked the next batter, Phil Ouellette. Desperate to get something going, the Giants sent up a pinch hitter, Harry Spilman. He grounded out to Bill Doran. Another pinch hitter, Mike Aldrete, flied to left. That made eight innings of no-hit ball.

Before the ninth inning began, Scott looked over at Craig in the opposite dugout. If it wasn't for Roger, he thought, I wouldn't be out here doing this now.

"Why did it have to be me who taught him the damn thing?" Craig was asking himself.

Dan Gladden, the leadoff batter, stepped in to start the ninth. He struck out. The crowd was on its feet, cheering every pitch. Robby Thompson, the San Francisco second baseman, also went down swinging. That made thirteen strikeouts for Scott. He wasn't just keeping the Giants hitless, he was overpowering them.

Scott needed just one more out. Will Clark, the rookie first baseman, was the batter. He was the last hurdle standing between Scott and the baseball record books.

Scott fired a fastball to Clark, right down the middle of the plate. It was the worst pitch he threw all day. Ashby saw the pitch hang out there, and he grimaced. He thought Clark was going to blast it. But Scott got lucky. Clark got on top of the ball and grounded it harmlessly to first base. That was it. A no-hitter!

Thirty minutes later, the crowd was still standing and cheering as a couple of Houston players paraded Scott around the field on their shoulders.

The real-estate world had lost a salesman, and baseball had gained a superstar pitcher.

◇ Mike Scott was a cheat. Gary Carter was convinced of it. And Carter, the National League's premier catcher and one of its top sluggers, figured he knew a cheat when he saw one.

"All of a sudden, he's developed into a three-hundred-strikeout pitcher," said Carter. "There has to be some reason."

Carter was holding court in Montreal, where the New York Mets were finishing their last road trip of the regular season. The Mets had long ago wrapped up the National League East title. They would finish the season with 108 victories, giving them a huge twenty-one-and-a-half-game cushion on their closest pursuers, the Philadelphia Phillies. For weeks, they had the luxury of thinking ahead to the National League playoffs.

And for Carter and many of his teammates, that meant an examination of the tactics employed by their playoff opponents, the Houston Astros. And chief among the suspected wrongdoers on the Astros was Scott.

"Sure, he's talented," continued Carter as the tape recorders rolled and the writers scribbled down his remarks, "and he developed a split-finger fastball. All in all, though, I think he's had a little help from his friends."

What friends might those be? Perhaps one of his fielders discreetly scuffing the baseball in a strategic location? Or a piece of sandpaper hidden somewhere on Scott's person or in his glove or clothing, allowing him to scrape a spot on the baseball before delivering it to the plate?

The charges first surfaced shortly after Scott began throwing the split-finger, and consequently striking out more batters, back in 1985. He beat the Chicago Cubs one day that June, and afterward Cubs first baseman Leon Durham claimed to have found a piece of sandpaper left on the mound.

Carter alluded to that incident.

"I don't think the groundskeeper left it there," he said with a knowing smile.

Roger Craig had warned Scott there would be accusations against him. But hadn't even Craig himself become one of the accusers in 1986? One game in June, he came out of the Giants dugout three times to demand that Scott be searched for illegal paraphernalia. Scott was stunned at the actions of his former mentor.

No evidence was ever found against him, but that didn't stop the complaints. A week after throwing his no-hitter, Scott faced the Giants again. He held them hitless until Will Clark led off the seventh inning with a double. It was the first hit he had given up in sixteen innings.

Craig could watch only so many of Scott's pitches veer off at crazy angles before storming out of the dugout to have the ball checked.

"How can a pitcher be this good?" he complained. "Nobody can be this good!"

Carter figured the same thing. No pitcher could throw the ball like Scott was unless he was breaking the rules. A lot of the New York players felt the same way. And Carter vowed he wasn't going to be shy about protesting to the umpires in the playoff series.

Nobody could be that good. But the more the Mets talked about it, the more they seemed to convince themselves that Mike Scott just might be.

◇ A nap and pasta. Those were Mike Scott's pregame requirements on days that he pitched. Sleep and eat. Nothing elaborate. He just wanted to be lazy. And he wanted to be left alone. He normally was an easygoing fellow, but game days found him in a foul mood.

He woke up from his short nap and checked the time. It was almost three o'clock. He was especially edgy on this day. It was Wednesday, October 8, 1986, the first day of the National League Championship Series.

He hadn't really been asleep, just catnapping. He had the ability to do that, just sit down anywhere and snooze for a few minutes.

His wife, Vicki, had the spaghetti waiting for him. After nine years as a baseball wife, she knew the routine.

Scott got to the Astrodome as late as possible for that night's game. That was another of his game-day customs. He hated to sit around an empty clubhouse, drinking coffee and staring at the walls for two hours while the other players took batting practice and shagged balls in the outfield. So, on days when he was scheduled to pitch, Scott showed up just in time to put on his uniform, do his stretching exercises and loosen his pitching arm.

There was a lot on the line that day. The Astros had been lightly regarded in the spring, and most observers had them tagged for fifth place in the tough National League West. Sure, Houston had a few good pitchers, but it relied on a popgun offense. There were few stars in the Houston lineup. Bill Doran was one of the league's best second basemen, and Jose Cruz was a solid, underrated performer in left field.

But few other Astros starters garnered much recognition. The only power hitter on the team was Glenn Davis, the young first baseman who had hit twenty home runs in half a season the year before. Pitching great Nolan Ryan seemed to be breaking down of old age at thirty-nine. Dave Smith was an outstanding relief pitcher, but there was little else in the bullpen.

But new manager Hal Lanier had turned the Astros loose on the base paths and added some spark to a lifeless offense. Ryan, who was as overpowering as ever, and Scott provided a solid one-two pitching punch, lefty Bob Knepper added seventeen victories and rookie Jim Deshaies was outstanding as the team's fourth starter. The combination of overpowering pitching, heads-up defense and a scrappy offense brought the Astros the division title and a shot at the first World Series in the franchise's twenty-five-year history.

The Mets were solid favorites in the series, with a pitching staff the equal of Houston's and a powerful offense to go with it. But with pitchers like Scott and Ryan and Smith, the Astros had a chance at pulling off the upset. Late in the season, they sent the Mets a message with an incredible three-game stretch which started with Jim Deshaies striking out the first eight batters and shutting out the Dodgers one night, Ryan following with seven innings of no-hit ball and a shutout against the Giants and Scott capping the streak with his no-hitter.

Scott went off to be by himself in the clubhouse. Normally, on days when he pitched he was so lethargic beforehand he could fall asleep three minutes before he warmed up. He would almost have to slap himself to wake up, but once he started pitching he was fine.

This day, there was no dozing in the clubhouse. Scott had been brilliant during the regular season. Now, he had to prove he could be just as effective in the pressure of the playoffs.

Scott was a little nervous, but he knew he could handle it. No game he ever pitched in 1986 or in the years to come could match the pressure he felt in those early years when he went to spring training fighting to earn a spot on the ball club. He would pitch a game late in spring, when the final roster cuts were being made and he was on the bubble, knowing that any pitch could make him or break him. Now that was real pressure.

Gary Carter was having a good day. There was nothing unusual about that. For Carter, every day was a good one.

He made his way through the visitors' clubhouse at the Astrodome, smiling and greeting everyone in sight.

"Hey, how you doin'?"

"Hey, man, have a good one!"

"Okay, baby, have a great day!"

Carter was one of those rare people who welcomed each and every day with enthusiasm and boundless optimism. Always smiling, always happy, always talking—that was Gary Carter.

There were those who suspected the smile was artificial and the cheerfulness an act, that Carter was in truth what could only be described as a "phony." Carter never let such talk bother him. If others didn't understand, that was their failing. Carter was just being himself. And with him, he steadfastly maintained, what you saw was what you got.

"You can't fake being nice, you know," he said.

In his dressing cubicle, his clothes were meticulously placed on hangers, his pants carefully folded on the creases. His shoes were lined up side by side, neatly and precisely. His valuables were arranged in orderly stacks on the shelf.

"Cleanliness is close to godliness" was Carter's oft-repeated philosophy.

The name "KID" was stenciled on his sweatshirts and wristbands. The nickname was a natural for the talkative, enthusiastic Carter, and he took pride in it. He had picked it up as a twenty-year-old rookie with the Montreal Expos because of his hustle and enthusiasm, and, according to some, his immaturity.

Now thirty-two, Carter was still the Kid, both on and off the field. When you called him on the telephone, his voice on the answering machine informed you, "The Kid'll get back to you." When you spotted him driving around town, you saw his personalized license plates that read "KID-8," combining his nickname with his uniform number.

The Kid had reason to be pumped up on this day. After twelve years in the big leagues, during which he had established himself as one of the game's greatest and most popular stars, he finally had made it to the postseason.

The playoffs, the World Series—this was what the Kid had dreamed about since he really was a kid back in California. Many ballplayers acquired a jaded edge when they reached the big leagues. Not the Kid. Why, he still collected baseball cards!

Carter kept up his chatter out on the field during the pregame workout. He stepped into the batting cage and punctuated his words with the sharp crack of his bat as he sent one line drive after another into the outfield.

He couldn't wait for the game to begin. It was going to be another good day. No, make that a great day!

Gary Carter blocked out the crowd noise as he stepped to the plate in the first inning. More than 44,000 fans in the Astrodome were still cheering Mike Scott's strikeout of Keith Hernandez in the top of the first inning. There were two outs. A runner was on first base. Carter had a chance to do some damage and get the Mets off to a fast start.

Carter was the anchor of the New York lineup, having hit 24 homers and driven in 105 runs from the cleanup position. He was more than a cheerleader.

He took a fastball for a strike. Scott delivered his next offering, and it shot to the plate like another fastball. Carter swung, but at the last split second the ball dived underneath his bat.

It had to be an illegal pitch. Carter screamed in protest to home-plate umpire Doug Harvey.

"Harvey, no way!"

He wanted the ball inspected. Harvey looked it over, found nothing wrong and tossed it back to Scott. The crowd shouted its approval.

Another split-finger roared to the plate, and Carter swung and missed. The side was retired. Scott had thrown eight pitches, all of them for strikes. The Kid walked away shaking his head and muttering to himself.

The Astros led 1–0 on a Glenn Davis home run when Carter batted again in the fourth. Another of Scott's split-finger fastballs exploded past him.

"How would you like to be hitting that stuff," he complained to Houston catcher Alan Ashby.

"No thanks," said Ashby. "I'll stick to catching it."

Carter swung and missed at strike three. He gave umpire Harvey a woeful look before marching back to the dugout.

The Mets took the field for the bottom of the inning, and Carter squatted behind the plate catching Dwight Gooden's warm-up throws and carrying on a running dialogue with Harvey.

"Those balls are unbelievable. What do they do? They started out on the plate and ended up out of the strike zone."

Harvey assured Carter he had checked balls thrown by Scott several times during the season. They passed inspection every time.

Carter just shook his head.

In the sixth, the Mets got a runner on with one out, but Scott struck out Keith Hernandez and Carter to end the threat.

Scott nursed the one-run lead into the eighth. The Astros were used to these types of games—low-scoring, tense. It was almost as if they lulled their opponents to sleep.

Then the Mets threatened again. There were runners on first and second with two outs, and the batter was Hernandez, the best clutch hitter in the league. Scott struck him out on a high fastball, and Hernandez flung his bat into the dugout in anger. The Mets were growing more frustrated as the game progressed.

Carter led off the ninth for New York, with the Mets still behind, 1–0. It was their last chance to do something. He hit an easy grounder for an out, and the crowd sarcastically cheered him. He had finally made contact with one of Scott's pitches.

Darryl Strawberry singled and stole second base, raising the Mets' hopes again. But Mookie Wilson was robbed of a hit when Glenn Davis speared his hard grounder and threw to Scott covering first for the second out.

With Strawberry on third, Ray Knight was New York's last hope. He argued for nearly a minute on a called second strike, then waved feebly at strike three. That made fourteen strikeouts for Scott, tying a National League Championship Series record. It also ended the game.

Scott not only had beaten the Mets 1–0, he had left them talking to themselves. Even Gary Carter was frowning.

◇ The Mets were a cocky ball club. They antagonized opponents with their swagger and their air of superiority. They celebrated their feats on the field with high fives and frequent curtain calls for their fans. Their all-out, cocksure style of play led to four on-field brawls during the season, and their arrogant manner created enemies around the league.

It also helped them play winning baseball.

They led 2–0 in the fifth inning of Game 2 when Lenny Dykstra hit a long foul ball into the upper deck down the right-field line. Houston pitcher Nolan Ryan retaliated by knocking Dykstra down with a fastball aimed at the head. Dykstra brushed himself, glared out at Ryan, and two pitches later lined a single into the outfield. The Mets weren't going to be intimidated.

A single and triple followed, and the Mets were on their way to a convincing 5–1 victory. The series moved to New York, tied at one game each.

◇ The Shea Stadium crowd for Game 3 on Saturday afternoon was loud and raucous. Bob Knepper, the starting pitcher for Houston, ignored the insults and jeers from the fans.

New York was not Knepper's kind of place. It was the epitome of all that was wrong in American society—the corruption of values, the violence, the sexual permissiveness, the lack of morals. Knepper was a man with strong Christian beliefs.

There were other born-again Christian ballplayers in the major leagues, but few were as outspoken in their beliefs and as zealous in their lifestyles as Knepper.

He was somewhat of a loner on the Houston team. Knepper was not the type to go out and have a beer with the boys. That was not to say he was not well liked. He had many friends in the clubhouse. But everyone knew Knepper was different.

Other starting pitchers retreated into solitude on days they were to pitch. Knepper sat in his dressing cubicle reading one of the many books or magazines he carried around with him. Other players might sneak a set of golf clubs along with their travel gear on road trips. Knepper carried empty suitcases which he loaded with books. Others played loud music on their portable stereos. Knepper listened to inspirational Christian tunes.

He also carried his Christian beliefs with him onto the playing field. His principles were such that he refused to throw at batters, as occasionally was required of a big-league pitcher. This sometimes led to clashes with his managers, but Knepper refused to compromise his stance.

In one game in Chicago, the Cubs tagged Knepper for back-to-back homers. Keith Moreland was the next batter, and he was so sure Knepper would knock him down in retaliation that he began to fall back as soon as Knepper delivered his first pitch. Instead, the ball went low and outside as Moreland sprawled in the dirt. From the Astros' dugout came the anguished voice of manager Hal Lanier: "Everyone knew you were supposed to throw at him. Even he knew!"

But Knepper, a left-hander who had made a successful conversion from power pitcher to finesse pitcher, had won seventeen games for Houston in 1986. On a staff of hard throwers who ruled by intimidation, he offered a striking and effective change of pace.

He kept the Mets off-balance for five innings on Saturday, allowing just one runner as far as second base. The Astros, pecking away at New York starter Ron Darling, built up a 4–0 lead.

But Knepper came unraveled in the sixth. Two hits and an error were followed by a homer off the bat of Darryl Strawberry, tying the score.

The Astros regained the lead with a run in the seventh. When the eighth inning began, Knepper retired to the clubhouse to ice down his arm. Astros manager Hal Lanier turned the game over to his bullpen.

The Astros were two outs from victory when Dykstra, only five-feet-eight and 165 pounds, blasted a two-run homer off Houston relief ace Dave Smith. That gave the Mets a dramatic 6–5, come-from-behind victory.

Bob Knepper, dressing quietly after the game, blamed himself for the crushing defeat, for not being able to hold the four-run lead. Dykstra's last-inning homer had capped the New York victory, but it was Strawberry's homer that had turned the game around. Next time, Knepper vowed, he would do better.

◇ It was a homecoming of sorts for Mike Scott. He went onto the field to begin his warm-up throws on Sunday, and looked around the familiar expanse of Shea Stadium.

This had been his first home in major-league baseball. This was where he broke in. It seemed like a lifetime ago.

The stands were already filling up. There would be another sellout, a far cry from the sparse crowds that had turned out when he was a Met, back when the ball club was losing. The New York fans were tough and loud, but when there were 55,000 of them in the stadium, it was just one giant roar. When there were only 5,000, you could hear every insult aimed your way.

Scott remembered the year after he left New York, when Keith Hernandez was traded to the Mets. Scott saw him one day during batting practice and asked how he liked it in New York.

"I hate it," said Hernandez. "First chance I get, I'm out of here."

But that was when the Mets were still near the bottom of the standings. The next year, they started winning and the atmosphere changed completely. Scott ran into Hernandez again, and asked, "Well, how do you like it now?"

"This is the best place in the league," said Hernandez. "You can't beat it."

New York was like that, thought Scott. If you win, there's no better place to be. If you lose, there's no place worse.

Scott finished throwing and walked back to the dugout. He was just getting ready to duck down the steps when he heard a fan call out to him.

"Hey, Scott. You used to suck!"

"Well, thank you."

This was the New York he remembered. Welcome home.

"You won't believe New York."

That's what everybody told Mike Scott back in 1979, when he earned his first promotion to the big leagues.

"Oh, it can't be that bad," he scoffed.

He had spent just three years on a rapid rise through the Mets' minor-league system before winning a spot on the New York roster that spring. It was an exciting time. He was one of the team's top pitching prospects. His career was ready to take off.

He and his wife, Vicki, arrived in New York that April and headed out to Shea Stadium for their first look at the ballpark. They drove their new van. They parked it outside the stadium, looked around and then boarded the team bus for the trip up to West Point for an exhibition game. They figured the van would be safe. After all, it was parked at the ballpark.

The team got back to Shea late that night, and the Scotts went out to look for their van. It was nowhere in sight. Their first day in town, and their van was stolen.

The police found it early the next morning, a burnt-out shell. It had been stripped down and set on fire. There wasn't even a doorknob left screwed in.

"That was our first meeting with New York," says Scott.

It made for a funny story, but at the time it wasn't easy to see the humor. The couple rented a place on Long Island. It was a modest apartment, but after paying the rent they couldn't afford furniture to put in it. They slept on mattresses on the floor, bought a cardboard set of drawers from Kmart and sat on a couple of beach chairs they owned. That was their home.

When Scott got sent back to the minors early in the season, it was almost a relief.

"Boy, at least now we know where we can stay with some decent furniture," he told Vicki.

Scott spent two years bouncing back and forth between the Mets and their Triple A farm club in Tidewater, Virginia. He finally made it up the majors to stay in 1981, but he continued to struggle. He was a fast-ball pitcher without a breaking ball. You couldn't get big-league hitters out on a consistent basis throwing the ball at just one speed.

The Mets liked Scott's arm, but they questioned his toughness. The knock on him was that he lacked the intensity to be a real winner.

"You've got to light a fire under your ass," Mets pitching coach Bill Monbouquette told him.

But that wasn't Scott. He was soft-spoken and undemonstrative. No gestures on the mound, no shouting and punching water coolers in the dugout. He was what he was—calm and reserved on the outside, yet still intense on the inside.

He pitched two full seasons in New York, with mediocre results. The Mets finally gave up on him after the 1982 season and swapped him to Houston for Danny Heep, a part-time outfielder. Scott had one year of modest success in Houston, going 10–5, but then fell to 5–11 in 1984.

But that was the old Mike Scott, the one who struggled to get his breaking ball over the plate in the summer and studied to become a salesman in the winter.

The Mike Scott who showed up to face the Mets in October 1986 was a new man with a new pitch. He was ready to conquer New York.

Game 4 started out much as Game 1 had. Mike Scott set the Mets down without a hit the first time through the batting order, and still had a no-hitter after four innings.

But Scott could tell a difference. He was throwing on only three days' rest, and his arm was not as strong. The first game, he threw a lot of fastballs. On Sunday, he relied more on off-speed pitches.

The Astros got a break in the second inning when Alan Ashby hit a pop fly foul down the left-field line and shortstop Rafael Santana called off Ray Knight, who was about to make the catch. The ball fell untouched into the temporary stands. Given a reprieve, Ashby hit the next pitch into the left-field bullpen for a two-run homer.

In the top of the fifth, Astros shortstop Dickie Thon blasted a homer over the left-field bleachers. Houston led 3–0.

In the bottom of the inning, Ray Knight grounded a single into left field. It was the first hit off Scott, but nothing came of it.

Scott began throwing almost all split-finger fastballs in the sixth. The Mets kept making outs, one after another.

Not a single New York batter asked the umpire to check any of the balls Scott threw. But over in the dugout, the Mets collected the balls that were hit foul and passed them around for inspection. Inevitably, they would find a scuff mark on each ball and would shake their heads in amazement. Later, they would have plenty to say.

In the eighth, an infield hit, a groundout and a sacrifice fly led to the first New York run off Scott. Trailing by only two, the Mets still had a chance.

Scott got the first man out in the ninth, but Lenny Dykstra slapped a single into left field for New York's third hit of the day. Maybe it was going to be another last-inning comeback by the Mets.

Keith Hernandez, always dangerous, was up next. He hit a weak grounder to second for the second out. A grim-faced Gary Carter marched to the plate. He had only one hit in sixteen at-bats during the series. His boundless enthusiasm was being put to the test.

Above the crowd noise, one fan yelled out: "Earn your money, Gary!"

Scott threw another split-finger, and Carter hit an easy fly ball to center for the final out.

Mike Scott had done it again, beating the Mets 3–1 this time. The series was tied at two games each.

Eighteen innings, eight hits, one run, nineteen strikeouts, one walk. That was Scott's pitching line for his two games. No one could be that good. Or could he?

◇ The writers and radio-TV reporters kept coming up to him, one after another, asking the same questions. There were media people from everywhere—New York, Houston, Boston, Los Angeles, Philadelphia, Chicago, and on and on.

The New York writers were especially insistent. They came at him in waves. Scott knew all about them from his time with the Mets.

On those few occasions when he did pitch a good game, he would return to the clubhouse afterward, sit in his chair in front of his locker and wait for them to come around to talk to him. "Great game, Mike. What were you throwing out there?" But it never happened. Then, he would go out and get knocked out in the first inning, and, zoom, there they were pressing around him, demanding to know what happened. It was hard to hold your composure at times like that.

But you learn how to do it. You figure out what to say and what not to say. And you learn to be careful. One slip of the tongue, one misplaced statement, and, boy, it is all over for you in New York. No one can stir up a controversy like those guys.

So, Scott knew how to play the game Monday when he showed up at the ballpark and saw writers all over the clubhouse, looking for something to write about.

Outside, it was raining, and the fifth game of the series had been postponed until Tuesday. With no game to write and talk about, the media had to seize on something else. And Mike Scott and his alleged "scuffballs" gave them plenty of ammunition.

Across the way, the Mets were passing around baseballs with large, brown smudge marks on them as evidence of Scott's alleged scuffing. This activity had gone on Sunday after the game, and it was continuing on Monday.

"I don't believe grass does that, do you?" they would ask, and the writers would scribble down their remarks and the cameramen would zoom in for close-ups of the balls.

And then the writers would come to Scott, asking for his reaction to such charges. Over and over, one reporter after another would ask the same question.

"Whatever the Mets are doing to the baseballs is their business," Scott would tell them.

And then another newspaper writer, or a radio reporter, or whoever, would come up wanting to know the same thing. Scott did the best he could to accommodate them. He knew they all had their stories to write and their reports to file back home.

But several times that day, he wished he could just sneak off into the training room and hide. He wished he could just tell his questioners, "Look, I'm not pitching today. Talk to somebody who's playing."

But Scott kept answering their questions, over and over. It was all very tiresome, but he figured the more this controversy continued, the more it worked to his advantage.

If the Mets went to the plate thinking, "Well, he's doing this, or he's doing that," the better it was for him.

Scott didn't say it at the time, but his advice to the Mets would have been, "Hey, just hit the ball."

Doug Harvey, the veteran umpire, stood behind a microphone and looked out at the crowd of reporters and cameramen before him.

Harvey had been a National League umpire for twenty-five years, and he was widely regarded as one of the best, if not the best, in the business. But he wasn't used to being on center stage like this. Umpires seldom were called into the media interview rooms.

But this was no ordinary championship series. This one seemed to revolve as much around talk of illegal pitches as it did around the plays on the field.

"Gentlemen," said Harvey, "I entered this game of baseball with nothing but my integrity, and I will leave with my integrity. I am here to tell you that I have worked behind the plate six times when Mike Scott has pitched this season, and I've probably checked about sixty-five or seventy of the balls he's thrown, and not a single one has had a mark on it. I'm telling you that he's clean."

Harvey was a neatly dressed, dignified man with silver hair and a reassuring tone of voice and manner.

"Dammit, guys, that ball comes in there hard! And other than the spitter, it's the most explosive pitch I've ever seen.

"But it is clean. And it just seems to me that nobody can accept the possibility that the man has just come up with one hell of a pitch."

Elsewhere in the stadium was a bag of twenty-five baseballs which the New York players had gathered as their evidence of Scott's cheating. All, they said, had been thrown by Scott on Sunday, and all had scuff marks on them.

The balls were presented to National League president Chub Feeney for his inspection. Feeney promised to look into the matter.

"We'll get to the bottom of it before he pitches again," vowed Feeney.

Everyone knew when that would be. Give Scott three days between starts again, and he would be ready to pitch the decisive seventh game. If the series went that far. The feeling among the New York players was that it had better not.

◇ Nolan Ryan went out to pitch Game 5 for the Astros. He was thirty-nine years old, but still threw ninety-five-mile-an-hour fastballs. He still was the Ryan Express, baseball's strikeout king.

Ryan already had more than four thousand career strikeouts and five no-hitters in his career, and when he was finished seven years later he would have 5,714 strikeouts and seven no-hitters.

Ryan also was a tough competitor. He had a sore elbow, and he hurt his ankle running the bases in the fourth inning. But he pitched through the pain, striking out twelve Mets and surrendering just two hits and one run over nine innings.

His counterpart, Doc Gooden, the young "Dr. K," was just as effective. He also gave up only one run, and the game moved into extra innings.

Ryan had gone as far as he could go, so the Astros brought in young Charlie Kerfeld. He retired the first six Mets he faced, but in the twelfth an infield single by Mets second baseman Wally Backman, a wild pickoff throw and an intentional walk put runners on first and second.

Gary Carter stepped to the plate. He had only one hit in twenty-one at-bats in the series—for a miserable .048 batting average—and was

0-for-4 in the fifth game. This time, he lined a single to center field, sending Backman home. The Mets were 2–1 winners. At last, Carter had reason to smile again. He had delivered the winning hit.

The Mets led the series three games to two. One more win, and they wouldn't have to worry about Mike Scott anymore.

◇ Bob Knepper's big day finally arrived on Wednesday. There would be no idle reading at his locker before this game. No singing opera pieces on the ride to the Astrodome with his friend and fellow pitcher Mike Scott. No turning to Scott while driving down the freeway on their way to the ballpark for a game he was to pitch and asking idly, "Who are we playing today?" No more Bob Knepper, the flake. No more Bob Knepper, the quiet, reserved pitcher who kept his emotions inside. No more Bob Knepper, the pitcher accused of fatigue late in the season.

This was judgment day for Knepper. Game 6 of the National League Championship Series. This was the day he proved himself as a tough, winning pitcher, the kind who could be counted on to come through when the pressure was greatest.

The Astros were backed up to the wall, trailing three games to two in the series. They needed a win today to force a seventh game. And if this series went seven games, Mike Scott would get to pitch again against the Mets.

Everyone in both locker rooms knew what that meant. The Mets couldn't beat Scott. The Astros knew it, and the Mets' posturing and protesting over scuffballs seemed to show they knew it, too.

But first the Astros had to force that seventh game. And Bob Knepper wanted to prove he was the man who could do it.

He sat in front of his locker and looked at the pictures of Mike Scott he had taped to the wall. Get the ball to Scotty, Knepper told himself.

Knepper barely noticed when Houston pitching coach Les Moss walked up to him.

"Pitch your game," Moss reminded him. "Forget the bad calls, the odd bad pitch, or the error that might happen behind you. Pitch your game and all of that will take care of itself."

Knepper listened quietly, but he didn't need to be reminded. He knew what he had to do.

He thought about his ten years in the big leagues and all the struggles he had endured. There had been losing seasons, the constant self-analysis and the many battles he had fought with himself to master his pitching mechanics. Most of all, there were the constant barbs aimed at him over his religious beliefs and how they affected his ability to succeed at this level of competition.

Knepper wanted to show he could be both a Christian and a winning pitcher. He felt he had a lot to prove this game, for himself and for other Christian ballplayers.

"Forget being your normal, reserved self," Knepper kept repeating. "Go out there and let it all hang out."

There would be no let downs today, he vowed. This would be Bob Knepper's day of redemption.

It had been a sleepless night for Billy Hatcher. He didn't mind. All he wanted to do was get back out on the field. He was counting the hours, and the minutes, until the start of Game 6.

The Astros had arrived from New York after midnight Tuesday, and Hatcher had tried to get some sleep. All he could think about was the ball game. He finally got up and got dressed to go to the ballpark.

He lived in an apartment a few blocks from the Astrodome, and the place was full of people. Friends and family were in from out of town for the playoffs. They had all come to root for Billy.

Hatcher wasn't used to the company. He liked to guard his privacy, and in the off-season he moved from place to place in his hometown of Williams, Arizona, to keep people from knowing where he could be found.

Too many people came around wanting things from him. So Billy liked to hang out where there was no phone and no way to be tracked down. Only his family knew where he was. And if someone else located him, then Billy moved on.

One day the previous winter, his solitude had been interrupted by a knock on the door at a trailer home outside town. Hatcher went to the door, and there was his brother bursting with news. You've been traded, he told Billy. The Cubs traded you to Houston.

Hatcher was stunned. He had come up through the Cubs organization, and he always thought he would be playing the outfield at Wrigley Field. And out of the blue, the Cubs had gotten rid of him.

He didn't know what to think. Had he done something wrong, he wondered.

It turned out to be the best thing that could have happened to him. The Cubs already had their outfield filled. Hatcher never would have played there. But the Astros needed a center fielder and a base stealer. Hatcher fit the bill.

He turned in a solid season, batting a respectable .258 and stealing thirty-eight bases while batting second, behind Bill Doran. He was fast enough to cover the massive expanse of territory in center field in the cavernous Astrodome.

Now, here he was in his first full season in the major leagues, and he had a chance to go to the World Series.

When it finally came time to leave for the Astrodome, several of Hatcher's houseguests decided they would stay at his apartment to watch the game on television rather than fight the crowd at the ballpark.

We'll be looking for you, they told him.

◇ Ground ball. Fly out. Pop-up. Three quick outs, and Bob Knepper ran off the mound with his fists clenched. Take that, Mets. One inning down, eight to go.

The Astros immediately began pecking away at Mets starter Bob Ojeda. It was a typical Houston rally. Single. Fielder's choice. Double. Single. Walk. Bloop single. Three runs crossed the plate, one at a time.

The Astros could have had more, but Alan Ashby missed the ball on a squeeze bunt, and Kevin Bass was hung up between third and home.

It didn't seem to matter at the time. Houston led 3–0, and Knepper returned to work.

One, two, three, the Mets went down in the second. And on it went, through three innings, then five, and on into the eighth. Knepper kept the Mets off-balance with his assortment of curveballs, change-ups and occasional fastballs, never giving the batter the pitch he was expecting.

And each inning, he ran off the mound, shouting and gesturing, while the crowd roared its approval. He punched his fist in the air to mark each out. He was pitching the game of his life.

The Astros were unable to add to their lead, but that had been their style all year. Scratch out a few runs, then rely on their pitching and defense to make them stand up.

The excitement and the noise in the Astrodome grew as the game entered the eighth. Ray Knight led off for the Mets. Knepper threw him an off-speed pitch, and Knight hit a harmless grounder. One out. Knepper shook his fist.

Tim Teufel rapped a single into center field, and the crowd stirred nervously. Knepper shouted for the ball. He stared in at the batter, Rafael Santana, then delivered another curve. Santana bounced the ball up the middle, but shortstop Dickie Thon was there to scoop it up, step on second for the force-out and throw to first to complete the double play.

Knepper leaped off the mound and ran toward the dugout as the crowd stood and cheered. He had pitched eight brilliant innings, allowing only two hits and no runs. One more inning, and the series would be tied.

"Scotty tomorrow! Scotty tomorrow!" the Houston players kept saying to one another as they came off the field.

The Astros went down one, two, three in their half of the eighth, but it didn't seem to matter. The fans rose to their feet cheering as the Houston players ran back onto the field for the final inning.

The reserves in the Astros dugout lined up along the railing, swept up in the excitement of the moment. Mike Scott felt his heart racing as he watched the drama and thought ahead to tomorrow.

"It's really happening," he thought. "We can do it. Three more outs, and they're going to be able to give me the ball tomorrow."

Pitch-hitter Lenny Dykstra led off for the Mets. Knepper got ahead of him one ball, two strikes. Dykstra drove the next pitch into center field, just out of Billy Hatcher's reach. The ball rolled all the way to the wall for a triple.

That brought up Mookie Wilson. Knepper threw two quick strikes past him. One more and he would have him. Knepper tried to slip a pitch just out of the strike zone, but Wilson lined the ball into right field, just out of the reach of a leaping Bill Doran. Base hit. Dykstra scored, and the Mets had their first run.

Kevin Mitchell grounded to third base for the first out. Two more to go. That brought up Keith Hernandez. He hit a shot into right center for a double, scoring Wilson. Suddenly, the Astros' lead was only 3–2.

That was it for Bob Knepper. He left the game to a standing ovation, while Dave Smith came on to protect the lead.

Knepper couldn't believe what had happened. Eight great innings, and then he fell apart. His masterpiece was ruined. He stood at the front of the dugout, his arms resting on the railing and his hands clasped, as if he were praying. He remained there the rest of the game, watching in a dazed silence.

Nothing seemed to go right for Dave Smith. He thrived on these situations, as his record showed. Thirty-three saves, a 2.73 earned-run average. Smith, free spirit and California surfer, was at his best with runners on base and the game on the line.

He ran the count to two balls, two strikes on the first batter he faced, Gary Carter. The next pitch caught the outside corner. Or so Smith thought. Fred Brocklander, the home-plate umpire, called it ball three. Smith angrily stomped around the mound. He threw two more balls to walk Carter.

The next batter, Darryl Strawberry, also walked on a full-count pitch. The bases were loaded, with only one out.

Smith threw a strike past Ray Knight on the outside corner of the plate. Knight griped to Brocklander about the call. Knight fouled off a pitch, and the count went to one-and-two. Smith decided to go back to the same location. He fired another fastball over the outside part of the plate. Strike three, he thought. Ball, called out Brocklander.

Smith came off the mound yelling at the umpire. Manager Hal Lanier ran out of the dugout to join the protest. Catcher Alan Ashby voiced his frustration.

"Stop umpiring!" Knight shouted at Ashby.

That brought Dickie Thon in from shortstop, yelling and pointing at Knight.

Finally, everyone returned to their places, the nerves on both sides still stretched thin. Knight fouled off a pitch, then drove a fly ball to Kevin Bass in right field. It was just deep enough to score Hernandez with the tying run.

When he finally got the third out, Smith stomped off the mound, yelling at Brocklander.

The 3–3 tie held up into the tenth, then the eleventh, without either team getting a base runner. The fans were on their feet, screaming on every pitch.

The twelfth inning passed with no scoring. Both sides went out in order in the thirteenth.

The standoff finally ended in the fourteenth. Aurelio Lopez was in to pitch for Houston. A single and a walk put New York runners on first and second to start the inning. One out later, Wally Backman lined a single to right to score Darryl Strawberry with the tie-breaking run.

It looked like the Astros were finished. They were down 4–3, and they hadn't scored a run in the past twelve innings.

Jesse Orosco, the Mets' relief ace, went out to nail it down in the bottom of the fourteenth. He struck out Bill Doran for the first out.

Billy Hatcher stepped to the plate. He had hit only six home runs all year, but he decided he would go for one here. What did he have to lose, he figured.

Orosco's first pitch was a fastball, and Hatcher drove the ball into the left-field stands, just foul. That brought the crowd back to life. Hatcher had come within inches of tying the game.

The count went to three-and-two, and Orosco fired another fastball to the plate. Same pitch, same location. Again, Hatcher put everything into his swing. He drove the ball high and deep to left field.

"Stay fair! Stay fair!" he yelled as the ball hugged the foul line.

This time, the ball hit high off the net marking the fair side of the foul pole. It was a home run. The noise in the Astrodome was deafening.

"We're going to win it! We're going to win it!" Hatcher kept repeating as he ran around the bases, his ears ringing. At that moment, he felt like he was the happiest man in the world.

The game was tied again, 4–4.

The two teams struggled into the sixteenth inning, longer than any two teams had ever played in postseason competition. Every pitch, every play was crucial.

Darryl Strawberry led off with a pop fly into shallow center. It fell just in front of Hatcher, who had been playing deep. Strawberry ended up on second.

Ray Knight was the next hitter, but before stepping into the box he went back to the dugout to check with manager Davey Johnson.

"Do you want me to bunt him along?"

"Hell, no," answered Johnson. "Drive it to right and get him home."

Knight followed his orders. He lined a fastball into right field for a base hit, and Strawberry scored standing up.

The Mets were back on top, 5–4, but they didn't let up. A wild pitch, a walk and another wild pitch scored the second run of the inning. One out later, Lenny Dykstra singled in another run.

It was 7–4. The three runs might as well have been a dozen, given Houston's lack of offensive firepower. It looked like the Astros were out of comebacks.

It was quiet in the Houston dugout. It got quieter when Craig Reynolds struck out to lead off the bottom of the inning.

Then came a walk to Davey Lopes and a stirring in the stands. Bill Doran banged out a single, and the stadium began to come alive with noise again. Billy Hatcher was back up. Could he do it again?

Orosco fidgeted on the mound. No more fastballs to Hatcher. Whatever else happened, Orosco had to keep the ball in the park.

He threw Hatcher an off-speed pitch. Hatcher lined it into left center. Another base hit. A run scored. It was 7–5, and there were runners on first and second. The stadium was rocking. Another comeback was in the works.

Orosco settled down to get Denny Walling on a grounder to Keith Hernandez for a force-out at second. Two down, runners on first and third. Only one more out to go.

Glenn Davis walked to the plate, praying he wouldn't be the one to make that final out. At third base, Knight prayed Davis wouldn't hit the ball out of the park.

Orosco threw another fastball, and Davis lined it softly over second base for another single. Doran scored from third, and Walling went to second. The Astros were still alive. It was 7–6, and there were runners on first and second.

The anxious New York infielders gathered around their pitcher. Gary Carter came out from behind the plate to join the conference.

"If you call another fastball," Keith Hernandez yelled at the catcher, "I'll kill you."

"No kidding," said Carter.

Orosco would throw only sliders the rest of the way.

Kevin Bass, another tough hitter, was up. Orosco threw him a slider, and he swung and missed. Strike one. Another swing and a miss. Strike two. The next pitch was a ball. Then another ball. The fans and players on both teams were hanging on every pitch. Another close pitch, ball three. The count was full.

Bass dug in, his fists squeezing the bat. Orosco threw one more breaking pitch, this one down and in. Bass swung, as hard as he could. He got nothing but air. Strike three. The ball game was over. The Mets had won, 7–6, for the National League title.

Orosco hurled his glove high in the air and sank to the ground in relief. Bass turned in anger and disappointment and thought about throwing his bat into the stands. Instead, he walked off. In the dugout, the Houston players stood and watched, unable to move. The fans were stunned for a moment, then began to applaud both teams. Win or lose, it had been a great game—some would say the greatest game ever played.

◇ Billy Hatcher sat in a chair in front of his dressing cubicle and stared at the pile of shoes in his locker. Earlier, when he had hit that home run in the fourteenth inning, he had been overcome with happiness. Now, in the wake of the Houston defeat, he felt like crying.

He barely noticed as Kevin Bass walked over and sat down next to him.

"Glad you were the one to hit that ball, Hatch."

Hatcher kept looking at the shoes. "What am I going to do with all this crap?"

He looked up, and he saw the writers and cameramen mingling among the players in the clubhouse. They would be over to talk to him, wanting to know what pitch he had hit for his homer, how he felt now, asking all the many questions that had to be asked. He didn't really feel like talking, not at a time like this.

"I feel, I feel like . . . I feel like I should just go into a room by myself, shut the door, drink two or three beers and pass out."

Bass understood. He felt the same way. He got up to leave and put his hand on his friend's shoulder.

"No use worrying about it no more," he told Hatcher.

Bob Knepper fought to hold back the tears. He had failed. He was going to pitch the game of his life, and for eight innings he had done so. Then, he had let it get away. The sense of failure and disappointment was overwhelming.

He replayed every pitch of the ninth inning in his mind. He had come so close. An inch here, a fraction of an inch there, and maybe things would have turned out differently.

"I never wanted to win a ball game so bad in my life," Knepper mumbled.

The pictures of Mike Scott stared back at him from his locker walls. It had been Knepper's job to get the Astros to Game 7 and Mike Scott, but he never got them there. Knepper shut his eyes and thought about the days to come.

"God, it's going to be a long winter," he said.

It was over. Mike Scott couldn't believe it. He stood in the locker room, numb, not knowing what to think or say. The playoffs were over. The Astros had lost. There would be no World Series.

It was strange, but he had never thought about the season ending, not when the Astros fell behind by a run in the fourteenth, not even when they were three down in the sixteenth. It wasn't until Kevin Bass struck out that it finally hit him. No game tomorrow. It was time to pack the bags and go home. It hadn't even crossed his mind before.

There were reporters and cameramen crowded around him, and he heard someone ask him about his award. He had been voted the Most Valuable Player of the National League Championship Series. Imagine that. All the great players involved in this series, and Scott had been singled out for the honor. Maybe he should have been more excited about it, but he wasn't. Not after a loss like this one.

"I guess I'll enjoy it more in a couple of years or a couple of months," Scott told the writers. "It's hard to celebrate right now."

He thought about packing his bags and going home tomorrow. Not to Arizona, but to California. He had finally bought his house in southern California, the one he had dreamed about for years. That was some consolation.

Scotty tomorrow. That had been the Astros' rallying cry throughout the day. But there would be no game tomorrow. There would be no chance to find out if Mike Scott could shut down the great New York Mets for a third time.

No one in the Houston clubhouse had the slightest doubt that he would have. Not the way Scott was pitching, and not the way the Mets had built him up in their minds. The New York players admitted as much in the victorious clubhouse.

"I feel like I've been pardoned," said manager Davey Johnson. "I really don't want to see Scott again until next April."

"We didn't want it to go seven. We didn't want to face Mike Scott," echoed Gary Carter.

Scott listened impassively as the comments were relayed to him.

"Who knows?" he responded. "We might have won ten-to-nothing or lost ten-to-nothing. We'll never know."

Scott spoke from experience. He had learned a lot in the past two years. You can't take anything for granted, not in baseball and not in life. That was important to remember. You never know what tomorrow holds.

3

THE ONE THAT GOT AWAY

Is this what I'm going to be remembered for? Is this what I've killed myself for all these years? Is a whole season ruined because of a bad hop?

—BILL BUCKNER

Two shoes. Both black, both high-topped. They didn't look like baseball shoes, but that is what they were.

Bill Buckner held them up for inspection. They were odd-looking, but he liked them. He liked the way they felt, and he liked the way they were designed. Most of all, he liked what they could do for him.

They had arrived the night before by rush order. Buckner had been excited to get them. You didn't think about baseball shoes being as important to a ballplayer as his bat or his glove, but for Buckner they were. Without these shoes, he might not be able to play against the New York Mets. Bill Buckner's World Series hopes rode on these shoes.

He slipped the right shoe on, and felt it wrap around his Achilles tendon, the one he had injured two nights earlier in the victory over California in Game 7 of the American League Championship Series. Buckner had been running out an infield hit, going full blast down the first-base line, the way he always did, when he felt the tendon pop. It had scared him. The tendon had been sore for a couple of years, but this was something different. He limped out of the game—and when

69

hard-nosed Billy Buck, the man with the incredible pain threshold, came out of the game, you knew it was serious.

He stood up and looked down at his new shoes. Black high-topped orthopedic shoes. Just his style.

Buck went outside in the early-morning darkness to test them out. It was five-thirty on Friday morning, one day before the World Series was to start. Thirty-eight hours before the first pitch between the Boston Red Sox and the New York Mets. That didn't leave much time for healing. For all practical purposes, Buckner had been scratched from the Game 1 lineup for the Red Sox. But no one who knew Billy Buck was counting him out yet.

He tried running in his new special-delivery shoes. He put his weight down on his right foot, to see if the injured Achilles tendon could stand the strain. Amazingly, it did. The new shoe, with its special support, worked! That was not to say there was no discomfort; but his right foot had no more pain in it than did his left, and Bill Buckner had played through ten years of grinding pain in that foot.

Buckner continued his run, like a kid trying out a new toy on Christmas. Normally, he hated to run. "I'd rather clean up dog biscuits than run," he liked to say. But this morning was different. The more he ran, the more convinced he was his Achilles tendon would hold up. He knew then that he was going to play on Saturday. They would have to drag him off the field to keep him out of the Boston lineup.

Later that Friday, Buckner showed up at New York's Shea Stadium for a workout by the Red Sox. He hobbled onto the field in his custom-made footwear and joked about his new look.

"It may become a trend," Buck said, showing off his new shoes. "Everyone may be wearing them by next year."

He stepped into the batting cage and began rattling line drives off the outfield walls. He stood there in his high-top shoes, waving his black bat and glaring out from behind his thick, black mustache, and hit one shot after another.

Billy Buck could hit, bad legs or not. New shoes, old shoes, high-top shoes, low-cut shoes, no shoes, it was all the same. Strained Achilles tendon, bad ankle, sore feet, standing on one leg, it didn't matter. Just prop Buckner up at the plate, and he could hit a line drive.

Buck finished batting practice and picked up his glove to field some grounders down at first base. There were writers all over the place.

Are you going to be able to play Saturday? they wanted to know.

"For me not to play, you'd have to get a gun and shoot me." Buckner laughed. He was in an upbeat mood. "And they might just do that here, too."

Someone pointed to his new shoes. Are you going to play in the high-tops, he wanted to know.

"I may even sleep in them," answered Buckner.

Bill Buckner and his orthopedic shoes. Not since Shoeless Joe Jackson would a baseball player become so identified with his footwear.

It started with a bucket of ice. Bill Buckner set it down in front of his dressing cubicle and placed his feet in it. The pregame routine had begun.

It was midday, Saturday, October 18, 1986. Game 1 of the World Series, Boston versus New York, would be played that night.

Buckner, the old warrior, was getting his body ready. It wasn't as easy as it used to be. "Until I get loose, I hobble around out there like I'm one hundred years old," he had said on more than one occasion.

He sat there soaking his ankles, a routine he followed daily throughout the baseball season. Ten years, hundreds of games and countless hours spent with his feet encased in ice. It was just a small part of what he went through to play baseball.

A timer went off, and Buckner took his feet out of the ice. An hour had passed. One hour before the game, and one hour after the game. That was the routine.

He made his way into the training room, walking gingerly on the left ankle, the one he had injured as a young ballplayer more than a decade earlier. He had caught his foot under second base on a slide, flipping him over and twisting the ankle underneath him. He came back and played too soon and never really recovered. He had surgery to remove a tendon from the ankle, and later doctors removed bone chips. A staph infection set in, and the joint never completely healed.

Buckner had seen X rays of the ankle. There was supposed to be about an eighth of an inch of separation between the bones. For him, it was virtually bone grinding against bone in there.

He had read about plastic ankles and ankle fusions. Maybe someday that is what it would come to. But not now. Not while he could still play baseball.

Buckner eased into the whirlpool. After that would come ultrasound treatment on his legs, followed by a rubdown.

Buck's day was just beginning. He didn't mind. All the hours soaking and mending, the many stretching exercises and the uncounted miles pedaled on the stationary exercise bike were a small sacrifice to make.

What Buckner didn't like were the shots and the drugs. He took numerous cortisone shots throughout the season for sore or swollen joints and muscles. He had taken nine such shots in 1986 alone. And they were painful shots, injected right into the area that was ailing.

Even worse was the anti-inflammatory medication. Two pills a day for ten years now. Buckner knew that wasn't good for him. There would be a price to pay somewhere down the line. But that was a decision he had made, and he was willing to live with it.

Other ballplayers had quit the game rather than risk long-term health problems. Not Buckner. He wanted to squeeze every at-bat out of his career. He didn't want to look back ten, twenty years from now and wonder what else he might have accomplished.

Billy Buck was quite a ballplayer. He was thirty-six years old and still going strong, bad legs and all. He was a batting champion and seven-time .300 hitter. Three times, he had driven in more than a hundred runs in a season. He had scored more than a thousand runs. He had even stolen 175 bases.

And Buck was just thirty-six hits short of twenty-five hundred for his career. He had an outside shot at three thousand. It was a goal of his. That would put him up there with the greats of the game, the Cobbs and Musials and Roses.

Not bad for a guy playing on one leg.

Buckner began wrapping himself in tape. Yards and yards of tape. Buckner wore so much tape he liked to say he looked like the Invisible Man out for a walk.

He got up and made his way across the locker room. By now, he had ice bags taped to his left ankle, right Achilles tendon, lower back, one elbow and one shoulder.

Red Sox manager John McNamara saw him coming. To McNamara, Buckner looked like a rodeo cowboy, limping to his pickup truck to throw his saddle in the back and drive off down the road to the next rodeo.

When Buckner hurt his Achilles tendon against the Angels, the early prognosis had been that he would be out of action for as much as a week. At best, the Red Sox hoped to have him back for Game 3 in Boston. With that in mind, McNamara had planned to move Don Baylor, the team's designated hitter, to first base for the first two games in New York. National League rules would be employed there, and the DH would not be allowed. Putting a healthy Baylor at first would keep his bat in the lineup and give Buckner time to mend.

But Buckner wanted no part of that. He wanted to play. He demanded to play.

I'm ready, he told McNamara on Saturday.

So, McNamara did what any manager would do: put Buckner at first base. If he said he could play, he could play. McNamara wrote his name in the lineup, batting third and playing first base.

That evening, Buckner stood in the dugout in his high-top shoes. Shea Stadium rocked with noise and anticipation as the pregame ceremonies began. Buckner soaked up the atmosphere.

It had been twelve years since his last World Series. It seemed like a lifetime ago.

Back then, Bill Buckner was a speedy young outfielder out to conquer the world. He batted .314 for the Los Angeles Dodgers in 1974, and was one of the cornerstones of what was shaping up to be the most formidable ball club in the National League. These were the Dodgers of Steve Garvey, Davey Lopes, Bill Russell, Ron Cey, Tommy John, Don Sutton. And Bill Buckner.

They lost the Series to the Oakland Athletics, but everyone knew there would be more pennants and more World Series games to follow. What Buckner didn't count on was tearing up his ankle. What he couldn't foresee was being discarded as damaged goods, swapped to the lowly Chicago Cubs to play out his career in pain, battling the drudgery of one losing season after another. It wasn't until the Cubs shipped him to Boston that he finally got to play on a winner again. The long wait made it all the more special.

Buckner listened as they introduced the ballplayers. His name was called and he shuffled awkwardly onto the field in his black high-top shoes. He stood there on his two bad feet as the introductions were completed and the national anthemn played.

Billy Buck had courage. You had to admire a man like that.

◇ The cold cut through Shea Stadium. Temperatures were in the low fifties, and there was a stiff nine-mile-per-hour breeze from the northeast. The conditions seemed more suited for football than baseball.

It was past eight o'clock when New York's Ron Darling finally delivered the first pitch of the 1986 World Series. Television was responsible for the late start. The money it paid to televise the games enabled it to dictate starting times. First had come nighttime starts for weekday games. The year before, 1985, even the weekend games had been played at night.

No one on the field was complaining. Players on both sides were glad to be here, still playing ball this late in the year.

The game began as a pitchers' duel. First, Darling would set down the Red Sox. Then, his Boston counterpart, left-hander Bruce Hurst, would dispose of the Mets hitters.

Groundout. Single. Double play. The Red Sox were gone in the first.

Strikeout. Strikeout. Fly out. The Mets followed suit in the bottom of the inning.

For six innings, the game followed this pattern. Darling struck out four Red Sox batters in a row in the third and fourth innings. Hurst pitched out of trouble in the third, fourth and sixth innings.

The tie was finally broken in the seventh, when a ground ball skipped under the glove of Mets second baseman Tim Teufel, allowing Jim Rice to score from second. It was a cheap run, but Boston led 1–0.

It stayed that way into the eighth. Bill Buckner limped into the dugout to await his turn at bat for the Red Sox. He was having trouble covering ground at first base. He went over to talk to manager John McNamara and second baseman Marty Barrett about it.

"Well, what do you think?" he asked. "Should I stay in or should Stape come in?"

Nearby was Dave Stapleton, the backup first baseman. He had been Buckner's late-inning defensive replacement in all four wins over California in the American League playoffs. Stapleton, a former second baseman and shortstop, was healthy and could cover more ground than Buckner.

For Barrett, the answer was simple.

"Well, we're up, and Stapes can make the plays you can't make."

That was all it took. Buckner grounded out to end the inning, and retired for the evening. Stapleton, the defensive specialist, would take over at first base to shore up the Boston defense.

The bottom of the eighth started, and Dave Stapleton ran out to first base. Just being on the field was a personal triumph. He had been a rookie sensation in Boston in 1980, batting over .300 and finishing second in the voting for the league's Rookie of the Year award. He moved from second base to shortstop to first base, where he was the starter until he tore up his knee so badly in 1984 it looked like his career was over. But Stapleton came back. He had to take a backseat to Bill Buckner when he did, but after a long, hard struggle he was playing again. And now he was in the World Series.

It was a one-run game, leaving no margin for an error or misplay. Strangely, Stapleton didn't feel as nervous out on the field as he had in the dugout watching. He was too busy playing ball to think about it.

It was another one-two-three inning for Hurst. Three fly balls, three outs. Stapleton never touched the ball at first base.

He would have to wait to get his baptism by fire.

The bullpen phone rang. Calvin Schiraldi knew what it meant. He was going into the game.

What a spot to be in, thought Schiraldi. A one-run lead in the ninth inning of the first game of the World Series. And he was taking over for a pitcher who had thrown eight shutout innings.

That showed how much faith John McNamara had in him. When Bruce Hurst had been due to bat with the bases loaded and two outs in the top of the ninth, McNamara had pulled him for a pinch hitter. The Boston manager hadn't wanted to pass up the opportunity to pad his lead. With Schiraldi as his "stopper," he had been able to make that move.

Schiraldi, a six-foot-four Texan, had come by such an important and high-profile job in a roundabout way. He had been a starting pitcher all his life, from his days as the ace of a University of Texas staff that also included Roger Clemens to his rapid rise through the New York Mets farm system. But then Schiraldi stumbled in his early trials with the Mets, and he was swapped to Boston for pitcher Bob Ojeda in a multi-player deal prior to the 1986 season.

Schiraldi showed up at spring training for the Red Sox with a sore arm and was sent to the minors to regain his strength. There, he was made into a relief pitcher, and after regaining his fastball he thrived in the role. A midseason promotion to the Red Sox followed, and every time the team had called on him he responded with one or two strong innings.

Eventually, Schiraldi moved into the closer's role, with phenomenal results. In one stretch through August and September, when the Red Sox were battling for the division title and the games counted most, Schiraldi appeared in seventeen games, saving nine of them and winning four others. All told, he pitched fifty-one and one-third innings and gave up only eight runs.

Calvin Schiraldi, only twenty-four, looked to be as big a prize in Boston as his Texas counterpart, Roger Clemens.

Out on the field, rookie Mike Greenwell lofted a fly ball to Lenny Dykstra in right center. The Red Sox had failed to score. McNamara's gamble hadn't paid off.

Schiraldi walked to the mound to pitch the bottom of the ninth. He didn't mind admitting he was scared to death. A 1–0 lead, bottom of the ninth and the Shea Stadium fans cheering for another of the Mets' many last-ditch rallies. This was no place for the fainthearted.

Schiraldi walked Darryl Strawberry to start the inning. The tying run was on base. The next batter was Ray Knight. He tried to advance the runner, pushing a bunt to the right side of the infield.

It wasn't a bad bunt, but Dave Stapleton pounced on the ball quickly and threw to second a split second ahead of the sliding Strawberry for a force-out. Bill Buckner wouldn't have been able to make that play. Dave Stapleton did.

A fly out and a strikeout ended the game. The Red Sox won 1–0.

Schiraldi, the young relief pitcher from Texas, had gotten a save in his first World Series appearance. Dave Stapleton, the backup first baseman, deserved one, too.

◇ Roger Clemens versus Dwight Gooden. The Rocket against Dr. K. A rematch of the starting pitchers in the All-Star Game. Game 2 on Sunday night figured to be another low-scoring affair.

It didn't stay that way for long. In the top of the third, the Red Sox scored three runs, the last on a sharp single to right by Bill Buckner.

Buck felt good when he went out for the bottom of the third. His movement was still restricted by his two bad ankles, but he was swinging the bat well. Maybe he was about to break out on another of his many batting tears.

The Mets got their first hitter on base, bringing up pitcher Dwight Gooden. He tried to bunt the ball, but instead popped it in the air toward first base.

Buckner scrambled forward, pushing himself on his two bad ankles, trying desperately to get to the ball in time to make the catch. At the last second, he lunged forward in a headfirst dive, his glove extended. The ball landed just out of his reach. All hands were safe. Billy Buck got up and shuffled back to first in his high-top shoes. The Mets went on to score two runs, cutting the Red Sox lead to one.

Dave Henderson led off the fourth inning with a home run off Gooden. Three innings later, Henderson added a run-scoring single as the Red Sox built up an 8–3 lead.

Since his dramatic two-out, two-strike, ninth-inning homer in the fifth game of the AL playoffs one week earlier, Henderson had become a hero in Boston. When he hit that home run, the Red Sox became a team of destiny. Now, he was adding to his heroics.

Bob Stanley went in to pitch the seventh inning for Boston. Stanley had spent a lifetime waiting for this moment. The World Series. Except for the birth of his three kids, it was the greatest thrill he had ever experienced.

Stanley had once been a favorite in Boston, but the past two seasons had been tough ones for him. He suffered through some injuries, he blew some leads and the fans turned on him.

He gave up singles to Lenny Dykstra and Wally Backman to start the inning.

"Here we go again," he muttered to himself.

The heart of the Mets' batting order was up: Keith Hernandez, Gary Carter, Darryl Strawberry. The fans were in an uproar. Boston's five-run lead no longer looked so safe.

The count went to one ball, two strikes on Hernandez. Stanley came back with a sinkerball. It was his bread-and-butter pitch, the one that had kept him in the big leagues for ten years. The ball got to the plate and dropped straight down, as if it had fallen off a table. Hernandez swung and missed. Strike three. One out.

Carter stepped in. Stanley gave him nothing but strikes. Three pitches, three misses. Another strikeout. Darryl Strawberry followed with a groundout. Side retired. Stanley was out of the inning.

The Mets went out in order in the eighth. Fly out. Groundout. Strikeout. That made six outs in a row for Stanley.

The Red Sox upped the lead to six runs in their half of the ninth. Henderson started things with a single, his fifth hit in nine at-bats in the Series. Wade Boggs drove him home with a double.

Stanley went back out to pitch the bottom of the ninth. Mookie Wilson flied out. Seven in a row. Stanley's streak was snapped when he walked Dykstra on four pitches. It didn't matter. Backman grounded out to Dave Stapleton, who had replaced Buckner at first base. Two down.

Stanley faced Hernandez for the second time. The Mets' first baseman drove a fly ball deep to center field. Stanley turned to see Dave Henderson glide back to the warning track, where he made the catch for the final out of a 9–3 Boston victory.

◇ All of New England was alive with excitement as Game 3 arrived Tuesday night. The Sox had won two in a row on the road to open the World Series. It was an incredible achievement. They came home with a chance to win the title in their own ballpark. They would have three tries to win two games.

The mood changed quickly. Oil Can Boyd started for the Red Sox. The third pitch he threw was drilled into the right-field stands by Mets leadoff batter Lenny Dykstra for a home run.

The next two batters singled, and Gary Carter drove them home with a double off the left-field wall. A botched rundown and a single produced another run. The Mets led 4–0 before the Red Sox even batted.

Still, Boston hung in there. The Red Sox trailed only 4–1 after six, and on several occasions had Mets starter Ron Darling in trouble. It wasn't too late for a comeback.

But in the seventh, Carter singled home two more runs, breaking Boston's back. The Mets went on to a lopsided 7–1 victory.

Carter continued the onslaught in Game 4 on Wednesday. He broke a scoreless tie with a towering shot that landed in the screen above the left-field wall. In the eighth, he drove a ball over the screen. Two home runs in one night. This was the Gary Carter who had terrorized National League pitching all summer.

The homer was the finishing touch on a 6–2 victory by the Mets. The Series was tied at two games each.

◇ Boston was damp and cloudy for Game 5 on Thursday night. This was the pivotal game. The winner here would be one victory from the title. Eight months of hard work, hundreds of hours of practice and thousands of miles of travel, and it was all coming down to these next two, maybe three, games.

Bruce Hurst opened on the mound for the Red Sox. Manager John McNamara had maneuvered his pitching brilliantly, setting it up for Hurst and Roger Clemens to pitch these next two games with four full days of rest. Everything was falling into place as planned.

The Red Sox led 1–0 in the second inning when Bill Buckner reached base on an error and went to second on a walk. There were two outs. The next batter, Dwight Evans, lined a hit into center field, sending Buckner running for home on his bad legs. He barely made it, throwing himself across the plate in a belly slide just ahead of the throw.

Buckner no longer could move like he used to, but his charge to the plate symbolized the all-out Boston effort. Two innings later, the Red Sox drove Dwight Gooden from the mound with two more runs.

It was 4–1 in the ninth when Dave Stapleton went out to play first base. Stapleton had a perfect record in postseason play: This was the seventh time he had taken over for Buckner in the late innings. So far, the Red Sox had won every game he had played.

The first two batters went out, but then the Mets staged another rally. A double and a single drove home one run. Finally, Hurst struck out Lenny Dykstra to end the game.

The Red Sox had their victory. Only one more and they would be world champs. But the Mets hadn't gone down easily, not even with two out and no one on in the ninth. They had fought back. You had to give them credit for that.

◇ Sixty-eight years without a World Series title. The long wait was coming to an end for the Boston Red Sox.

They gathered in the visitors' clubhouse at Shea Stadium on Saturday, ready for the clincher. One more victory. That was all they needed. One more victory and all of New England would celebrate. The Sox hadn't won the Series since 1918, back when a young Babe Ruth played left field and pitched for the Sox, before he went to New York and began belting home runs in record numbers.

From Babe Ruth to Bruce Hurst and Roger Clemens. From Harry Hooper to Dwight Evans, Stuffy McInnis to Bill Buckner, Everett Scott to Spike Owen. From baggy wool pants to bright, snug uniforms. From the Dead Ball Era to the TV Era. Seven decades. It had been a long time.

There was a quiet confidence in the room. These Sox had knocked down every obstacle in their way. They were written off in the spring as too old and too slow. Not enough pitching, said the critics. When a midseason slump threatened their perch at the top of the American League East standings, they were branded as chokers. "Poised for another El Foldo?" read the headline in one national magazine. When they fought their way down the final weeks and days of the pennant race, they were hounded by reminders of past Boston failures. The negativity and sense of doom was overwhelming.

But these Sox never choked. They never folded. Don't blame us for past failures, they raged. This wasn't Johnny Pesky holding the ball while Enos Slaughter scored the decisive run to beat Boston in the 1946 World Series. This wasn't Mike Torrez giving up a cheap homer to Bucky Dent to blow the 1978 playoffs to the Yankees. These weren't the overpaid, underproductive Sox of past years.

They had prevailed in a tough race to win their division title. They had picked themselves off the deck to beat the California Angels in a dramatic league championship series. And now they were on the verge of winning the World Series.

These Sox didn't pay attention to history. Not yet, anyway.

Bill Buckner finished tying his black high-top shoes. He was taped up and iced down. He was ready to go.

The feet felt better, he thought. He had almost improved to the point to where he was limping normally.

Buck went outside for the pregame drills. The field was crawling with reporters and cameramen. The World Series atmosphere was a madhouse.

The writers weren't allowed on the playing field, but it was hard to tell it by the condition of the Shea Stadium infield. It was bumpy. It had holes in it. On a field like this, you never could tell where a ball might bounce. "It looks like a grenade went off out there" is how Bruce Hurst described it.

Buckner knew all about Shea Stadium. He had played fifteen years in the National League before joining the Red Sox. This was familiar terrain.

It wasn't one of his favorite stadiums. The wind could be brutal here. Buck remembered his rookie year with the Dodgers, when the team arrived in New York and was unable to play that night's game because a hurricane had blown through. With no game on tap, Buck went out drinking that night. He didn't get in until six the next morning. Two and a half hours later, he was roused out of bed by the traveling secretary, who informed him there would be a doubleheader that day. Buckner, hung over, had to face fastballers Nolan Ryan and Tom Seaver. He almost died afterward.

Maybe Shea Stadium would hold fonder memories after tonight. Maybe it would be the place where Billy Buck won a World Series championship ring.

He went out to first base to field some grounders. He scooped up the balls, one after another. Buck didn't have the range he once did, but he was as sure-handed as ever. Hadn't he set a major-league record with his 184 assists in 1985? That was his second record, breaking the mark of 161 he had set three years earlier.

Buckner was producing the same steady results in the World Series. He had handled forty-five chances in five games against the Mets and hadn't made a single error.

That was Bill Buckner. Just call him Mister Dependable.

◇ The Red Sox started the game with a bang, scoring once in the first. They added another run in the second and had two runners on with two outs. Another hit might break open the game. The batter was Bill Buckner.

He drove the ball deep to right field, high into the night air. It looked like it had a chance to go out, but Darryl Strawberry reached up and caught it just short of the fence. A long out, that was all.

Still, the way Roger Clemens was pitching, the two-run lead looked imposing. He struck out six batters in the first three innings and shut out the Mets through four.

Buckner batted again in the fifth. Another runner was on base for him. He lashed another long fly ball to right field. Strawberry caught this one two steps in front of the fence. Buck was 0-for-3, leaving four runners on base.

The Mets tied it in the bottom of the fifth. Ray Knight singled in one run and later scored on a double-play grounder.

It stayed that way into the seventh. You could feel the tension on every pitch. Roger McDowell came on to pitch for the Mets. He walked the first batter, Marty Barrett. Buckner, batting once more with a runner aboard, grounded out, moving Barrett to second.

Jim Rice was the next hitter. He hit a grounder to third, right at Knight. It was a routine play, one Knight had made thousands of times in his career. He fielded the ball cleanly and threw to first. But he got too much on the ball, and watched in horror as it sailed high and bounced off Keith Hernandez's glove. A throwing error. Rice was safe at first, and Barrett advanced to third.

Dwight Evans followed with a groundout, allowing Barrett to hustle home. That broke the tie. The Red Sox led 3–2.

When the inning ended, Knight said a silent prayer, asking for a chance to redeem himself.

Roger Clemens was hurting. He had torn a blister on one of his pitching fingers throwing a pitch to Mookie Wilson back in the fifth. In the seventh, he tore the fingernail off the middle finger on the same hand.

Boston manager John McNamara decided to pull him for a pinch hitter in the top of the eighth with a runner on second and one out. The move backfired when Mike Greenwell struck out.

But the Mets weren't out of trouble yet. Two walks loaded the bases for the Red Sox. McNamara told Don Baylor, a right-handed hitter, to get ready to bat for Bill Buckner if Jesse Orosco, a left-hander warming up in the bullpen, was brought in to pitch for New York.

Baylor quickly slipped into the clubhouse to take a few practice swings. While he was there, Orosco was waved into the game. The situation was right. Baylor, a right-handed batter, could face the left-hander with the bases loaded. Afterward, Dave Stapleton, the defensive specialist, could take over at first base. It was all set up.

Baylor came back to the dugout ready to hit. He looked out to see Buckner hobbling up to the plate. McNamara had changed his mind. Baylor went back to the bench and sat down. He didn't bother to ask McNamara what had happened.

Orosco threw Buckner one pitch. Buck lofted it into center field, an easy fly out. That was the end of the threat.

Buck grabbed his glove and went back out to first base. He was having a tough night. He had batted five times with eight runners on base. He had made five outs and failed to advance any of the runners.

Calvin Schiraldi took over in the bottom of the eighth for his fellow Texan, Roger Clemens. Schiraldi had been in this spot before. A one-run lead, six outs to go.

But this was the World Series, not just another Saturday night ball game. He gave up a single to pinch hitter Lee Mazzilli. The next batter, Lenny Dykstra, bunted. Schiraldi fielded the ball and pegged it toward second. In his haste, he rushed his throw and bounced the ball there. Everyone was safe.

The Mets' fans were in an uproar. Another bunt moved the runners to second and third. Schiraldi walked Keith Hernandez, loading the bases.

Gary Carter was next. Schiraldi seemed rattled. He threw three pitches out of the strike zone. Three balls, no strikes. One more bad pitch would force in a run. Schiraldi grooved a fastball down the middle. Carter hammered it into left field on a line. Jim Rice made the catch, but Mazzilli tagged at third and ran home with the run the Mets needed.

The score was tied, 3–3.

Neither side scored in the ninth. The game went into extra innings.

Dave Henderson made his way to the plate to lead off for the Red Sox in the top of the tenth. Rick Aguilera, a hard-throwing right-hander, was on the mound for the Mets. The New York pitching coach, Mel Stottlemyre, went out to talk to him before he threw his first pitch to Henderson.

Stottlemyre knew all about Hendu. He had been the minor-league pitching instructor for Seattle when Henderson started out in Class A ball for the Mariners in 1977.

"This guy's hot," warned Stottlemyre. "Don't give him anything good to hit."

Aguilera threw his first pitch past Henderson for a strike. Hendu dug in for Aguilera's second pitch.

It was a fastball. Henderson hit it on a line to left field, deep, deep, and over the fence. He had done it again. Another home run. Hendu pranced around the bases flashing that big smile of his. It was like a fairy tale, he kept thinking. The homer against the Angels. Another homer in Game 2 of the Series. Ten hits and four RBIs in the World Series. And now he had struck the most dramatic blow of all, the one that looked to give the Red Sox their long-awaited World Series title. The fans back in Boston must be dancing in their living rooms, watching the game on TV. This was history being made. The Sox had the lead.

The next two batters struck out. It didn't seem that important. The Red Sox were anxious to nail it down.

Then Wade Boggs lined the ball off the wall in left center for a double. Marty Barrett bounced a single up the middle, and Boggs chugged home ahead of Lenny Dykstra's throw for yet another run. Icing on the cake. Boston led by two. The Red Sox fans in the crowd were going wild.

Aguilera was rattled now. He hit Bill Buckner with a pitch, putting two men on base. Finally, the inning ended when Jim Rice lined to Lee Mazzilli in left.

The Sox bounded out of the dugout and fanned out on the field, ready to finish it off. The score was 5–3. The big moment was at hand. Calvin Schiraldi marched out to the mound. Dave Henderson, the Cinderella hero of the postseason, ran to his position in center field. Everyone got ready for the celebration that was to follow.

Back in the dugout, Dave Stapleton, backup first baseman, stood with his glove in hand. He waited to see if he would be summoned to play defense, as he had been in the past seven postseason victories by the Red Sox. Instead, he saw Buckner take up his position at first base. Billy Buck would be on the field for the celebration. After ten years of pain, he wasn't going to miss this moment.

Stapleton stayed in the dugout with the other reserves to watch the final drama unfold.

Calvin Schiraldi completed his warm-up pitches. He could tell his fastball didn't have its usual zip. It had been a long season. Maybe his arm was tired. It didn't matter. He still had to get the job done.

Throw strikes. Don't walk anyone. Don't get in another jam. He had been struggling since he entered the game in the eighth. The first two batters had reached base that inning, and one of them scored. There were two men on when he finally got the last out. He had put the first two runners on again in the ninth. Again, he pitched out of a trouble.

Schiraldi didn't want a repeat of those performances. He would go right after the Mets.

The first batter was Wally Backman. Schiraldi threw the first pitch past him for a strike. Backman fouled off the next one. No balls, two strikes. Schiraldi came right back at him, and Backman lofted a fly ball down the left-field line. Jim Rice ran over and made the catch. He gave his glove a shake for emphasis. One down.

Keith Hernandez was next. Schiraldi threw a strike past him, then two balls. The next pitch was a fastball, and Hernandez drove it to deep center field. Dave Henderson roamed back just short of the warning track and hauled it in. You could hear the shouts coming out of the Red Sox dugout. Two outs. Schiraldi took the ball and turned back to the plate.

It was quiet in the New York dugout. For once, the Mets didn't seem so cocky. Hernandez veered off the field after his out and angrily retreated to the clubhouse. He opened a beer and sat with coach Darrell Johnson to watch the final out on a screen. It looked hopeless.

Up and down the bench, the New York players glumly stared out at the field. A great season ruined by a loss in the World Series. It was hard to comprehend what was happening.

Gary Carter stepped in. He wasn't smiling now. He was in the toughest spot a ballplayer could be in. He could be the last out in the last game of the World Series.

The count went to two balls, one strike. Schiraldi grooved a fastball down the middle of the plate. He could afford to gamble. A home run wouldn't hurt him, not with a two-run lead. Make Carter hit the ball, that was all he had to do. Carter hit a soft liner into left field for a single. He clapped his hands as he rounded first base. He had done his job. He hadn't made the last out.

Kevin Mitchell, a rookie, stepped in. A few minutes earlier, believing the game was lost, he had been in the clubhouse undressed, calling to make reservations for a flight back to California. When someone yelled at him that manager Davey Johnson wanted him to pinch-hit for pitcher Rick Aguilera, Mitchell had to throw on his uniform and run back to the dugout to grab a bat.

Mitchell fouled off the first pitch. Strike one. The next pitch was a slider, low and outside. Mitchell reached out with his bat and lined the ball into center field. Another base hit. Carter stopped at second. Mitchell, representing the tying run, arrived safely at first. The Shea Stadium fans were on their feet yelling for more, battling along with their heroes.

Bill Fischer, the Red Sox pitching coach, hurried to the mound to talk with Schiraldi. The organist played "New York, New York." The Mets no longer were sitting on the bench. They were on their feet yelling and clapping. The players in the Boston dugout watched nervously.

Ray Knight was the next batter. A few months ago, the Mets' front office had tried to ship him to any team that would have him. There were no takers. He was the player the Mets didn't want and couldn't get rid of. Now, he was all that stood between the Mets and defeat.

Schiraldi threw a fastball for a called strike. Knight bounced the next pitch down the third-base line, foul. No balls, two strikes.

One more strike. One more pitch. That was all the Red Sox needed. They were as close as a team could get.

Schiraldi threw another fastball, this one on the inside part of the plate. It was a good pitch. He could tell that as soon as it left his hand.

Knight swung and hit the ball off the handle of his bat. It wasn't a well-hit ball, but it was well placed. It flew over second base and landed in short center field. Another base hit, the third in a row.

Carter ran home, clapping and pointing to Mookie Wilson, the on-deck hitter. Mitchell raced to third base. The fans were in an uproar.

Suddenly, it was a one-run ball game. There were runners on first and third. That last out was proving to be the toughest out of all for the Red Sox.

Bob Stanley ran to the mound. How many times before had he made this same hurried journey in his baseball career? How many miles must he have traveled from the bullpen to the mound, hurrying to the rescue of a fellow pitcher?

But Stanley had never been in a situation like this one. He had never pitched in a game of this importance. He had never been called on to save not just a game, but a World Series title.

He felt good warming up. He was throwing the ball well, and had been the entire Series. He had been up and down in the bullpen, but that hadn't bothered him. Stanley had been told he would pitch the tenth, but after the Red Sox took the lead, Schiraldi went back out for one more inning and Stanley stayed in the bullpen. It was an emotional roller coaster for a relief pitcher.

Like the other Boston players, he had stopped to watch after Schiraldi got the first two outs of the inning. Stanley was ready to take part in a celebration. And then, without warning, Schiraldi gave up the three hits, one-two-three. Just like that, Stanley was in the ball game. Now he was the guy on the hot seat.

Tying run on third. Winning run on first. No room for mistakes. Stanley threw his first pitch to Mookie Wilson, a switch-hitter batting from the left side of the plate. Mookie fouled it off.

It was funny how things worked out. Stanley used to play a make-believe game while playing catch with his son Kyle out in the yard. "Okay, seventh game of the World Series," Stanley would call out. "Two outs in the ninth. Here's a pop-up!" He would toss the ball in the air, and Kyle would chase after it. If Kyle caught it, he was the hero. If he missed, well, it was a foul ball, and he would get another ball to catch. But this was a different sort of game. If you missed here, there were no second chances.

Stanley threw two pitches high for balls. Wilson fouled the next one in the dirt, making the count two balls, two strikes. Once again, the Red Sox were one pitch away.

It was only right that Stanley would be the one to throw that last pitch. Hadn't he vowed months ago to be on the mound when the Red Sox finally won the World Series? He deserved it, after all he had gone through—all the boos, all the angry taunts, all the years of service to the ball club.

Wilson fouled off two more pitches. What a duel. Six pitches, and neither Stanley nor Wilson had budged.

Catcher Rich Gedman crouched behind the plate and flashed his sign. Stanley reached back and threw once more, but this time the ball took a different path. It sailed inside, forcing Wilson to scramble out of the way. Gedman lunged for the ball but missed. It shot past his glove and toward the backstop.

There was a roar from the stands as Gedman scrambled after the ball and Wilson bounced up frantically waving Mitchell home from third. Stanley ran to cover the plate, but it was to no avail. Mitchell hesitated, then ran home, well ahead of Gedman's return throw.

All around Stanley, there was pandemonium. The fans were screaming and cheering, and the New York players were hugging one another in the dugout. The game was tied. The Red Sox had let their victory get away.

The players in the unlikely drama returned to their assigned places. Bob Stanley went back to the pitching mound. Mookie Wilson stepped back in the batter's box. Rich Gedman squatted behind the plate. Ray Knight led off second base, where he had advanced on the wild pitch.

And Bill Buckner, wearing his black high-tops, stationed himself next to the first-base bag. With a left-handed batter at the plate, he was playing deeper than normal.

The duel continued between Stanley and Wilson. Two more foul balls went off Wilson's bat. The count remained full.

The players were hanging on every pitch. The confrontation had lost none of its importance. If the Red Sox could get this final out, they still would have a chance to win the game and the World Series in the innings that would follow.

Stanley fired the ball to the plate once more. It was the tenth pitch he had thrown to Wilson. This time, Mookie swung and topped the ball down the first-base line.

Buckner saw the ball bouncing down the line, and he moved to his left, behind the first-base bag. Wilson charged down the base path, head down, running as fast as he could. Stanley broke from the mound to cover first. It was Buck's play now. All he had to do was field the ball and hope Stanley could beat Wilson to the bag. If he did, the side would be retired.

Buck got in front of the ball and reached down for it, just like he had done thousands of times over twenty years of professional baseball. Get in front of the ball. Get your glove down. It was the most basic play in baseball, one ballplayers learned in Little League.

The ball bounced, and it bounced again, right under Buckner's glove and through his legs. It rolled into right field, and with it went Boston's World Series title.

Ray Knight rounded third base, saw what had happened, and ran home holding his hands to his head, overwhelmed by what had just transpired. He jumped onto the plate into the waiting arms of his teammates. The Mets had won. Down to their last out, their last pitch, they had rallied for three runs and victory.

Down at first base, Billy Buck stood with his hands on his hips. He looked up at the sky in disbelief. He couldn't remember the last ground ball he had missed. But he never would forget this one.

◇ It rained on Sunday. It seemed fitting. You don't expect to be greeted by sunshine the day after letting the World Series slip through your fingers.

The commissioner finally called off the game. It would be played on Monday.

Bill Buckner was in his hotel room when he got a call from Reggie Jackson of the Angels. Reggie knew what the Red Sox were going through. He knew what it was like to have a title in your grasp, be one out from the clincher, and then see it snatched away.

The Angels never recovered from the loss in Game 5 of the American League Championship Series, Reggie told Buckner. They were beat before they went back to Boston for the final two games.

The Red Sox were too good to let that happen to them, Reggie said. You've got to come back and take it to them. Hang in there, he told Buckner.

Buck thanked him for the call.

◇ Game 7 was finally played Monday evening. Boston manager John McNamara took advantage of the one-day delay to pitch Bruce Hurst in the decisive game. Hurst had three days' rest since his last start. He had already beaten the Mets twice. Maybe he could do it again.

Fifty-six thousand fans braved the chilly weather to turn out at Shea Stadium. Another fifty-six million watched on television.

The pregame introductions were made, and when Bill Buckner was announced, the New York fans gave him a standing ovation. Someone held up a sign that read, "Nice legs." Buck didn't laugh.

Mets starter Ron Darling retired the first two Red Sox hitters of the game. More derisive cheers greeted Buckner as he made his way to the plate. He answered with a hard grounder up the middle for a base hit.

In the second inning, Dwight Evans led off with a drive over the fence in left-center field for a home run. Rich Gedman followed with a blast over the wall in right center for another homer. Boston led 2–0.

The Red Sox kept up the pressure. A walk, sacrifice and single by Wade Boggs scored another run, making it 3–0. A bunt single by Marty Barrett put runners on first and second with two out.

Buckner stepped to the plate. There were no taunts now, not with the Red Sox up by three and threatening to break open the game. Buck hammered one of Darling's pitches to deep center field. It was the best he had hit a ball since the Series began. Buck ran to first base, convinced he had an extra-base hit that would score the two base runners.

There was a roar, and Buckner looked up to see a streaking Mookie Wilson reaching up to make a running catch. It was just another long out. Buck shouted in anger. He wasn't having much luck with Mookie.

The Boston lead stayed at three runs.

Bruce Hurst made it stand up through the fifth inning. He ran out of steam in the sixth. After thirty-seven brilliant innings in postseason play, his left arm finally gave out.

Hurst got the first batter out, then gave up a single, followed by another. He walked a batter to load the bases. Keith Hernandez lined another single to left center to score two runs. Gary Carter followed with a blooper that eluded Evans in right field, allowing the tying run to score.

Calvin Schiraldi took over for Hurst in the seventh. The day of rest on Sunday had helped Schiraldi, both physically and emotionally. His fastball had recovered some of its pop. He felt confident walking onto the field, not nervous as he had been on Saturday.

Ray Knight was the first batter. The count went to two balls, one strike. Schiraldi's next pitch was an inside fastball. Knight drove it over the fence in left-center field. Knight pumped his fist in the air and skipped around the bases. Schiraldi hung his head. The Mets had the lead, 4–3.

The dazed Schiraldi gave up a single to the next batter. He threw a wild pitch. Another single followed, scoring the second run of the inning. A sacrifice bunt moved the runner to second.

That was it for Schiraldi. He left the game a beaten pitcher. Two more walks loaded the bases, and a sacrifice fly scored another run, giving the Mets a 6–3 lead.

The Red Sox came back with two runs in the eighth, and had the tying run on second with no outs. But they were out of comebacks. Jesse Orosco came on to pitch for the Mets. He retired Rich Gedman on a line drive. Dave Henderson, no heroics left in his bat, struck out on three pitches. Don Baylor grounded out.

The Mets scored twice more in the eighth to make it 8–5. That was how it ended after the Red Sox went out one-two-three in the ninth, the end coming when Orosco threw a third strike past Marty Barrett.

Orosco hurled his glove high in the air in celebration before being mobbed by his teammates. New York players ran onto the field, hugged and shouted, and rolled on the ground in celebration. The Boston players sat in their dugout and watched. It was the kind of celebratory scene they had envisioned for themselves just two nights earlier.

◇ Two years passed after the World Series and Bill Buckner returned home following another baseball season. He still lived in the Boston area, but he no longer played for the Red Sox.

The parting had come in July 1987, when Buck was cut loose by the Red Sox with the team buried in fifth place, fourteen-and-one-half games out of first. He was batting a respectable .273 at the time, but it had not been a happy season, neither for him nor the Red Sox.

Buckner had limped into spring training following yet another operation on his ankle in the off-season. He had booted a ground ball on opening day in Milwaukee, bringing back memories of Mookie Wilson's grounder bouncing through his legs in the World Series. The Red Sox returned to Boston for their home opener, and when Buckner was introduced before the game he was greeted with a mixture of boos and cheers. Buck heard only the boos. It was hard not to.

Later, when he got two hits and made a daring run from first base to third on one play, the boos turned to cheers. "Wait until I make an error," Buckner noted cryptically.

He was a thirty-seven-year-old ballplayer, and when Boston started losing and fell from the pennant race, there was no point in keeping him. So the Red Sox gave him his release, and Buckner signed with the California Angels. He knew it was time to go. Things had been good for him in Boston up until that sixth game in the World Series. After that, everything changed.

When Buckner made his first trip back to Boston in a California uniform, he was booed again.

The next year, 1988, Buck was released by the Angels, and he caught on with the Kansas City Royals. He finished the season with a modest .249 batting average, not bad for an aging ballplayer who could not run; but it was the lowest output for Buckner in thirteen years.

That fall, Buck went to the University of Massachusetts Medical Center for treatment of his bad ankle. It was the same hospital where he had driven himself two years earlier, after the 1986 World Series, for surgery to clean out his left ankle. Back then, other drivers had honked and waved at him, and yelled encouragement to him. Back then, a boy came to Buckner's hospital room to tell him, "You'll always be my inspiration."

This time, there were no young admirers to greet him or cheering fans to encourage him. There was only an attending nurse, who saw his name on the chart and looked up at Buckner quizzically. The name seemed familiar, yet she could not quite place it.

And then it came to her.

"Hey," she said, "aren't you the guy that let that ball go between your legs?"

PART II

THE PLAYERS

4

DONNIE MOORE:

IT WASN'T JUST A GAME, IT WAS HIS LIFE

Tonya Moore shut her eyes and thought back to that afternoon. She could see everything very clearly. The California players leaned forward at their positions on the baseball field. The fans at Anaheim Stadium were on their feet cheering. And there, at the center of this drama, was her husband, her Donnie, standing on the mound, the ball in his hand. He glared at the batter, Dave Henderson of Boston. Tonya remembered how proud she was that day, and how happy she was for her Donnie.

She was wearing a black hat. It was a special occasion, and she wanted to look her best for the TV cameras that sometimes focused on the wives of the ballplayers. She was a pretty woman, tall and slender with loosely curled hair.

It was an exciting moment in Tonya's life. The Angels were one out, one pitch, from the World Series. All Donnie had to do was throw one more strike past the batter. Like everyone else in the stadium, Tonya was on her feet, waiting for that final out. All around her, the fans shouted words of encouragement to her Donnie.

She clapped her hands and smiled. Donnie was doing so well, and everything seemed so perfect. He was just one out from the World Series. That was his dream, to pitch in the World Series. To stand out there on the mound and know that he had reached the mountaintop—the World Series. It wasn't the money, or the fame. It was knowing, "Hey, I am the best." It was every ballplayer's dream.

And then he threw that pitch.

The ball flew off Dave Henderson's bat and toward left field. It carried deeper and deeper until it cleared the fence and landed in the bleachers. Tonya watched in disbelief. It was like a nightmare. A home run, and now Boston led. She put her head down and tears rolled down her cheeks. She looked up to see the expression on Donnie's face, to see if he was all right. When she saw him through her tears, she knew he wasn't.

He seemed to be in a daze, standing there on the mound while Henderson gleefully circled the bases. Donnie looked so helpless and lost. Tonya wanted to leave her seat, jump over the railing onto the field and run out to tell him it was all right. He just wanted some reassurance. Her Donnie wanted the reassurance that nobody ever gave him.

There was nothing she could do but cry. Nearby, the Boston wives were jumping up and down, hugging each other and screaming happily. Why did the wives of the opposing teams have to be seated next to each other? Didn't anyone understand how painful that would be, with one group rejoicing while the other suffered? It was a horrible experience.

Two innings later, Tonya watched numbly as Donnie walked off the mound, a beaten man. Even after he had thrown the home-run pitch, the Angels had had chances to win. They had the bases loaded with only one out in the bottom of the ninth. A fly ball would have scored the winning run. They didn't get the fly ball. They failed to score in the tenth inning. None of that mattered now. The Red Sox had scored a run in the top of the eleventh inning, and everyone in the stadium knew the Angels had blown the game.

The fans booed her Donnie as he left the field. They yelled insults and curses at him. He kept his head up as he walked. The expression on his face never changed.

At home that night, Donnie didn't talk much. The house was full of people. The three kids were there. There were family members and other relatives from out of town. Donnie didn't say anything about the home run. He showed no emotion around the others. It was as if he was saying, "Okay, I made a mistake. That's all."

He didn't act angry or try to blame anyone else. "I made a mistake." Nothing more.

That was the way Donnie was. He was a quiet man. He never talked much.

Donnie drank more than usual that night, and he and Tonya had words. Donnie often got mean when he was drinking, but nothing happened on this occasion. Just some harsh words.

The next day, the team traveled to Boston. Tonya and the other wives went with the players. The trip turned into a cruel ordeal. The fans were loud and mean and taunting. It was cold. Nothing seemed to go right for the Angels. They lost both games, and the pennant. Maybe it wasn't meant for them to win.

Donnie never blamed anyone but himself for what happened. He was the one who threw the pitch to Henderson. He accepted the responsibility for California's stunning loss in the series, for blowing the lead in Game 5 when the Angels were just one out from victory. Donnie didn't second-guess his catcher for the pitch he called. He didn't criticize his manager. He didn't use his bad back, or his sore ribs, or his bad shoulder, as an excuse for his performance.

But Donnie couldn't get that pitch out of his mind. He brooded over it all winter. Sometimes, he mentioned it to Tonya. They would be sitting and talking, and Donnie would wonder out loud if he should have thrown a fastball or some pitch other than the split-finger fastball which Henderson hit over the fence. Maybe he should have shaken off the catcher's sign. Things might have turned out differently. He couldn't help but wonder.

But even then, Donnie didn't duck responsibility for what happened. He threw the pitch and he would take the blame for the loss, he would tell Tonya.

"Well, it's not just your fault," she would snap.

It made her mad to hear him talk that way. One man doesn't win or lose a game singlehandedly. There were other people involved. The catcher tells the pitcher what pitch to throw. Isn't that right? And during that same game, weren't the bases loaded with only one out and the score tied in the bottom of the inning? That game still could have been won. And didn't the team need to win just one of the two games in Boston? What happened to all those other players? But people didn't think about that. All they thought about was that one pitch.

"That's okay," said Donnie. "They want to blame it on somebody, they can blame me."

And they did. The fans, the writers, the people on the radio talk shows. Worst of all, Donnie seemed to blame himself. That one pitch was always on his mind. He knew he had made a mistake. And he didn't know if he would have another chance to be in the World Series, ever again. He didn't know if he would ever get that World Series ring. And that ring was very special to him.

It was a terrible winter. And things only got worse the following season. Every time Donnie stepped onto the field, the fans booed him. Every time they saw him walk out to the bullpen, they booed him.

It made you wonder. Did these people have any feelings? Did they have any heart? Did they know what this individual was going through? Didn't they know they affect the ballplayers? Some of the ballplayers were strong enough to let the boos and the criticism pass them by, but there were a lot of them who couldn't take it.

There were times when Tonya wanted to turn around in her seat at the ballpark and yell back at the fans who booed. She wanted to hit them with her purse or curse at them the way they cursed at her husband. But she was a lady, and a ballplayer's wife. She was not allowed to strike back at those people.

So she sat and listened to them boo and criticize her Donnie, and she said nothing.

Donnie never said what he thought about all the criticism. Tonya would look at him and wonder what was going through his head. What was he thinking? He seemed to have so much on his mind. Donnie never said. He wouldn't talk about it. He never talked about his feelings. He kept them all locked up inside. But one day, they would have to come out.

Tonya was not one of those wives who just popped in after her husband had already reached the major leagues, making big money and enjoying his celebrity status. She was there from the beginning. She had started at the bottom and gone all the way to the top with Donnie.

She knew what a struggle it was to make it in professional baseball. She knew about the good times, and she knew about the bad times. Like Donnie, she had paid her dues.

Tonya went everywhere with Donnie on his long climb up the baseball ladder. The minor leagues, the Instructional League, the winter leagues, spring training. Key West, Florida. Midland, Texas. Wichita, Kansas. Puerto Rico. Venezuela. You name it, Tonya was there.

You get used to the travel. Donnie would get word that he was being promoted, and he would leave immediately for his next assignment. It was Tonya's job to pack their belongings, load them in the car and drive to the new destination. You didn't think about it, you just did it.

Tonya felt it was important that she do more than just stay home and visit Donnie here and there during the baseball season or wait for him to return from winter ball. She was always there for him. She knew that Donnie needed the support. He always had her to encourage him and take care of him. That was important.

The minor leagues were fun. There was a special camaraderie among the players and their wives. Everyone wished good things for everyone else, and they all shared in one another's happiness and success. The wives would do things together. In Midland, they formed their own baseball team. They had pot-luck suppers. It was like family.

Baseball was Donnie's career, but he didn't look at it that way. He wanted to keep advancing and make it all the way to the major leagues, but there was more to it than that. Playing the game was what really mattered. Donnie loved baseball. Standing on the mound, pitching the ball, the competition, earning the respect of his manager and teammates—that was what it was all about. It wasn't the money or the fame. It was playing baseball.

Baseball had been a part of Donnie's life for as long as Tonya had known him. They met as teenagers when Tonya was attending a family reunion in Lubbock, Texas, where Donnie lived. Shortly afterward, Tonya's mother moved the family from Los Angeles to Lubbock. It was a shock, moving from southern California to west Texas. But knowing Donnie made it worthwhile.

Donnie was a great guy. He was funny, engaging, personable, considerate, caring. He was popular wherever he went. It was fun being with Donnie. Tonya thought he was a real sweetheart.

Tonya went to Lubbock's Estacado High School, which had a large black and Hispanic population among the student body. Donnie went to the city's other high school, Monterey, where he was one of the few blacks among two thousand students. It was difficult for him at first, but soon he fit right in. Donnie loved Monterey. He became one of the most popular kids in school. Everybody loved Donnie.

Even then, Donnie was serious about baseball. He was a superstar, and he could throw the heck out of the ball. His senior year, Monterey won the state championship.

But things weren't always what they seemed with Donnie. There was a dark side to his personality. He was a nice guy, but he had a mean streak in him.

One Saturday, when she was nineteen years old and she and Donnie already had a one-year-old daughter, Demetria, Tonya was at her house getting ready for a party. Donnie was playing ball for nearby Ranger Junior College and was not supposed to be home that weekend. Most of Tonya's friends were men, and one of them was with her that day while she was preparing to leave. And then Donnie unexpectedly showed up at her house, and he saw the other man in Tonya's room.

That was the first time Donnie hit Tonya. He hit her hard with his fists, over and over again. She remembered bouncing off the bed as the blows rained down on her, and her brother running to call their mother on the telephone. Tonya doesn't know what happened to her friend. All she knows is that Donnie beat her senseless.

By the time Tonya's mother arrived at the house, Donnie was gone. Her mother was furious. She put Tonya in the car and drove straight to Donnie's house. There, she confronted Donnie's mother and told her Donnie better not lay a hand on her daughter again. She would not bother to have Donnie arrested, she said. There was a threatening tone in her voice.

Tonya let herself believe it would not happen again. She thought Donnie had learned his lesson, that he would be embarrassed by what he had done.

She came to find out otherwise. Once a man hits you, he will always hit you. Don't ever let him tell you that he won't. Once they start hitting you, they always will.

Tonya doesn't know if it is a sickness or what. She is no doctor. But she does know that once a man hits a woman, he will always hit a woman.

Donnie was what they call a "journeyman pitcher." He spent five seasons in the minor leagues. After he reached the big leagues in 1977, he spent the next six seasons bouncing from team to team, back and forth between the majors to the minors, up and down, always trying to hang on.

Once a player has made it to the top, the minor leagues are no longer fun. It was a frustrating experience, and at times Donnie got discouraged. He didn't always understand why he was sent down. He couldn't believe what people told him.

Someone in management would tell him, "You're going to make the team, you're going to do this, you're going to do that," and then a few days later, Donnie would be sent to the minor leagues.

It would be better if they didn't say anything to the ballplayers, because anything could happen. It was a day-to-day process. Someone else might start playing better than you. Or the team might need a left-hander instead of a right hander. You never can tell. The ballplayers know who has to make the team and who already has made it. They know what is going on.

So, why tell them something that isn't true? That messes with their minds. And if a person doesn't have a strong mind, that can mess him up. That was the way Tonya felt, watching Donnie and seeing what he was going through.

But she never said anything about it. She was just a wife. She didn't know everything that was going on. She didn't know what was being said in the clubhouse. And Donnie never talked about it. What happens in the clubhouse stays in the clubhouse. That was the ballplayers' world. They took care of each other. That was the way it was.

When Donnie did come home, Tonya did everything she could to make it pleasant for him. He had enough problems at the ballpark. If she gave him trouble also, then he would be getting it all the way around.

But even when he was being shipped from Chicago to Wichita to St. Louis to Springfield to Milwaukee to Richmond to Atlanta, one thing about Donnie never changed: He could pitch the ball. Put him on a pitcher's mound, and he was a thing of beauty.

Tonya loved to watch Donnie pitch. He could pitch the heck out of the ball. He had such a graceful motion and fired the ball to the plate with such power. And he didn't care if the batter was a lefty or a righty or whatever. Once a man stood at the plate, Donnie was ready for him. It was one-on-one. Either the batter beat Donnie, or Donnie beat the batter.

Donnie knew he was good. In his mind, he had always been a super-star. He just needed someone to believe in him. That was all.

When he got to Atlanta, he finally found that person. Joe Torre, the manager of the Braves, gave Donnie the chance he wanted. He gave the ball to Donnie in crucial situations. He showed that he trusted Donnie, that he valued him. If Donnie gave up a walk, Torre didn't pull him out of the game. He let Donnie pitch out of the jam. Torre believed in Donnie, and that made all the difference in the world. Donnie, relying heavily on his split-finger fastball, had his first big year as a relief pitcher, saving sixteen games.

That was the turning point in Donnie's career. He had proved him-self. Suddenly, Donnie was a very valuable commodity. That winter, the California Angels acquired him from the Braves in a special compen-sation draft. The Angels immediately installed him as their No. 1 reliever, the man who was counted on to come out of the bullpen with the game on the line and nail down the victory.

Donnie thrived in the high-pressure role. His first year in California, he earned thirty-one saves and had an earned-run average of under 2.00. He was named to the American League All-Star team, and he pitched two shutout innings in the All-Star Game.

Gene Mauch, the California manager, was a tough, demanding man-ager, but he believed in Donnie, the same way Joe Torre did. Donnie was intensely loyal to Mauch. He would do anything for his manager. He would run through a brick wall for him, or pitch with his arm hurting—whatever Mauch asked of him.

That was the type of ballplayer Donnie was. He wanted the respect of his teammates and his manager. That meant everything to him.

Donnie never hit Tonya in the face. When he struck her, he did so where it would not show. There were no marks on her face nor any other visible signs of the abuse she suffered at his hands. No one else knew. No one could tell what was going on.

From all outward appearances, Donnie and Tonya had an ideal life together. After the 1985 season, Donnie signed a three-year, $3 million

Donnie Moore couldn't deal with the criticism from the fans and some members of the Angels organization after he gave up the home run to Dave Henderson. "I think a lot of people owe him an apology," says Moore's widow, Tonya. *Photo courtesy California Angels.*

contract with the Angels. He and Tonya moved out of their condominium and into an $850,000 house in Peralta Hills, an affluent community in Anaheim.

It was Donnie's dream house. It sat on an acre and a half of land that included a swimming pool and a private lake. You drove in, and it was secluded. You didn't have to worry about people. You could go in the backyard and swim in the pool. The kids could jump on the trampoline. Donnie stocked the lake with catfish and fished there. It was a paradise.

Donnie also bought Tonya a new Mercedes. Otherwise, the money didn't change things that much. The more money you have, the more you spend, so it was really about the same. More bills. More responsibilities. You pay more in taxes. You sign for a million dollars, but Uncle Sam gets half of that, so it really is no big deal. People fail to realize that.

Donnie let Tonya buy anything she wanted. He always was good to her that way. She could have whatever she wanted, or needed. It didn't matter. That was the way Donnie was.

But Donnie was a jealous man. Sometimes, that was what prompted his outbursts of violence and the terrible beatings he inflicted on Tonya. She took steps to prevent his rages. She stopped talking to other men. She stopped wearing bikinis.

Still, Donnie hit her. Sometimes, Tonya prayed that she would get beaten for something that she did. It wouldn't have been so bad if she got hit for something she really did. A "justified ass whipping," she called it. But it never happened that way.

Donnie was also a possessive man. He wanted to know where Tonya was at all times. She wasn't allowed to leave the house without his permission. A simple trip to the grocery store became an escape for her. She clipped coupons out of the newspaper and saved them for her shopping excursions. It always took longer when she used her coupons. She would spend hours in the grocery store, roaming around with her coupons and searching for the items, having a great time. Donnie would hit her when she got home, but that didn't stop her. Sometimes, she just needed to get out of the house.

Tonya doesn't know why she took so much abuse, why she endured so many beatings. She knows that Donnie loved her. She is sure of that. Nobody can tell her any different. When he wasn't drinking, he was a real sweetheart. He was a good guy, but when he started drinking that

Jack Daniels, he got real mean. He was just a man with a real temper. Donnie never hit her when he wasn't drinking. Never. But when he was drinking, well . . .

Why did she stay? It wasn't the money, because there were times when they didn't have any money.

Tonya can't say for certain. Donnie needed her. And she wanted to be there for him. She was married to him. It was her duty to be with him. She wanted her kids to have their father. She didn't want a bunch of different men in her house with her kids.

Why did she stay? She thinks about it a lot, and she doesn't know. She can't say. She doesn't know for sure.

A few times, Tonya did think about leaving Donnie. But whenever she did, she wanted to die. She couldn't stand thinking about it.

Donnie wasn't a bad person. If anybody met him, just met him, he was a sweet, gentle, kind, giving, considerate man. He was all of those things. But then he could turn around and be mean and evil and cruel. The same probably is true of just about anybody on this earth. Anyone can be nice one minute and mean the next. That doesn't make him a bad person.

People think when a player makes a big salary, he is playing for the money. It wasn't that way with Donnie. He loved the game. The money was good, but the game was what counted. That and his teammates, his manager, his coaches.

If it was just the money, Donnie wouldn't have gone out there when he was hurt. Why would you have to go out there when you are hurt? All you have to do is say, "I'm hurt," and sit on the bench.

But Donnie played the game because that is what he wanted to do. People depended on him. That made him feel good.

That is why Donnie went out there and pitched in 1986, even though his arm hurt and his back hurt. That is why Donnie took all those shots and endured all that pain. He wanted to pitch. He had to pitch.

Tonya went with him when he got the cortisone shots in his back. The Angels would send him to a doctor, and Tonya would be with him, holding his hand. Not if a team doctor gave Donnie a shot in the clubhouse, but when they sent him here and there around town to get his shots. Tonya always went with him. She was there. She had to be there. When Donnie got his knee drained, she was there. She always was there.

Sometimes, Donnie would get a shot in his back, go to the ballpark and then turn around and pitch that night. A couple of times Tonya didn't think he was supposed to pitch, but Donnie pitched anyway. He didn't care. All he wanted was to get out there and pitch.

Tonya did what she could to help. She massaged his back and put heat on it. Later in the season, Donnie had migraine headaches. He was in a lot of pain that year, but he never complained. He just kept pitching. He pitched in forty-nine games that season and earned twenty-one saves. It wasn't as good as the year before, but he helped the Angels get into the playoffs. A lot of people forget that. If it wasn't for Donnie Moore, California might not have been in the playoffs. He pitched his heart out for the Angels that year.

Donnie was still hurt when he pitched in the playoffs. It didn't matter. He would have gone out there with his leg in a cast. Maybe if he wasn't the type of player he was, if the game hadn't meant so much to him, what happened later wouldn't have been so hard on him.

He was hurt when he threw the pitch to Dave Henderson. But Donnie could deal with that. He could endure the physical pain and the shots. It was the emotional pain he wasn't equipped to handle.

People are so quick to blame someone. After that pitch, Donnie couldn't go onto the field without the fans booing him. He couldn't hold his head up high. He tried, but they wouldn't let him.

Maybe if the fans had stood and clapped for him, it would have been different. They could have let him know it is okay to make a mistake. A man is entitled to make one mistake in his lifetime, isn't he?

But the fans didn't clap for Donnie. They didn't stand and applaud him. Instead, they held up angry signs insulting him. They jeered him. They booed him. Those same people who once cheered him went to the ballpark and booed him. Loud, taunting, mean boos.

And then those same fans had the nerve to want his autograph when he stepped outside the clubhouse. The fans! They pay their money to get into the ballpark, they drink their beer, they criticize you, and then they ask you for your autograph.

Donnie didn't say anything about the booing. All he said was that it didn't bother him, that he could handle it. Everyone knew he was a tough guy, but he wasn't that tough. No one is. It had to hurt him. Everyone on the team could see that.

Tonya was the one who showed her anger. It made her mad to see her Donnie treated that way. She had to sit in the stands and hear the boos and the insults directed at her husband. Donnie didn't talk about it, but sometimes when he came home after pitching in Anaheim Stadium, he would cry.

Donnie stopped signing autographs that year. He would sign his name for the kids, but that was all. No adults. Not after the way the fans treated him.

One day in late May, he gave up two runs in the tenth inning to lose a game to the Yankees. Donnie walked off the field with the boos ringing in his ears. It was too much for him. He had heard enough. He looked up at the fans and angrily waved an open palm at them. That made them boo even louder.

The pain in his back would not go away. He worked with weights to strengthen his shoulder, but the back problem persisted. The Angels left on a road trip, and Donnie stayed behind in Anaheim. He was placed on the disabled list to give his back a chance to heal.

He had to sit at home and watch the games on television. He wanted to be with the team. Even if he was hurt and couldn't pitch, he could at least sit on the bench with his teammates and take his therapy and exercise with the other players. He was the closer. He should have been with the team. But the Angels were on the road and Donnie was at home with his family, seated in front of a television set.

It was difficult for him. And it was miserable for his family. Donnie was moody. He was irritable. He used to be a positive person. That year, he became very negative. He walked around with a chip on his shoulder. Every little thing bothered him. He always seemed to be irritated, even over the little things around the house.

Donnie kept telling the team his back was hurt. He was having problems with his back, and he kept telling them, but the doctors couldn't find anything wrong. Maybe they didn't believe him. Maybe they thought he was full of crap. He kept going to doctors and getting cortisone shots so he could pitch for the Angels. That wasn't good enough for the people who doubted him. They wondered if Donnie really was hurt.

The Angels entered September with a chance to defend their West-
ern Division title, but they lost fourteen of their next eighteen games.
They fell all the way to last place before the season ended. People were
angry. They needed to blame someone.

One day, Donnie picked up the newspaper and read a comment by
Mike Port, the team's general manager. Port called Donnie a "malingerer." He said Donnie should "get out there and pitch."

"Instead of whining about hurting his rib cage, he should have been
out there earning his money," Port said in the newspaper. "What do we
pay him $1 million for? . . . He's supposed to be in shape. We should
be getting our money's worth."

Donnie couldn't believe it when he read that. He freaked out. He
felt betrayed and humiliated. How could Port say that? How could anyone say that? Donnie didn't understand. He had been out there pitching in pain. He was hurt in 1985, when he was the team's best pitcher.
·He was hurt in 1986, when he helped the Angels get into the playoffs.
He blocked out the pain so that he could pitch. He tried to keep pitching in 1987 despite the pain. And then Port had the nerve to say he was
what, a "malingerer"? Donnie never got over that.

Things got so bad, Donnie even tried acupuncture, where they stick
all those needles in you. He and Tonya did this on their own, because
Donnie's back was still hurting and he wanted to fix it so he could
pitch. But the needles didn't solve the problem, either. That is when
Donnie was told he had a problem with his spine. The man who did
the acupuncture told Donnie something was wrong with his spine.
That was why the needles didn't work.

The season was over when a back specialist finally discovered the
problem. He found a bone spur the size of a dime near Donnie's spinal
column. Donnie was in surgery for five hours while they cleared the
calcium deposit and relieved the nerve irritation.

Mike Port visited Donnie in the hospital and tried to make things
better between the two of them. But there was no apology in the newspapers. Tonya thought Port owed Donnie that much. He should have
made a public apology for calling Donnie a "malingerer." Donnie
could have been paralyzed by the bone spur. He was fighting for his life
in surgery. And Mike Port had the nerve to make Donnie look like a
piece of garbage to the whole world. Donnie never forgave Port.
Neither did Tonya.

People believe anything they read in the newspapers. Tonya knew
better. A lot of that stuff is untrue. If only people knew. You can't
believe everything you read in the papers.

To be an athlete, you need to have a lot of people behind you. It's just like anything else. If you want to be a singer, you have to have people behind you. If you want to write a book, you have to have people behind you. Even though it's your job, you wouldn't do as well with people criticizing you all the time.

You can't do as good a job when you don't have any incentive. Why should you go out and do something when everybody is going to criticize you anyway? You work your ass off, and then it's still not good enough. Why should you keep trying? What is your reward?

Donnie was not the same pitcher in 1988, after his surgery. He felt good physically, but he had trouble getting anyone out. He kept blowing leads late in ball games. The Angels had to stop relying on him. He was demoted from his job as the team's closer.

Donnie walked a lot of batters. It used to be when he was on the mound, he very seldom walked anybody. When Donnie walked too many batters, Tonya knew something was wrong. She could see something wasn't right.

Maybe it was because of the back surgery. That affected Donnie. But the criticism had a lot to do with it, also. Tonya knew that if Donnie felt the fans, his teammates, his manager and his coaches were behind him 100 percent, he would have had more willpower, more energy to take his therapy, to work out and get himself back into A-1 shape.

Donnie pitched poorly that year, and he suffered other injuries. The Angels put him on the disabled list again. After he came back that August, the ball club turned him loose. Suddenly, Donnie was a thirty-four-year-old pitcher without a team.

Tonya used to tell him: "When you stop playing baseball, you know you can be a coach. You can work in the front office. I mean, there are other things to do besides pitching the ball."

Baseball was Donnie's life. The whole time he and Tonya were married, Donnie only had one other job. That was when he was twenty years old, and he worked on a street-paving crew one winter. Baseball was all he knew.

Donnie got a chance to make a comeback in 1989. The Kansas City Royals signed him on the recommendation of Bob Boone, Donnie's catcher with the Angels. Donnie was assigned to the Royals' top minor-league club, in Omaha, Nebraska.

He kept to himself. He paid extra to have a room by himself when the team went on the road. Donnie wasn't used to having roommates. You didn't have roommates in the big leagues.

It was tough on Donnie, being back in the minor leagues. Baseball players can be real cruel. The minor leaguers kidded him about the big contract he had. They called him "Million Dollars."

Donnie wasn't himself, pitching for Omaha. He wasn't the same pitcher he used to be. On June 12, the Royals gave Donnie his release. His baseball career was over.

Tonya knew that once Donnie was out of baseball, he would take it out on her. She knew her life would be miserable. Donnie would be drinking more and trying to kick her ass more. So she moved out. After sixteen years of marriage, she got her own apartment nearby. She still did the family laundry, but she and Donnie were separated.

Tonya knew that if she stayed, sooner or later Donnie would end up hurting her. It was bound to happen someday. That was why she left. Tonya still loved Donnie. But she didn't want to be hit anymore.

She was tired. And once a battered woman gets tired, she is tired.

Baseball and Tonya. That was Donnie's life. And he was losing both of them.

They talked about getting back together. It was an on-again, off-again sort of thing. They argued a lot. They were both headstrong people.

"I will stay with you if you keep your hands off me," Tonya told Donnie. "I'm never going to get my ass kicked again."

"I'll keep my hands off you," he promised.

But Donnie didn't keep his hands off her.

They decided to sell the house. They were having some financial problems, and they needed the money. They had been late making their mortgage payments. They had a large tax bill due. And Donnie's agent, David Pinter, claimed Donnie owed him more than $75,000.

That was why they made the decision to sell the house—money and uncertainty about whether they were going to be together.

In early July, Donnie called a real-estate agent he found through an advertisement in the newspaper. Donnie seemed very anxious to sell.

A week later, on Tuesday, July 18, 1989, a prospective buyer was supposed to look at the house. Tonya showed up to help, but the buyer never arrived.

Donnie and Tonya talked some more. They became angry, and there were harsh words. Then Donnie hit Tonya. He had promised never to hit her again, but he did.

"If you're trying to work things out," Tonya said to him, "why are you doing the same thing you've always done to me? That's not going to work."

The argument lasted most of the morning. Then things calmed down. Donnie said what he had to say, and Tonya said what she had to say. That was all there was to it.

That afternoon, Demetria arrived in the Mercedes to pick up her mother.

"Okay, let's get the hell out of here," said Tonya.

The whole family was there. Tonya. Donnie. Dee, who was seventeen. The two boys, Donnie Jr., who was ten, and Ronnie, who was eight.

Tonya turned to leave. That was when she saw Donnie sitting at the kitchen table with a semiautomatic .45-caliber handgun, the one she had given him for Christmas. He pointed the gun at his head.

"What, in front of your kids?" she said.

Donnie slowly turned the gun away from himself and aimed it at her. Tonya didn't move.

"You're not going to do that," she said.

There was a loud explosion, and Tonya went numb. She could see smoke, and she heard her kids screaming. She was in shock.

"My God!" she thought. "This man has shot me!"

The first shot hit Tonya in the neck, and the bullet came out the back by her spine. She ran from the kitchen into the laundry room, and Donnie chased after her with his gun. He fired four more shots. One bullet hit her just below the chest and passed through her midsection. Another hit her in the chest and went through one of her lungs. Two other shots missed.

Tonya staggered outside, and Dee tried to help her into the car. Dee opened the back door of the Mercedes, and Tonya fell into the seat. She was wearing a white blouse and white skirt, and they were covered with blood from the six bullet holes in her body.

Tonya thought she must be dying, because she was spitting up blood. She was in the backseat bleeding to death, and her daughter would not stop screaming.

"I'm dying here!" yelled Tonya. "Could you calm down please!"

Dee pulled out of the driveway and sped down the street.

"What hospital are you taking me to?" asked Tonya.

Dee answered that she was going to Anaheim's Kaiser Permanente Hospital. It was just minutes away.

"Oh, I'll die for sure there," said Tonya. She had been shot three times, and she was coughing up blood, but she still was able to make a joke.

When they got to the hospital, Tonya got out of the car. Dee held her head up, and Tonya walked to the emergency room. She refused to sit out there in the car and die. There was no way in hell she was going to die like that.

After he shot Tonya, perhaps while she still was getting into the car, Donnie pointed the gun at himself once again. His two boys were still in the house with him when he fired the last bullet into his head.

Ronnie had to lean over his father's body to pick up the phone and dial 911.

"My dad's been shot!" he yelled into the phone.

When the police arrived, they found no suicide note—just some letters to Donnie asking for autographs, a baseball from the 1985 All-Star Game in which Donnie had pitched and a ball signed by Reggie Jackson.

But there was no reason for them to think it was anything other than an attempted murder and suicide.

Tonya lost consciousness after she arrived in the emergency room. She was lucky to be alive. The three bullets that had passed through her body had just missed her arteries, organs and spinal cord. Miraculously, she had not suffered any fatal or crippling injuries.

When she woke up, she asked for Donnie. She remembered hearing four shots, but she knew that only three bullets had hit her. There actually had been six shots fired, but she remembered hearing only four. She wanted to know about Donnie.

"Just worry about yourself," she was told. "Worry about yourself."

Tonya had lost a lot of blood, and she was fighting for her life. She was in critical condition, but the doctors were able to stabilize her wounds. Afterward, she was put in the intensive-care unit, and there was a television on. Tonya looked up at the screen, and she saw her house and the authorities carrying out a body in a green bag. She started shaking.

"He's dead, isn't he," she said.

Someone quickly turned off the television set and told Tonya to worry about herself. That was when she knew her Donnie was gone.

The three children stayed with friends and relatives after the shooting. It was difficult for the boys to understand what had happened. They kept asking about their dad.

The next day, they were taken to the hospital to see their mother. They went back and forth from the intensive-care unit waiting room to the lobby. Ronnie, the youngest child, bought his mother a necklace at the hospital gift shop.

The boys played with some of the other children who were present, running around the room and into the hallways. Ronnie ran past a newspaper rack, where he saw his father's picture on the front page of a newspaper. He stopped and pointed at the photo.

"See, he's on the cover of the newspaper."

Tonya was too weak to attend a memorial service held for Donnie in nearby Santa Ana, California, or to travel to Lubbock, Texas, for his funeral. She still was in the hospital, with tubes running from her body and a respirator hooked up to her lungs. She vowed she would attend the wake one way or the other, so arrangements were made to bring

Donnie's body to a private room in the hospital. There, Tonya would be able to see him one last time. She would get to say good-bye to her Donnie.

When she was taken into the room where Donnie was, she saw that he was in a suit she had not wanted him buried in. She was unhappy about that. Donnie's hair was messed up, so Tonya tried to fix it. She sat in the room and cried and talked to Donnie and fumbled with his hair, and there were tubes hanging out of her and police all around. It was a mess.

She told Donnie she loved him, and she forgave him. She asked him why. Why did he do it? What made him do such a thing?

After she was well enough to leave the hospital, Tonya spent two months in a treatment center. "The cuckoo house," she called it.

People think the cuckoo house is a bunch of crazy people running around, but it isn't. It's like a big hospital, with little kids downstairs, and a wing for people who are being treated for drug abuse or alcohol abuse, and another for sexually abused people, and one for obese people, and so on. There are all kinds of people there, not just a bunch of crazy people.

The cuckoo house is there to help people understand, and to figure out what they are going through, and to accept it. To realize that they are not the only ones who have gone through what they are going through, that other people have similar problems.

When Tonya got out of the cuckoo house, she returned to the house in Anaheim Hills. It was important to her to be in that house, and to go through it again.

She wanted to see pictures of the house after the shooting, and she wanted Donnie's gun, the one he had used to shoot her. She wanted it because it was the last thing Donnie touched.

She got home and sat in front of the house, and she could feel Donnie inside. People thought she was crazy, but she could feel him in there. When she slept in her bed at night, there was nobody in heaven who could get her to go into the kitchen without the lights on. She was never in the house alone at night after that. Never.

She knew Donnie was there. He wasn't trying to hurt her, but he was there. One time, Tonya was asleep and she felt Donnie rubbing her ponytail. He was doing it to let her know everything was all right, that he was watching over her. It was weird.

Sometimes, she could see Donnie walking through the house in the purple Puma pants he used to wear. Donnie had a contract with Puma, and he had purple pants and purple shoes. She still saw him in those purple pants.

Donnie wasn't there to hurt her. He was just there to let her know everything was okay.

Tonya bought a Ouija board for the boys. She called it a "squee-gie" board. Ronnie got it out one day and said: "We never told Daddy good-bye. Let's tell Daddy good-bye."

So Tonya and the boys tried the Ouija board. They held their hands over the Ouija, placing their fingertips on it as instructed, and the Ouija started moving across the board toward the different letters. It moved on its own power—no one there was moving it. It scared Tonya, and she jumped up from the table. The boys got mad at her, but she didn't care. She took the Ouija board and threw it away.

Later, Ronnie retrieved the Ouija board from the trash. Tonya found it and wouldn't let the boys bring it back into the house. If they wanted to do something like that again, she told them, they would have to have a séance, or something with someone who knew what they were doing. There are good spirits and bad spirits, and you don't want to release the wrong ones. You need to be careful about such things.

A couple of years after the shooting, Tonya sold the house and moved to another in the same area, about ten minutes away. She didn't need the big house anymore. And it was time to move on. There were too many memories there.

She still drives by the house, though. It isn't far away, so she will drive by every once in a while. When she does, she can still feel Donnie's presence there. She knows he is still in that house. It was his house. His spirit is still there.

◇ It used to be difficult for Tonya to talk about Donnie and what happened. It got easier with time. As the years passed, she could talk about it better.

She sat in a small hotel room on the outskirts of Fort Worth one day in the spring, and she recalled her life with Donnie, the shooting and its aftermath. She was in town to visit her mother, who was ill. It had been four years since Donnie's death, and talking about it brought back painful memories. But it was important for Tonya to talk about it.

"I have a lot I want to say. But due to the fact that I want to write a book, people tell me I shouldn't say much."

Tonya sat cross-legged on the bed.

"But there's a lot I need to say. A lot I need to say. A lot. A lot."

She spoke slowly, choosing her words carefully.

"What I want this book to be about is Donnie Moore . . . me . . .baseball . . . the front office . . . fans . . . players . . . the writers. Um, and also I'm going to write a book about battered women . . ."

Tonya's voice was barely audible over the steady drone of the air-conditioning unit in the room. It was a warm, sunny day outside. Another baseball season had begun. Tonya still followed baseball, and when she picked up a newspaper she always read the sports pages first, "like I'm some kind of man or something." She always looked for the familiar names of the players she had known when she was in baseball. But that had been a long time ago, and now there were very few names she recognized. Still, Tonya faithfully read the box scores and statistics each day. It was a habit. She had been in baseball since she was nineteen years old, and old habits were hard to break.

". . . battered baseball women," she concluded. "I'm sure I'm not the only one."

Tonya also wanted to appear on some television talk shows to talk about these things. There was so much that she could talk about.

"How people sit in the audience, or sit wherever they are sitting, and make judgment." Her voice rose in anger. "How they criticize and they don't know SHIT about what they're talking about! Have never experienced, and don't know why, but they always got something to say about the situation. I would love to be on talk shows about this situation here.

"Um, it's just like, people are so . . . people are so critical! I can understand kids being critical. But adults? I mean, goddamn, use your brain!"

She had so much to share. She could talk about sexual abuse, and battered women, and what they must go through.

"You know how people don't believe. How people are always trying to put the blame on the person that it is happening to. Or how to cope with your life once it's happened to you. Most people that are abused sexually, mentally or physically think it's their fault. How to accept that it is not your fault."

Tonya paused and took a deep breath. She still had to take short, quick breaths sometimes because of the damage the bullet had done to her lung. Sometimes, her neck, where she had also been shot, felt numb, as if it were not alive. The doctors called her "Miracle Girl," she said. She had six bullet holes in her, and should have been dead or paralyzed. But she had made a full recovery physically. The emotional wounds were taking longer to heal.

"It was difficult for me to watch a movie that had shooting in it," she said. "Especially if somebody shoots theirself in the head, I just freaked out. But now I can handle it sometimes. It depends on how much shooting. Because usually when I hear gunshots, it's like I can feel myself being shot again."

She seemed lost in her thoughts. "Yep, being shot is an experience. It didn't hurt. It's just an experience."

Tonya's voice had lost its anger. She was subdued, and she sounded weary.

"I've been through so much in my life," she said softly. "Being shot by my husband was the icing on the cake. But I'm still here. I'm here for a reason.

"I should be dead. So why am I here? Am I here to help others? Am I here—I know I'm here for my kids. Am I here to talk to people about my life, what I've been through? How I survived—barely?"

She was quiet for a moment. She closed her eyes. "Um, I know I'm going to make it. I mean, there's just steps I have to go through to make it. It's a difficult task sometimes. Sometimes, I don't think I can go on.

"But, like they say, God puts no more on you than you are able to deal with. But, I don't know. Life is hard. I know I'm not the only one out there who has been through all this shit."

"How'm I doing emotionally?" Tonya said, repeating the question. She thought about it a moment.

"Hmmmm. They tell me I'm a strong female. I've been through a lot. I used to never cry. I refused to cry. There's no tears in these eyes. It's like I'll just block out the pain. And I've got so much pain. But now I cry."

She laughed at herself. It was a short, sad laugh.

"Tears just roll down these eyes sometimes, you know, and sometimes it hits me, like when I look at my kids and what they're going through, and sometimes I wonder if I'm being a good enough parent for them. I mean, sometimes I wonder, do they blame me for their father's death?

"It's difficult for me to leave them. My kids used to think I'd never come back."

There were times when things got so bad Tonya wanted to kill herself. But then she would think about her kids, and how her problems would go to them, like Donnie's problems went to her. How would her kids go on with two parents who'd killed themselves? Thinking about her kids made her realize she had to be strong enough to deal with her problems, to work them out, whatever it took. It was hard, but she had to do it.

Tonya smiled when she thought about her children.

Ronnie, who was twelve now, looked exactly like his father. He had his legs and his body. And he pitched like him, too. The first time Tonya saw Ronnie pitch, she almost passed out. He had the same form, the same movement, the same everything as his dad. He was just a miniature Donnie Moore. Tonya watched Ronnie pitch, and she saw her husband pitch all over again.

Ronnie was named after Donnie's half brother, who was killed when he and Donnie were young boys. When Tonya got pregnant the third time, Donnie asked her, "If it's a little boy, can we name him after my brother?" That is how he got his name, Ronnie Ray Moore.

He was the neat one in the family.

"His room is perfect," said Tonya. "He collects baseball cards, basketball cards. He puts a lock on his door so his brother's friends don't come in the room. He kicks their ass if they do."

Tonya remembered the time, more than three years after Donnie's death, that Ronnie went on a field trip to Anaheim Stadium, where his dad had pitched. Tonya went also, because she was worried about her son. It was the type of field trip where you went into the clubhouse and the dugout and onto the field, all the places where the players went. Tonya wanted to be there to help support her son, in case he needed her.

"I'm so worried about Ronnie," she recalled, "and we go down to the clubhouse, and we start going toward where Donnie was—used to be. I totally freaked out. I had to go to the escalator and go to the top. I was shaking and tears were running down my eyes. It was like—it was like déjà vu. I mean, it was a mess.

"But Ronnie was okay. He's always okay. They're always okay. I mean, I guess one day they're going to break down. Maybe they're just stronger than I am. I don't know."

Donnie Junior was fourteen. He was the quiet one.

"Sometimes, I don't even know he's there." Tonya smiled. "I'll go in there and he be talking to those girls."

Donnie was also a pitcher, but he was taking a break from playing ball. People depended on him in sports. Maybe he was tired of it. Tonya didn't know. She didn't know what was going on in his head.

Was it because Donnie felt the pressure of trying to live up to his father's reputation in baseball? Other people must expect the sons of famous players to be superstars.

Tonya shook her head. "It doesn't bother them. No, it doesn't bother them.

"Like Donnie, this year he was in class, and I believe they were talking about suicide. And there was a new little boy that came to his school, and he was saying, 'Oh, do you remember that ballplayer Donnie Moore who killed himself?' and such-and-such and such-and-such.

"And everybody looked at Donnie. And then they looked at the boy. And he said to him, 'Oh, you're that Donnie Moore.' And Donnie didn't look at him. And Donnie didn't say anything. No reaction, no nothing.

"Then the teacher explained to the little boy what was going on. They handled it well. They probably handled it better than I would have."

Dee was twenty-one. She and Donnie Junior looked like her mother.

"Miss Dee Moore," Tonya said proudly. "She's working part-time and enjoying life. She was thinking of being a model. That's a difficult task, but she's got the body. Now she wants to be a lawyer. If she can't model, she wants to be a lawyer.

"When she was in the mental institution, she was a senior. She had a partial scholarship to Yale, but she decided not to go. And she was good in sports, too—basketball, tennis. She was all-American in basketball."

Dee still went to the Angels games after her father's death. It didn't seem to bother her. Nothing seemed to bother her.

"Oh, Dee's so headstrong. After it happened, she was going in the house, she was doing this, she was doing that. I don't know. I don't know. I don't think nothing bothers her.

"I mean, I don't even know if she broke down and cried about the situation. She was mad at me because I put her in a mental institution. She told me, 'I saved your life, and this is what you did to me.'"

Sometimes, Tonya and the boys joked about the cuckoo house. They might be walking in the mall and one of the boys would start cutting up, and Tonya would laugh and tell him, "They're going to put you back in the cuckoo house."

His answer would be, "You're the one who needs to be in the cuckoo house." And they would all laugh some more.

It had been almost four years since the shooting, and the wounds were slowly starting to heal.

"We talk about it a little bit now," Tonya said. "But it takes time. It's getting easier and easier."

Tonya was still trying to decide what she wanted to do next.

"I'm thinking about going back to school," she said, and her voice picked up. "I got to do something. I love music. I've always wanted to be a singer. But that was a long time ago. I'm almost forty years old now."

Forty is still young, she was told.

"I don't know." She sounded tired again. "You got to have somebody behind you to push you. Like my husband. I was always there for him. Always."

She did not have a job, she said. But she kept busy.

"I work out. I cook. I clean. I take care of my baby."

Tonya stopped and thought. "I stress out," she added.

She threw back her head and laughed. "Ohhhhhh!"

"Excuse me," she said, still smiling at her private joke.

And how was she doing financially?

"So-so. I'm making it. Donnie owes back taxes, and I have to pay that crap."

There also was the matter of paying off Donnie's debt to his agent, David Pinter. Donnie had not gotten along well with his agent, said Tonya, and Donnie still owed him money from his contract.

"They didn't have a good relationship. Usually, I did all the talking. At first, they had a good relationship. But later on, they didn't."

"Maybe David said something to him wrong or made a wrong opinion. I don't know what happened between them. It might have been money. Money makes people act crazy."

Tonya did not like Pinter, either. Anytime his name was mentioned, she replied with obvious disdain, "Oh, Mister David PINTER."

She believed Pinter had misled her in their dealings after Donnie's death. He had tried to trick her into signing some papers, she said, and she no longer trusted him. He had made what she considered inappropriate remarks to her. Plus, Pinter had sued to get the money he was owed by Donnie, and now Tonya had to pay him.

"Somehow I was advised when Donnie passed away, I didn't have to pay his bills," she said, "but I do."

But Tonya also had some money due her. After Donnie had his outstanding season in 1985 and became a free agent, California was the only team to offer him a contract. He signed the $3 million deal with the Angels, but he never got the chance to see how much money he could have commanded on the open market. Later, it was ruled the major-league owners had illegally conspired not to sign other teams' free agents that year. The owners were fined, and that money was being disbursed to the players affected by the collusion. Tonya would receive the $264,000 awarded Donnie.

She wished she had more of Donnie's belongings: his baseball souvenirs, his old uniforms, his gloves, his caps and other momentos. All of that had been in the house when Donnie died, but it was not there when Tonya returned home from the hospital. There had been so many people in the house, so many family members, and someone took these things. Tonya wanted them to give to her children, but now they were gone.

Tonya lost so much more than these keepsakes. She also lost her relationship with Donnie's family. After Donnie's death, her in-laws no longer wanted anything to do with her, she said. She felt betrayed.

"It's like, uh, I think they blame me because their son shot me. He tried to kill me, I didn't try to kill him."

She ran her hand through her hair. "It hurts, because I was close to them. At least I thought I was. I guess somehow I needed their love, their understanding. But I got none of that shit! All I got was criticism, hatred, meanness, evilness!"

There had been an article about Donnie in *Gentlemen's Quarterly* magazine in February 1990. In it, some of Donnie's family members speculated that Tonya had arranged her husband's death, perhaps bringing in a third person to shoot him and make it appear to be a suicide.

Tonya's voice rose in anger. "Yeah. Or maybe I shot him and then shot myself. Right, I'm going to shoot myself three times. I mean, no one—why are they going to make accusations?

"Thank God my kids were there, because I'd probably be in jail or prison, or still going through court, or God knows what. I mean, all they have to do is ask their grandkids. Their grandkids saw everything."

Tonya thought about it some more, and it made her sad. "I used to want their love. Now, I have accepted that either they hate me or they blame me for what's going on, and they don't want anything to do with me.

"I feel sorry for them, because they had only one child. I didn't destroy his life. He destroyed his own life."

It was getting late in the afternoon. Tonya would be leaving the next day to return home to California. She was looking forward to getting home and seeing her children again.

She thought about the summer and what the boys might be doing when school was out. She still toyed with the idea of taking singing lessons. And she thought about the book she wanted to write.

"It will have a lot to do with what I think about men." After Donnie's death, she would not look at another black man, she said. If two men were sitting in a room, and one was white and the other black, she would talk to the white man but not the black man. But that had changed. She no longer was wary of black men, or afraid, or whatever it was that caused her to feel the way she had.

"At least I don't hate men," she added.

In her book, Tonya said, she will try to make people understand what Donnie felt, and what he went through. She wanted people to understand.

And how did she want Donnie remembered?

Tonya thought for a moment before answering. "I want him to be remembered as a nice, thoughtful man. An excellent pitcher. I'm not sure how his teammates think about him. I think he was a great person.

"Although he killed himself, he ended his life when he thought that has to be it. And I can kind of relate, because when it seems like nothing is going right, and my problems are getting stronger and stronger and stronger, and no matter what I do I can't make them go away, I can't make them right, I just want to die. So, I want him to be remembered as a great person and a very good athlete."

Tonya blinked back the tears. "I think a lot of people owe him an apology," she whispered.

She had a lot of bitterness in her, she admitted. But she could not be blamed for that.

"All those people that booed him, I wonder how they feel. Do you think that they had anything to do with my husband being dead? Is that bothering their conscience? I think it might have something to do with it. Can they live with theirself, knowing each and every day that Donnie Moore might be dead because they didn't have enough courtesy to give him a hand?"

She clapped her hands together several times to demonstrate what she meant, and in the tiny hotel room there was the sharp sound of the applause that her Donnie never heard after he gave up that home run.

Tonya still went to visit Donnie's grave in Lubbock on occasion. The first time she did so was a year and a half after his death.

"Why do you want to go see him?" her mother asked her. "He tried to KILL you."

But Tonya still went. Other people didn't understand, but she knew she had to go.

She went to his grave, and she sat and talked to Donnie. She talked and talked and talked.

"Donnie, what the hell is going on?" she asked. "WHY?"

Why did he do it? That was the question Tonya kept asking. But she never got an answer. Donnie was the only one who knew, and he couldn't tell her.

5

MIKE WITT: WITT'S END

It was the most controversial move of the 1986 American League Championship Series. California manager Gene Mauch pulled his best pitcher with a one-run lead and two outs in the ninth inning of Game 5.

Mike Witt, the six-foot, seven-inch right-hander with the ninety-three-mile-an-hour fastball and the "Mercedes bends" curveball needed just one more out to put the Angels in the World Series. He had faced thirty-four Boston batters and gotten out twenty-six of them; surely he could retire one more. He had thrown 121 pitches. He was bound to have at least one more in his powerful right arm.

But Mauch played it by the book. There was a left-handed hitter, Rich Gedman, coming to bat. Mauch chose to bring in a left-handed pitcher to face him.

Witt was standing on the mound, waiting to pitch to Gedman, when he saw someone coming out of the California dugout. It wasn't Mauch, who normally made the pitching changes. It was Marcel Lachemann, the pitching coach.

"I thought we were going to discuss how to get Rich Gedman out," remembered Witt. "He had had a good day off me."

For eight innings, Gedman had been the only Red Sox who had done any damage against Witt. He had three hits, including a home run.

Lachemann arrived at the mound, and Witt waited for instructions on how to pitch to Gedman. "Tell me what to do and we'll get this guy," he thought. "Then we can start celebrating."

Instead, Lachemann took the ball from Witt and signaled for a new pitcher. That was how Mauch wanted to play it.

A few minutes later, Witt was sitting in the clubhouse, stripped down to his underwear, an ice pack strapped to his right arm. He watched on a television monitor as California's once-certain victory unraveled. Gary Lucas, the left-handed reliever, hit Gedman with a pitch. Donnie Moore came in to relieve Lucas. He got two strikes on Dave Henderson.

"Don't throw him a split-finger!" someone in the clubhouse yelled.

Moore threw the split-finger, and Henderson hit it over the left-field fence for a home run. The Red Sox won the game, and the Angels never recovered. The playoffs would not end until the Red Sox won two more times in Boston to complete their comeback, but for all practical purposes the pennant was decided that Sunday afternoon in Anaheim Stadium.

The Angels let the game, and the league championship, slip away from them. They had their best pitcher on the mound, but they took him out one batter too soon.

Afterward, Gene Mauch went up to Mike Witt to tell him why he had felt it necessary to pull him when he was so close to the victory.

"I didn't want him to get you," said Mauch, referring to Gedman. "I didn't want him to get you."

Witt nodded. He understood. Still, he couldn't help but think, "Then come out and tell me how to get him out, and we'll get him out."

But there was nothing Witt could do about it.

"They took the ball," he said, "and that's it."

It was a spring day, and Mike Witt, then thirty-two years old, once again had an ice pack attached to his right arm after pitching in a ball game. This time, the scene was Fort Lauderdale, Florida, not Anaheim, California. The uniform that hung in his locker was that of the New York Yankees, not the California Angels. And the game still in progress outside was a meaningless exhibition, not a postseason playoff game.

Witt reached above his locker and pulled down a baseball card of himself.

"I've got to look at the card," he said. He glanced at the statistics printed on the back. "It was in '90. I hurt my arm in '90."

He had trouble remembering the year, but not the situation. It was the second inning of a game in Baltimore. There were two outs, and Greg Walker was the batter. Witt threw a pitch and immediately felt "a pop" in his right elbow.

And that was the beginning of his troubles. He left the game and the next day was placed on the disabled list for the first time in his career. He would spend the next three years trying to overcome problems with the elbow.

Witt used the years listed on the baseball card as a checklist of his medical history.

"I rehabbed for two months in '90. I came back for spring training here in '91 and hurt the elbow again. That was the worst. I tried to rehab all of '91, pitched a couple of games and had surgery in July."

It was a complicated procedure. The ulnar collateral ligament in Witt's right elbow was reconstructed, using a tendon in his left leg to replace the one in his elbow. He was not able to pitch until June 1992, eleven months later. Witt pitched three games for the Yankees' Rookie League team in Tampa, Florida, and developed tendinitis in the elbow. Once again, he had to stop throwing.

"I guess it survived '92." He smiled, holding up the elbow.

The process of rehabilitating the elbow was slow and often discouraging. Weeks turned into months as Witt struggled to regain the ability to throw a baseball. Finally, in the spring of 1993, he was able to test his elbow in a "Grapefruit League" game against the Mets in Florida. Witt pitched two scoreless innings. It was a significant step in his comeback, and in the clubhouse afterward he was encouraged by his performance.

Witt had been with the Yankees three years now and had pitched in only eighteen regular-season games. He had just five victories in pinstripes. It wasn't much of a return on the three-year, $7.7 million contract he signed with the team in January 1991.

"It's been tough not being able to earn my keep," he said. "But when you hurt your arm, there's nothing you can do about it. You just let the doc do what he has to do and you do what you have to do to get back. Hopefully, everything will work out and you will get back in there."

But even before he hurt his elbow, Witt had not been the same dominating pitcher he had been in that memorable 1986 season. The year after the playoffs, he gave up more than four earned runs a game, and he slumped badly in the second half of the season to barely finish above .500 with a 16–14 won-lost record. He had losing records in 1988 and 1989 and was demoted to the bullpen the following season. Witt started the 1990 season in spectacular style, pitching the final two innings of a combined no-hitter with Mark Langston against Seattle. But a month later, Witt was traded to the Yankees for Dave Winfield.

Witt can't explain what caused the sudden turnaround in his fortunes, from one of the league's best to a losing pitcher.

"In '87, I was ten-and-five at the break and ended up going six-and-nine after the break," he began. "And I'm trying to put my finger on what happened myself. To go ten-and-five and six-and-nine is just ludicrous.

"And the next year, I just followed the same pattern. Thirteen-and-sixteen. I pitched a lot of innings and struck out a lot of guys, but I wasn't getting the results.

"I don't know if it was an arm problem I didn't know about, or I just physically couldn't do it, or what. But I was pitching, and obviously getting guys out, because I was pitching a lot of innings. But I gave up a lot of hits and runs, and just wasn't as good a pitcher as I was before then. I still can't figure out what was going on."

Those were rough years. He had enjoyed pitching in southern California, where he lived, but once he started losing, the fans began to turn on him. Suddenly, Witt, the hometown hero, was becoming the target of the fans' boos.

"It hurt," he said of how the fans reacted. "But, you know, it's a business. And maybe it was a change of scenery I needed.

"I came over here and had some success after I was traded. They signed me to a three-year deal after that first year, and then I hurt my arm."

He laughed. "So, here I sit."

Had he learned any lessons in all of this, he was asked.

"Well, I've learned to be persistent and to persevere through a few things, whether it is the fans booing or the media getting on you or whatever. You've just got to keep going."

Mike Witt pitched the California Angels within one out of the World Series before manager Gene Mauch lifted him for a reliever in Game 5 of the AL Championship Series. "I don't hold anything against him for doing what he did. . . . He just thought that was the best move to make at that particular time. I can't fault him for that," said Witt. *Photo courtesy California Angels.*

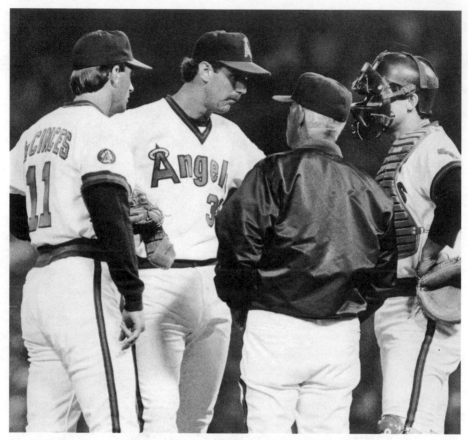

From left, Angels Doug DeCinces, Mike Witt, Gene Mauch and Bob Boone confer on the mound. "Playing with Gene," said DeCinces, "sometimes he controlled the pitchers to the point where it was difficult to deal with." *Photo courtesy California Angels.*

Mike Witt is not a man to dwell on the past. Ask him about the 1986 American League playoffs and his role in that famous fifth game, and he will tell you he can't remember the last time he gave it so much as a passing thought.

"It's got to be at least two years," he said. "Somebody probably brought it up and I thought about it for a while.

"Every now and then, I'll run across something in the house, like in the attic when I'll go through some things looking for something else and I'll see a baseball or some articles about my games. But it never runs through my mind just sitting around."

Mostly, he remembers the postseason for other reasons. It was on October 6, 1986, the day before he was to pitch the opener of the American League Championship Series in Boston, that his second child, Justin, was born. And four years earlier, when California played the Milwaukee Brewers in the 1982 playoffs, Witt began dating Lisa Fenn, who worked in the Angels' marketing department.

"I knew her before then," he pointed out. "But we really got together during the playoffs. That was when we made an item of ourselves."

The couple were married the following year, in November 1983. By then, Witt, only twenty-three years old, already had spent three full seasons in the major leagues. He had a tremendous amount of talent, but he was young and inexperienced, and he struggled to gain the confidence and concentration it took to win at baseball's highest level.

Looking back, Witt admits he might have been in over his head, but he had no regrets, then or later.

"In a baseball sense, it was difficult coming up at such a young age," he said. "But in my career and my life, it was great. I was twenty years old and making a lot of money and playing in the big leagues. I wouldn't change it for anything.

"People said I needed to go down to the minors and learn how to pitch, and I thought, Oh, please don't do that, I'm having too much fun here. But it took me three years before I figured out what the heck to do up here. Maybe the three years could have been better spent in the minor leagues, but at the time California didn't have anybody, so I was it."

Witt's breakthrough came in 1984, the first season after his marriage. He won fifteen games and lost eleven, struck out 196 batters in 246 innings and ended the season by throwing a perfect game against the Texas Rangers.

"That was my first good year," he said. "I struck out a lot of guys and got a lot of innings in. I think that whole year was more of the thing that got me going. If I had got ripped that last game, I think I still would have had confidence going into the next year. But the perfect game was like an exclamation point on that whole year, which was a turning point in my career. It carried over for the next four or five years, and I threw pretty well for a long time there."

In a four-year stretch, Witt won sixty-four games and pitched more than a thousand innings for the Angels. But the 1986 season was his masterpiece. His won-lost record of 18–10 did not reflect his true dominance, as Witt posted a brilliant 2.84 earned-run average and struck out 208 batters. He was especially overpowering in the month of August, when he won five games and allowed just one earned run in forty-three innings.

On a team of superstars and famous personalities, it was Witt who was selected California's Most Valuable Player as the Angels won the American League West Division title.

And when the playoffs opened in Boston, it was Witt who pitched a five-hitter for an 8–1 victory over the Red Sox and Roger Clemens, who had won both the American League Most Valuable Player and Cy Young awards.

"I hadn't been in that situation before," recalled Witt. "I was on the team during the '82 playoffs, but I was a bullpen pitcher. In '86, I remember getting up the day of the first game of the playoffs and reading *USA Today* and all the other papers and seeing my name and Clemens' name together. It was a good feeling to see that.

"For some reason, I was relaxed that day. I was just really relaxed. And I knew I was going to pitch a good game. I didn't know if I was going to win or not, but I knew I was going to pitch a good game. I knew if we got some runs, we had a chance to win.

"Even though that was Clemens' MVP and Cy Young year and all that stuff, he had gotten hit in the arm his last start. He was hurting a little bit, and we jumped on him quick. After we won, I had to get up at something like five in the morning or four in the morning the next day to be on *Good Morning America*. But I had no problem getting up."

Five days later, Witt drew the starting assignment in the fifth game of the playoff series. This time, the stakes were even higher. If the Angels won, they would advance to the World Series for the first time in the franchise's history.

It was the most important game of Mike Witt's career. There was a sell-out crowd in Anaheim Stadium. A national television audience was watching. The Angels were coming off an emotional victory the night before, when they rallied for three runs in the ninth inning against Roger Clemens and eventually prevailed in extra innings for a three-game-to-one lead in the series. Witt had the chance to add the finishing touch to California's dream season.

He had no trouble remembering the feelings of that day.

"It was a big, emotional game. In Game 4, we came back against Clemens, and we were riding high. Just one more game. That was what we were thinking.

"I had the same feelings I did the first game. I was real confident. I knew what I could do. I knew I could get them out, because I had done it before. And I went out there and threw great the first eight innings. Everything was going our way.

"The ninth inning came, and we needed three more outs. We were winning, what, five–two? Then Buckner got a hit, Baylor hit a home run, and it's five-to-four. I had two outs when Dewey Evans popped up, and they took me out. The rest is history."

Witt shrugged his shoulders and laughed. He long ago had come to grips with the events of that day. He had wanted to stay in the game to get that final out, but even as he walked off the field, looking tired and angry, Witt understood Mauch's logic in making the pitching change.

"I felt, 'Lefty against lefty, Lucas against Gedman, and let's get out of here.' So, I was waiting for it to happen. I was waiting for everyone to come in the clubhouse and yell and scream.

"But Lucas hits him. So, they take him out and bring Donnie Moore in. That's not the whole game right there, but Dave Henderson hits a two-run home run and they take the lead."

Witt stopped to adjust the ice pack he was wearing.

"I was icing my arm just like this in the clubhouse," he continued, "and watching on TV. The pitch Moore threw Henderson was a real similar pitch to what I had thrown Baylor. A nasty, nasty pitch. I could not believe the ball went out of the ballpark when Baylor hit it. I still can't. And seeing the pitch Donnie Moore threw Henderson, I couldn't believe that ball went out of the ballpark. It was a good pitch.

"It was a split-finger, right? Location-wise, it was just too good a pitch to hit out of the ballpark. A base hit or whatever, but not out of ballpark.

"I threw Baylor a curveball, not a split-finger, but what I'm saying is the pitches were so similar as far as being nasty. That was Moore's out pitch. The curveball is my out pitch. It just had to be an out."

And what about Rich Gedman? Why was he, alone among the Red Sox that day, able to hit the ball so hard and do so much damage against Witt?

"I still can't figure that out," said Witt. "He hit fastballs that day, I believe. The first time up, I threw a pitch that almost hit him in the belt. He hit a homer off it. That gave them the lead. Then we got the lead off Hurst. The second time up, Gedman hit a double off the wall. The third time, he hit a single.

"So, when he came up for the last out, I'm thinking we need to try something different here to get him out."

Witt never got the chance because of Mauch's decision to pull him. In light of how the game and the playoffs turned out, that move drew a considerable amount of criticism.

But no matter how much he wanted to stay in the game, Witt never joined in the criticism of Mauch. Immediately afterward, his comment had been: "He made the right move. In that spot, bringing in a lefty makes sense. Anyone who second-guesses the move is using twenty-twenty hindsight."

With time to think about it, Witt still professed to have no qualms about Mauch's decision.

"I always got along with Gene," said Witt. "He treated me real good. He thought a lot of me, I know that. And he taught me a lot, so I probably wouldn't have been in that situation if it weren't for him.

"I still respect him. I don't hold anything against him for doing what he did. That was just his style. That was his way, and that's how he wanted to win that game that day. He definitely didn't want to lose. I mean, whoever would think that is kind of nuts. He just thought that was the best move to make at that particular time. I can't fault him for that."

A bell went off on the timer attached to the ice pack on his arm. Witt loosened the strap and removed the bag. He felt his rebuilt elbow with his left hand and turned his thoughts back to his chances of pitching in the big leagues again. As for the 1986 playoffs, well, maybe when he was older he would spend more time reminiscing about them.

"But I'm hoping something else happens between now and then to where I can talk about that more than I talk about losing a game or a World Series I didn't make. If I do my part here and help us get into a World Series, I would much rather talk about that."

Witt flexed his right arm and smiled. It was the future he was thinking about, not the past.

6

DOUG DECINCES:

NO HANDSHAKES, JUST A PIECE OF PAPER

The Boston Red Sox intentionally walked a batter to pitch to Doug DeCinces with the bases loaded in the bottom of the ninth inning of Game 5 in the 1986 American League playoffs. The score was tied. All DeCinces had to do was hit a long fly ball, and the Angels would win the pennant.

But he didn't do it. The first pitch was a fastball, and he popped it up into shallow right field. The Angels never did get that run home, and Boston went on to win the pennant.

DeCinces took a lot of heat for swinging at the first pitch in that situation. He should have taken a pitch, said the second-guessers.

"I've heard some writers be critical of swinging at the first pitch," said DeCinces. "But I've gotta tell you something. . . ."

He mentioned a game that was played the following spring. The same two teams were playing, again in Anaheim Stadium. The same situation arose. The Angels had runners on second and third, and once again the Red Sox walked the next batter to pitch to DeCinces.

"The first pitch was a fastball," he said, "and I hit it out of the ball-park for a grand slam. So, you tell me."

He let out a loud sigh. "No, they don't second-guess when you hit it out."

They should have held a ceremony for Doug DeCinces after he played his last game for the California Angels. He deserved a day in his honor, with speeches on the field and accolades by the ball club. The owner should have been there to bid him farewell.

He had been that kind of ballplayer. He was a local boy who made good, the player who succeeded the immortal Brooks Robinson in Baltimore and then came home to southern California to finish his career with six outstanding years with the Angels.

He hit 130 home runs for California, and he thrilled the fans with his spectacular plays at third base. He was a team leader, both on the field and in the clubhouse.

He played through the pain of chronic back problems and seven broken noses in his career. When he had good years, the Angels had good years, winning division titles in 1982 and 1986. He helped Baltimore win a pennant in 1979. Doug DeCinces was a winner.

He should have gotten a hero's send-off when the end came. Instead, the Angels gave him nothing more than a slip of paper.

The club didn't even have the decency to wait until the end of the season to let him go. It cut him with one week to play in 1987 in order to save $141,000 on the buyout clause of his contract.

The end was as swift as it was cruel. Two hours before game time, general manager Mike Port called DeCinces to his office and handed him a form to sign. It was a statement notifying him of his release by the team.

That was it. That was what Doug DeCinces got for the 482 runs he drove in as an Angel, for the fourteen cortisone shots he took one year to mask the pain in his back, for all the sweat and tears he gave the team, for the two division winners he played on. Not even a handshake; just a piece of paper to be signed.

That was the way it was in baseball. It could be a cold business.

The back pain was still there. More than five years after he played his last game of baseball, Doug DeCinces continued to have to deal with it. He had bad days, and he had good days. But always, the back was liable to give out on him.

"I still have problems with it," he said. "That and my hip. It affects me on the fifteenth hole now."

DeCinces laughed at his little joke. He had a deep, hearty laugh that must have been a good antidote for all the discomfort the bad back had caused him over the years.

"Sometimes, my back will really lock up still," he continued. "I never had the surgery, and I have to be very careful. It feels better on a consistent basis, because I'm not out pounding it all the time playing baseball.

"But by the same token, there are times I still hurt it. For instance, I was back East last week, and I rode the train from Baltimore to New York for a meeting. The next day, I hardly could move. Just from that constant vibration or whatever. So, I still have to be careful."

DeCinces had been traveling on business. He was president and chief executive officer of DeCinces Properties in Newport Beach, California, and in the fall of 1993, the real-estate slump that had plagued California showed signs of ending.

"Things are starting to pick up now," he said. "We represent a few people, we buy and sell some things and we also have our own properties that we handle as far as managing them.

"One of the largest industrial parks we have, we're trying to sell. That was one of the reasons I was back East, and now they're coming back out here. Hopefully, tomorrow we can finalize that deal. I do that, and I represent a couple of players that I send overseas, to Japan."

His ties to Japan stemmed from the season he played ball there, the year after the Angels let him go. His time in Japan, like his final days as an Angel, was not pleasant.

He encountered resentment because he was a "gaijin," or foreigner. Opposing pitchers threw at him. The fans booed him when he failed to deliver a hit. As a ballplayer, he could endure the hardships and the abuse on the field. But as a father, it was difficult for him to handle the treatment endured by his wife, Kristi, and his two children, Amy and Tim. They were stared at on the street, and ostracized by the neighbors. They sensed the resentment directed toward them as outsiders.

One rainy night in Tokyo, DeCinces slipped on the wet turf and injured his back again. That was when he knew it was time to hang up his glove. Two days later, he and his family were on a plane back to California. DeCinces was ready to build a life after baseball.

He and his father founded the property company after his retirement from baseball. When business slacked off, he formed a marketing company, DeCinces Sports Productions, which was involved in coordinating sporting events, consulting and dealing in sports memorabilia. It was a welcome change of pace, but by 1993 most of his energies were once again focused on the property company.

"I still have both companies, but the sports-production business is really down to nothing but finishing out some problems," he said. "I formed that business when I had a contract with Upper Deck [card company] to be a consultant with them. Since then, our consulting contract has ended, and I really don't have any other things.

"I do, like I say, represent a couple of players, but I really don't run that through the production company. That sports-production company really was set up to do memorabilia and consulting agreements, and we sold a lot of stuff on Home Shopping Network."

DeCinces lived in the Newport Beach area, about sixty miles from the San Fernando Valley, where he grew up and played ball. He had come full circle, starting his baseball career on the East Coast, ending it in the Far East and returning to his native southern California.

His son, Tim, was now the ballplayer in the family. He had just completed his first year at UCLA, and he was going to be competing for the starting catcher's job as a redshirt freshman the following spring.

Tim, who was six-feet-two and 195 pounds, was the same size as his father. "But he's a left-handed-hitting catcher," said DeCinces with a laugh. "And I don't fit that mold."

But the father and son had more in common than their stature. Tim, like his dad, played baseball with a passion. "It's exciting to have a son that loves the game of baseball," said DeCinces. "I mean, absolutely loves it."

And what did the future hold for him? Was there going to be another DeCinces in the major leagues someday?

"I think he has a chance," said DeCinces. "I think what happens— and I tell this to everybody—there's no shoo-ins. I've seen kids that I think are outstanding athletes that will never make it. It's just a matter of the makeup of the player and being in the right place at the right time.

"I tell him to put his nose to the grindstone and keep on going. That's his dream, to play in the big leagues. You just keep working, working, working, and you never know.

"I wasn't even drafted out of high school. I'm sure a lot of people were surprised that I made it. I didn't necessarily fit the perfect mold, you might say. But because of my determination and my desire, I worked on my physical attributes, and I got stronger as I got older. And it worked out for me. Nineteen years playing professional ball it worked out."

Now, middle age was upon him, and he had a bad back as a reminder of the nearly two decades he played pro ball. The doctors told him that surgery to correct the degenerative disks in his back was inevitable. "Double fusion, if not a triple," he said.

Had it been worth it, all those years of playing ball, knowing the damage he was doing to his back?

DeCinces did not hesitate in giving his answer. "Well, I had the back problem anyway, so yes, it was worth it." He laughed again. "I would assume that I would have had a back problem whether or not I played baseball. I don't know.

"The condition I have is a degenerative disk. I have bone on bone in three different spots in my back, and I'm sure I enhanced its progression by doing what I did. I paid a big price as a player because there were lots of times it was very difficult to play, and I think it affected my performance.

"But," he added, "the important thing is that I played."

There are times when Doug DeCinces reflects on his baseball career and wonders what he could have accomplished if he had been healthy all those years, with no bad back to hamper his swing or send him to the sidelines for weeks at a time.

Perhaps the 1982 season, his first with the California Angels, provides some insight into what might have been. DeCinces had spent the previous seven seasons in Baltimore, trying to fill Hall of Famer Brooks Robinson's shoes at third base. It had been an impossible task, and

DeCinces never got full credit for his outstanding play for the Orioles. Finally, he was traded to the Angels. That first year in Anaheim, free of back pain and out of Robinson's shadow, DeCinces enjoyed his best season, batting .301 with thirty homers and ninety-seven runs batted in.

"I never really had any problems with the back in 1982," he said. "Until the end of the season. It was late in August, and I was swinging the bat real well. We played one of Billy Martin's teams up in Oakland, and it was typical Billy Martin. They just kept throwing the ball at me either until they hit me or I went out and hit them. We had a little fisticuff deal, and I strained my back in a fight.

"But that year was about the only time I didn't have major problems with my back. Then I turned around the next year, in 1983, and everything was going along great, and then I miss fifty games and end up having fourteen different injections in my back, trying to play all the time. It was just, you know, off again, on again with the back."

There were other injuries, too. The broken noses, the pulled muscles, the separated rib, the sore legs. And early in the 1986 season, when he, like so many other Angels veterans, was in the final year of his contract, DeCinces injured his shoulder.

"I had a real tough month of May," he recalled. "I separated my left shoulder, my back was bothering me and I tried to keep playing. I remember Gene Mauch begging me to play. 'Hey, you got to be out there, you're the main part of our team. I know you're not one hundred percent, but just try to play.' So, I went ahead and did that, and wasn't very successful.

"And the next thing I know, they bring up Jack Howell to play third base every day. I looked at Mauch and went, 'Wha-a-a-t?'" DeCinces snorted incredulously. "He knew that I was playing hurt, he didn't want me to sit out five days like the doctors told me to do, and I went out and played that way for, like, fifteen days. And the next thing I know, I was sitting on the bench. I had some problems there.

"But when I got healthy, I came back and took my job back and had a decent year."

DeCinces paused to reflect on his old manager. Mauch had been a tough, demanding boss, but he always knew how to win. DeCinces had gotten along well with Mauch and respected him—until the manager benched him in 1986.

"From a player's perspective," said DeCinces, "Gene was great to play for at times because once he got confidence in you as an individual, there wasn't really a problem. I mean, he would put you into positions that he knew he didn't have to worry about you.

"But playing with Gene, sometimes he controlled the pitchers and he controlled the game to the point where it was difficult to deal with. But every player has different feelings about his manager at different times. I think there were times when I played for Earl Weaver that he and I never saw eye to eye, but we went out and won. The important thing is you go out there to win, and you produce the best you can. And each manager has got to do what he's got to do to get the best out of his team.

"But asking me to do something and then me doing it and getting punished for it, that stepped over the line for me. So, in 1986, when I came back and really played well, I wasn't playing for Gene Mauch, I can tell you that.

"I was playing for the team and myself. I was a free agent at the end of the year, and I figured I had to perform to my maximum with what was going on with the collusion and whatever. And my whole career, I've always been a second-half player. And it was second-half time."

DeCinces actually began his hot streak that year in June, when he hit five homers and drove in twelve runs in thirteen games. He kept hitting after the All-Star break, and was named the league's Player of the Month for August. After his slow start and early-season benching, he provided the Angels with a dependable run-producer in the middle of their lineup during the heat of a pennant race.

"It's funny how certain players perform better at certain times of the year," he said. "I usually always had a decent April and then got into May doing okay. Then, the end of May and June were always bad months for some reason. But then July, August and September were always months throughout my career that I did well. I wish I could explain it."

Doug DeCinces knows firsthand about the old baseball adage "It ain't over 'til it's over." He played for the Baltimore Orioles in 1979, when they fell to the Pittsburgh Pirates in the World Series after leading three games to one. He was a member of the Angels team that squandered a two-game lead in Milwaukee to lose the American League playoffs in 1982.

But none of those experiences compared with 1986. The Angels had won three of the first four playoff games against Boston. They had the lead in the ninth inning of the fifth game and their best pitcher, Mike Witt, on the mound.

"Mike Witt was one of the best pitchers in the league that year," said DeCinces. "And he definitely was the guy we looked to on our staff. He was as dominant in the league as Roger Clemens was."

And then, with victory so close, Witt was taken out of the game.

"Oh, let me tell you," DeCinces said sadly, "him getting pulled out of that game was probably the single most difficult thing I look back at.

"I can recall that instant so vividly. It was a tough game, anyway. I had had a couple of hits, and I was on base when Bobby Grich hit that ball that Dave Henderson jumped up on and knocked over the fence. Things were coming along great, and Mike Witt was cruising right along.

"And then in the ninth inning, there was a little ground-ball base hit up the middle, and then Donnie Baylor hit a down-and-away curveball over the fence. But it was a good pitch. It was a sharp-breaking pitch, but Don Baylor can do that, you know. You have to accept that. He was the type of hitter in a game situation, if he got a pitch he was looking for, it didn't matter where it was or how sharp it was, he had the ability to hit it. And he hit that pitch.

"The next hitter was Dwight Evans, and he hits a pop-up, skies a pop-up to me. I remember catching the ball, and of course there's sixty-three thousand fans screaming. That's the second out of the ninth inning, and I remember when I caught the ball Mike Witt was just ten, fifteen feet from me. He had come all the way over to get the ball, and he was zeroed in. You could feel it. This game was over.

"I flipped him the ball and said, 'Hey, this is the one we're looking for.' You could tell: He had it, this was it. It was his game to win—he was our ace the whole year.

"And as he's walking back to the mound, I remember seeing Marcel Lachemann jump out of the dugout. I said to myself, 'Oh, don't talk to him here. Leave him alone. We're zeroed in. Don't disrupt this right now.' So, Lachemann gets to the foul line, and all of a sudden I see

Bob Boone starting to walk out a little quicker than normal. So, I kind of trot in, and as Lachemann gets to the mound, he reaches for the ball and raises his left hand to call for the reliever.

"Boone and I just jumped on Lachemann. We said, 'What?! WHAT?! You can't do this! What's going on?' Lachemann turned around and said, 'It's not my move. Gene's already making the move. Now, just calm down.'

"Boone and I looked at each other, and we went, 'Oh, shoot!' Mike Witt was so disgusted. He walked off the mound and stared into center field. I mean, here's a guy who had carried us all the way, and he was so prepared mentally and physically to get this next out.

"He turned around, and he flipped the ball. He looked at Boone and me—he didn't even look at Lach—he just looked at us and said, 'Make sure you get this out.' Then he walked off the field.

"History tells the rest. And I don't think Mike ever came back from that. I think it broke his spirit a little bit. He had given everything he had. It was his time to do what he had to do."

DeCinces thought back on the ensuing events of that memorable inning. He could still see Gary Lucas, the left-handed reliever, coming out of the bullpen to take Witt's place on the mound.

"You know Lucas wasn't even warmed up," said DeCinces. "He was sitting there watching like everybody else. Next thing he knows, he gets called in to be sent into a position that—well, first of all, he's been a setup man his entire career. And he has done an excellent, excellent job at that, as a left-handed setup man.

"Occasionally, he would close a game, if things were going along great. But he's certainly not a closer. And the next thing you know, he's going from sitting on the bench to being in the game with sixty-three thousand fans jumping down his throat. The electricity on the field was incredible. And the first pitch, he hits Gedman.

"Gary Lucas was a control pitcher. It wasn't a flagrant pitch, it was just a fastball in. It just kind of nicked him. That was the only pitch he threw."

DeCinces shook his head and laughed, not from amusement but disbelief. All these years later, and it was still hard to believe.

He thought of the next California pitcher, the late Donnie Moore. Poor Donnie Moore. He was in no shape to pitch that day.

"Donnie Moore had a cortisone injection the night before," said DeCinces. "He wasn't supposed to pitch. He was NOT supposed to pitch.

"So, when we see this coming in, all the players on the team went, 'Oh, my gosh. What are we doing here?' Anybody who has had an injection, you know what you feel like the next day. It's extremely uncomfortable, and very sore to move the area. And you're extremely weak because of the medicine working on the muscles. It takes about forty-eight hours to recover.

"But Donnie was such a competitor. And sometimes, competitors like that aren't always intelligent, if you know what I mean. They're never NOT going to take the ball. It's that thinking, 'Hey, sometimes you have to bite the bullet, just go out there, give it your best and whatever happens, happens.' But this was not the situation or the time to do that. But there was nobody else, so in comes Donnie.

"I remember [catcher] Bob [Boone] telling me, 'You know, he had no forkball whatsoever.' Because to throw the forkball, you need arm velocity. The ball was just tumbling up to home plate.

"Henderson missed the pitch before. It was a fastball, and Bob said, 'There's just absolutely no way I can come back with a fastball here. This guy is going to kill this.' And Donnie just kind of hung a nothing forkball, BP [batting practice] speed, right down the middle of the plate. No movement, no anything."

DeCinces never will forget that pitch. It was the one Henderson hit over the left-field fence for his famous home run. Seeing that ball sail into the stands, giving the Red Sox the lead, DeCinces sank into a crouching position, almost as if he had been punched in the stomach.

"I don't think I've ever been at such a high and such a low in a matter of seconds. It was draining. To be on that field and then to just have somebody cut your legs off, it was incredible. It was an incredible flow of emotions. You could feel it. All of a sudden, everything there was just gone. You have everything, and to have it yanked away like that was difficult."

And then the final crushing disappointment for DeCinces. It was another scene he replays often in his mind. He comes to bat in the bottom of the ninth, after the Angels have tied the score and loaded the bases with one out. It is up to him to get the winning run home.

"I remember that so clearly, let me tell you," he said. "There's many times I remember that. I wake up many times remembering it.

"I remember Gene Mauch and Reggie [Jackson] on the bench, telling me, 'Just nice and easy, hit the fly ball. You can do this, you know how to do this.' And then I remember the thought process, and one of the things if I could take that swing back again, I would have gone back to my aggressive style of hitting. I could drive in the run by being aggressive.

"The first pitch, I'm looking fastball, and he throws a fastball. I figure I'm in the driver's seat because the last thing he can do is not throw a strike. If he throws a ball on the first pitch, he's dead. And I'm an aggressive hitter, and I've been very successful in bases-loaded situations, so I went up there looking for a fastball that I could drive.

"But instead of being as aggressive as normal, I was just looking to hit a fly ball and drive in the run. The infielders were in except for the double-play situation, and all I was trying to do was make solid contact up the middle.

"I remember the contact being right in the meat of the bat. But when you're trying to hit a fly ball, you drag your barrel just a little bit. You know, you get your hands through with the barrel back just to try to hit through to right center. And I could do that. I could do it nine out of ten times. But this time the barrel was just a little back, and I hit a high fly ball to shallow right.

"I hit it to the wrong guy. Ironically, it was Dwight Evans. You know, he and I grew up together. He and I played together in Pony-Colt League. My dad coached us. If it was somebody else, you may take a chance and try to score. But you're not going to do that with Dwight Evans."

The telephone in his office rang, and DeCinces excused himself while he answered it. He was working on a deal with some investors in Arizona, and there were some last-minute details to be worked out.

When he returned, he apologized for the interruption. "I'm trying to take care of some things so I don't have to go to Arizona tomorrow," he explained. If he could take care of business, he could save himself a trip.

That was what the Angels had thought that Sunday afternoon in 1986. Win that game, and they wouldn't have to go back to Boston to close out the series. But they didn't take care of business. They let the game slip away, and that failure traveled with them back East.

"That game carried over," said DeCinces. "It was incredible the next day. Everybody felt terrible. I felt terrible. I felt absolutely terrible. And I also felt, 'Hey, we've got to go out here in Game 6 and win. Let's tee it up.'

"But when you've got all the front-office people not talking and being absolutely critical of what happened on the field and things like that—you know, we were still ahead three to two. All we had to do was win one game. But it was like it was over."

There were more lost opportunities in Boston in Game 6.

"In the first inning, we could have closed off that game. Somebody led off with a hit, Reggie hit a double, then I doubled off the wall and knocked in those two guys. It was off of Oil Can Boyd. I got to third, and Grich was on, then we had a pop-up and a groundout. If we could have continued what we were doing, we could have knocked Oil Can out. He was maybe a pitch away from being removed. But the next thing you know he settles down, and McCaskill went out and had a tough game."

It was another demoralizing setback. But the worst was yet to come.

"What was really difficult was the seventh game," said DeCinces. "Mauch left [pitcher John] Candelaria in there for seven runs. The guys on the field were going, 'You've got to be shitting me. Let's go.'"

Was there no one else to put in? he was asked.

"Somebody would have been better than what we had. Candelaria was a big-game pitcher, but he didn't have it that day.

"If you don't have it that day, you just don't have it," he repeated. "And I think that was Candelaria's deal. He just didn't have it."

It was like 1982 all over again for the veterans on the California team. Two playoffs, two losses. Two teams to the brink of success, only to be denied.

"That was a very difficult blow in '82," said DeCinces, "and then to have to do it again. But you know what: There's only one team that gets to go to the World Series from each league. The most difficult thing in sports to comprehend is you're there with the opportunity. You didn't get there by mistake. You don't play all year to get there by a mistake. But only one of those teams is going to win.

"And let me tell you," he added, "that '86 series was pretty impressive to watch."

Things were not the same in Anaheim after that loss in the playoffs. Two days after the final game of the 1986 American League Championship Series, Doug DeCinces returned to Anaheim Stadium to clear out his locker and say his good-byes to his teammates. It should have been a happy time of reflecting on the accomplishments of the season. But not in this clubhouse, and not on this ball club.

Doug DeCinces, now a successful California businessman, still recalls his failure to drive home the winning run in the bottom of the ninth inning of Game 5: "I remember that so clearly, let me tell you. . . . I wake up many times remembering it."
Photo courtesy Doug DeCinces.

"I remember Grichie [Bobby Grich] was in there packing up his stuff because he had formally told them he was going to retire. So, he was getting his stuff and he wanted to take a couple of uniforms with him as mementos. And the Angels said no. Mike Port said, 'No, you can't take them. You have to pay for them.'

"I just sat there in amazement. Here's a guy that played ten years for this team, and they're not going to let him take one home uniform and one away uniform with him. And they wanted him to give them back his suitcase and his travel bag and all that kind of stuff. I just looked around and said, 'Wow, is that weak.'

"I remember Grich arguing with the general manager right in the middle of the clubhouse on the phone, telling him what he thought about it, that another reason why he didn't want to be around the organization anymore was these kind of cheap tactics.

"That kind of set the tone. We had about six or seven guys who were free agents that year. It was Brian Downing, myself, Boone and Reggie. Geez, who else was a free agent that year?"

He stopped to check the names: DeCinces, Downing, Boone, Jackson, Rick Burleson, Don Sutton, Ruppert Jones, Doug Corbett. The heart of the ball club. Two division titles in five years. One second-place finish. No other group of ballplayers had brought so much glory to the team.

"And we were all instructed, 'You are not allowed to be in here, so remove your stuff. Take your stuff out of the clubhouse. You're not allowed to come in for medical treatment.' The trainers were told they were not allowed to touch us. We had just killed ourselves for the year, and we weren't allowed to rehab or do anything inside the stadium."

DeCinces shook his head in disbelief. "That was two days after the playoffs.

"I had taken care of my trainers and my people before," he continued, "and they were embarrassed. They apologized, and I said, 'Hey, I fully understand. I'm not here to cost you your job or whatever.' I just got my stuff and left.

"We were omitted from any connection with the ball club whatsoever. We didn't get invitations to the Christmas party or whatever. We were just gone."

The first time he heard from the team, said DeCinces, was December 22, when it had to make a contract offer to him or lose its rights for compensation should he go elsewhere. The Angels offered him salary arbitration, and he turned them down.

On January 4, 1987, four days before he would become a free agent, DeCinces was offered a three-year package "at major cuts each year."

He thought about all he had done for the ball club, the numbers he had put up, the leadership he had provided. "And I was just getting slapped to death," he said.

Even that offer was withdrawn by the Angels, said DeCinces. As the signing deadline neared, he was a player without a team, facing an uncertain future as a free agent in a year when free agents were, in effect, being blackballed.

"All of a sudden, twelve hours before the January eighth deadline, they mail this contract to my agent. It was a two-year contract at major cuts. So, basically, they didn't want to sign me. But we made the decision that collusion was in full swing and there were not going to be any free agents offered contracts that year. We made the proper decision, because history showed that Tim Raines and Andre Dawson and all those guys did not get offered any contracts.

"So, my agent just called up the Angels with forty minutes left before the deadline, and Mike Port wouldn't accept his phone call. My agent, being intelligent as he was, accepted the contract with the secretary because she was an officer of the corporation.

"She said, 'What? You accept this? I'll have to go get Mr. Port.' And my agent said, 'No, we'll accept.' He finalized that deal right there. We made the right choice at the time because of collusion. And when the final payoff comes for that, I'm going to get what was due me."

DeCinces had his contract, but there was a catch. It included a clause that allowed the team to buy out the second year of the deal if it released him before the end of the season. The buyout would cost the Angels approximately $141,667, or one-sixth of his $850,000 salary.

"We tried to get that removed," said DeCinces. "Mike Port said, 'No way.' We said, 'What are you telling us?' He said, 'We're not telling you anything.' And I said, 'Yes, you are. You're telling me I'm not going to be here by the end of the year, period.' He just said, 'No comment.'

"So, I knew at the start of the season I was going to be released before the end of the year if the team wasn't in first place."

The hard feelings carried over to spring training. Gene Mauch wanted the players to report a week before the required reporting date, but DeCinces refused unless the buyout clause was removed from his contract. It wasn't, so he did not show up at camp until the March 1 deadline.

"I remember going down there, and Mauch was incredible. He had a meeting, and he goes, 'I hope all that stuff is behind you.' I said, 'What stuff?' He said, 'Well, your contract stuff.' And I go, 'Well, how much input did you have with that?' "

"He just looked at me kind of funny. I said, 'You really wanted me around here, huh, Gene. You really fought for me, like you fought for Carew.' Because he had done the same thing to Rod Carew the year before.

"I said, 'That's incredible. Here I busted my butt for you and when it came time for you to stand up for the type of player you wanted, you just walked away.'

"And so we had our few little quiet words there," DeCinces added with a chuckle.

"The next thing you know, Gene has a meeting with the team. He said, 'Last year, we did it your way. This year, we're going to do it my way.' Brian Downing and I looked at each other and went, 'Last year we did it OUR way?'

"We were trying to figure out what he meant. What did we do? If it was our way, Mike Witt would have stayed in the game."

DeCinces laughed at the thought of it.

"I'll never forget that. So, we did it his way and we finished in dead last."

There was bad chemistry on that California team, said DeCinces. Too many veterans were gone, replaced by too many young faces. Bobby Grich had retired. Reggie Jackson was let go over the winter. So was Bob Boone. And there were other factors at work. That off-season was the year of collusion, when the baseball owners conspired not to sign each other's available free agents. Salaries were down, and ballplayers were unhappy over their treatment.

"With all the collusion that was going on, the players that weren't there anymore, the influx of major youth and the front-office problems, that team was destined for failure," said DeCinces.

So, the Angels went from first to worst in one year. From the penthouse to the outhouse.

As that final, unhappy season drew to a conclusion, DeCinces knew his time with the Angels was coming to an end. He was willing to leave the team on good terms, he said. "They could have approached me and asked, 'What's the best way to do this?'"

Instead, DeCinces suffered the indignity of being pulled for a pinch hitter in his last game as an Angel.

"Jack Howell pinch-hit for me," he recalled. "I turned around and looked at Gene Mauch and went, 'What?' I didn't say anything, I just looked at him and left. I couldn't believe this had happened.

"After the game, a reporter came up to me and said, 'Nobody else knows this, but the rumor is they're going to release you tomorrow. What do you have to say about it?' I looked at him and said, 'The RUMOR is? I guess you're the messenger boy. I guess that's what happened on the field today, huh.'

"It was a Mike Port deal. See, Mike Port didn't like any of the veteran guys around. As you saw in the following years, he removed everybody that was there before, even Brian Downing. You know, just flat out removed him. Because the veterans were a threat to his ability to control the younger kids.

"And I was considered one of the leaders of the team, so they were going to show everybody right up front, 'Hey, this is what happens.' That's how I got treated.

"The next day, I was in the clubhouse before the game and I get a phone call that Mr. Port would like to see me before I get dressed. I walk in his office, and his whole desk is clear. There's just a piece of paper there, and he flips it across the desk.

"'These are your release papers,' he says. He wouldn't look at me. 'These are your release papers; we ask that you sign them. The club is releasing you.' And he turned and looked away. He was trying to ignore me, because Mike Port could not handle any one-on-one confrontations. He couldn't negotiate or discuss a problem one-on-one. It always had to be through a phone or through a message. That was the type of person he was.

"I sat there and looked at the paper. There was a moment of silence, and he's looking out the window. I just walked over and shut the door behind me, and he turned around and looked at me.

"He goes, 'Look, this can be real easy. Why don't you just sign this stuff and get out of here?'

"I said, 'You know what, Mike? I'm going to sign these papers, but not until you have enough balls to look me in the eyes and tell me why this is happening, and not until I finish telling you what I think about you. And as long as you keep looking out the window and not looking at me, the longer I'm going to be in this office.'

"It was tough for him. At one time, he started looking back, so I moved my chair over to the window. I just said, 'This has been a pre-planned deal from way back when. I assume you're going to do the same thing to the rest of these guys who have come through and given their blood and guts to this team. And you wonder why this organization never wins.' I said, 'It doesn't win because of people like you who can't understand what it's all about.' "

DeCinces said the final words slowly and emphatically.

"Oh, it was incredible," he added.

That was the day Doug DeCinces walked away from the California Angels. But the thing was, a part of him never really left. He still bought season tickets to the game. And later, he got along well with the new club president, Richard Brown. He even got back on friendly terms with team owners Gene and Jackie Autry.

"Richard Brown has tried to mend the fences a little bit," said DeCinces. "He's done it with some of the other players, too. I can go in and talk with Richard Brown, and I'll sit in his box. I'll sit with the Autrys now."

Doug DeCinces gave six years of his life to that team. You can't take that away with a piece of paper.

"I still think of myself as an Angel," he said. "I'll always think of myself as an Angel."

7

BOB KNEPPER:

STANDING IN THE GAP

I looked for a man among them who would build up the wall
and stand before me in the gap. . . .
—EZEKIEL 22:30

One ball, two strikes on the batter. The next pitch was a slider. Lenny Dykstra hit the ball to center field, where it barely eluded the grasp of Billy Hatcher and bounced away for a three-base hit.

Weeks later, driving down a road on his ranch in Oregon, Bob Knepper still was thinking about that pitch.

"Maybe I should have thrown a fastball," he thought.

In his mind, he could see the next batter, Mookie Wilson. The count was no balls, two strikes. Knepper threw a low, inside slider. Wilson hit a soft liner just over second baseman Billy Doran's outstretched glove. Another cheap hit.

Knepper shook his head in frustration. So it went, batter by batter, pitch by pitch, inning by inning, as he replayed Game 6 of the 1986 National League Championship Series.

And suddenly, Knepper looked down to see that as he was driving his hands were gripping the steering wheel as tightly as they could. His jaw was clenched and his body tense as he relived that day one more time.

It was a scene repeated over and over that off-season. Knepper would replay that game in his mind while lying in bed awake at night. He would be sitting at the table when he would suddenly close his eyes and start to think back on it again.

What had happened? A shutout for eight innings. A three-run lead in the ninth. Only three more outs and the Astros would have been victorious, forcing a decisive seventh game for the pennant. How did it all fall apart so unexpectedly? How could the Mets have scored three runs so quickly to force extra innings? How did Knepper pitch so brilliantly for so long, only to end up sitting on the bench watching as the Mets prevailed in extra innings?

That game was going to be the pinnacle of Knepper's career. He had been branded as a pitcher who couldn't handle the pressure. He had carried the label of a Christian ballplayer who wouldn't "kill to win." That game was going to disprove all those stereotypes. That game was going to be Bob Knepper's vindication—as a pitcher and as a Christian ballplayer.

Instead, it ended in defeat and disappointment and a terrible, lost feeling. Why had it happened? What could he have done differently?

Those were the questions that haunted Knepper that off-season. That was what led him to replay those events so many times that one day he caught himself thinking he really could go back and pitch that game over again.

Late one summer, on that same cattle ranch, Bob Knepper was up early on a Friday. He had much to do that morning.

Time was running out on him. He had sold the ranch, and in less than three weeks he would close the deal and vacate the premises. Gone would be the ranch he had dreamed about all his life. Gone would be the home where he and his wife, Terri, had raised their three children—Jacob, now eleven; Tyler, eight; and Heather, six.

"It's supposed to close here September first, I think it is," said Knepper. "So, although we still have it, we're losing it quickly."

He had bought the ranch a decade earlier as a refuge for his family. He and Terri wanted a secluded place where they could raise their children according to their Christian beliefs, away from the drugs, violence, sexual promiscuity and other ills that plagued society.

"We wanted a place that was totally isolated," he said.

They had searched Utah, Montana, Idaho and Oregon before finally finding these thirteen hundred acres in the southern Oregon community of Wilbur, population 47, situated in a valley between the Coastal Range and the Cascades.

Knepper did not know where he would go next, or how he would make a living. He was thirty-nine years old with a wife and three children, no job, no home and no plans, but he was not worried. He knew where to turn for guidance.

"We're not sure what we're going to do," he said. "One of the things we've been trying to figure out is just what we're supposed to be doing. My wife and I are very committed Christians, and what we have been trying to do since we decided to sell the ranch is to really pray and seek God's will and direction and find out what He wants us to do with our lives."

Knepper had been out of baseball for three years, since the Giants had turned him loose in June 1990. He thought he had the rest of his life planned out when he left baseball. He and his wife had their ranch in Oregon, and they would just settle down there and become ranchers. It was what they had talked about for years. But now they were getting ready to just walk away from it.

What happened? he was asked. Had ranching lost its appeal?

"Well, it's more of a spiritual reason," said Knepper. "Because I love to ranch. I really enjoy working the cattle, and I've really enjoyed the room and working outside.

"But the last three or four years, since I've been out of the game—in fact, even before that—I've just come to the realization that I feel God's calling in my life is not to just be a rancher but to be other things and do other things.

"We've gone beyond the point of just realizing that we're able to give up the ranch, which has been a lifetime dream of mine. We're willing and happy and anxious to do so and see what else God has got in store for us. We've realized a spiritual need in our lives to do something different. We've also come to the place where ranching does not hold the same appeal to us that it once did."

It had been the same way in baseball. Knepper pitched fifteen years in the big leagues and won 146 games. Twice, he pitched in the All-Star Game. But at some point baseball had ceased to be fun for Knepper. He began to distance himself from the game he had loved all his life.

When Houston released him in 1989, he knew that because of the problems he had endured in his nine years there he was getting mentally prepared to leave baseball. He returned to San Francisco to pitch the remainder of the 1989 season and the first part of the 1990 season. By then, he realized he no longer had the necessary enthusiasm for the game.

"I don't know if God was shaping me and changing the priorities in my life, or if it was just a natural progression of the struggles I had in baseball. If I was just getting tired of fighting it all the time. But by the time the Giants released me, I just didn't have the desire to do whatever it was going to take to stay in the game.

"I really believe that I still had enough ability. But I just lost too much desire, too much drive."

Outside the window, the cattle ranch stretched off into the distance. What was beyond those hills? Where would those roads lead Bob Knepper, former big-league ballplayer and former rancher?

These were questions he could not answer.

"My wife and I have gotten very involved with marriage ministries," said Knepper, "and we're looking to pursue some sort of ministry in marriage. It might be baseball players and their wives getting out of the game, the trauma that ballplayers and their wives face. I think it's going to be something along those lines, whether it's in baseball or through a local body church."

It was still too soon to know for certain, he added. Nor did he know if he was going to stay in Oregon or move elsewhere, perhaps to Colorado. There was so much yet to be decided, but he was not concerned. Things would work out. Bob Knepper had faith.

"A Christian ballplayer." That was the tag Knepper carried with him throughout most of his major-league career.

It had not always been that way. At one time in his life, Knepper explained, baseball was his religion.

"Yeah, I grew up thinking that baseball was all that life was about. I went to a small high school, so I was able to play four sports a year. But I really loved baseball the most. I just grew up, in grammar school and high school, thinking that baseball was the only thing in my life that was really important.

Astros pitcher Bob Knepper spent years trying to come to grips with his failure to win Game 6 of the NL Championship Series: "I put a lot more pressure on myself because people had criticized a lot of Christian ballplayers for not having the killer instinct." *Photo courtesy Houston Astros.*

"So I pursued it with a passion."

He was drafted by the Giants in 1972, after his senior year at Calistoga High School in California. He won his first game in the big leagues five years later, at the end of the 1976 season. His first full season in the majors, 1977, he won eleven games.

It was the culmination of a lifelong dream. Knepper was in the major leagues, playing alongside all the famous players he had followed, performing in front of huge crowds in spacious stadiums and earning big money. And for the first time in his life, he looked around at the glamorous world he lived in and wondered, "Is this all there is?"

"I got to the big leagues at a time with the Giants where some players that I had played with earlier in the minor leagues got there a year or two ahead of me," he remembered. "One of the things that people don't realize is that when you have a dream like that, and you buy into it like I did baseball, and you achieve those goals, you find out that those goals and those dreams don't give you lasting peace of mind and contentment.

"That's why so many ballplayers who make big-league baseball their goal get there and then they've got to do something else. They've either got to make more money, or they get into drugs, or drinking, or chasing women. They keep searching for that happiness.

"I got to the big leagues and I saw all these other guys ahead of me who got there and just like me had made baseball their god. And baseball won't give you complete satisfaction. There's got to be something bigger in life."

While searching for answers, Knepper came in contact with Gary Lavelle, a left-handed pitcher and one of the Christians on the San Francisco ball club. At the time, Knepper considered himself an atheist, and he enjoyed challenging the religious beliefs of his Christian teammates.

It was a much different Bob Knepper from the one who was seated at a ranch house in Oregon, waiting for God to lead him to the next phase of his life.

"It's kind of hard to remember all those years," he said, thinking back. "I just did not believe in God. And I used to love to debate Christians, because they couldn't even show me what they really believed in. Which is one of the real weaknesses of the Church today. Most Christians don't know what they believe in, and they can't give a good defense of what they believe in. Because most Christians are lazy when it comes to studying Scripture.

"Gary Lavelle was the first Christian that I ever played ball with that knew his faith well enough that when I would debate and talk with him, I couldn't beat him. Going up through the minor leagues, I used to win almost all the arguments. No one could ever convince me they knew what they were believing in.

"But Gary was the first guy that when I would argue and debate with him, he had the answers to my questions—and questions that I couldn't answer."

Knepper recited other factors at work in his life at this time. His father suffered a near-fatal heart attack in September 1976, when Knepper made his big-league debut. For the first time, Knepper began to confront the issue of life and death. In spring training 1978, he heard a chapel speaker "give a testimony that just blew me away." That year, Knepper decided if he was going to be "an honest atheist" he should investigate what the Bible had to say and decide if it was true or not.

"To me, it was just a matter of common sense," he explained. "I said, 'Okay, I'll look for God. I'll use the word of God—supposedly the Bible—and look for God. And if I don't find God, I can say the Bible is a lie, and therefore God is a lie.'

"So, I went to Gary and told him, 'Help me search the Scriptures. I want to find God and see if He really is true.' It came down to the point one night in my hotel room in Pittsburgh—I was rooming by myself—that I prayed for the first time in my life.

"I said, 'God, if you are real, if you're who the Bible says you are, I want to know you. But, God, I don't believe in you. I think I'm talking to the ceiling. I don't think there's anybody here. If you really are who the Bible says you are, if you really are God, then I know according to your word that I need you in my life as my lord and savior.'

"And I prayed for about ten minutes, being very honest, and when I got done, I broke down and started crying, because I came face-to-face with the holiness of God and the sinfulness of Bob Knepper.

"And for me, that was a major deal. Growing up as an athlete all my life—playing football, offense and defense; playing basketball; running track; playing baseball; being an all-around jock—you never show your opposition your pain. You never show tears. And to just break down like that . . . "

He left the sentence uncompleted.

"I had a spiritual experience right there in my bedroom," he added. "That is where I changed my life around, in May of 1978."

That was a landmark year for Knepper on the field, also. He won seventeen games, six of them by shutout, and helped a youthful San Francisco team make a surprising run at the pennant. In the flush of success surrounding the Giants, Knepper and the other Christians on the ball club were dubbed "the God Squad."

But in the fast-paced world of baseball, today's winners are tomorrow's losers. The Giants fell back in the standings in 1979. Knepper slumped to a losing record that season and the next. The God Squad fell out of favor.

Knepper's embrace of Christianity was fine as long as he was producing on the field. Once he faltered, it became a target of criticism. He was perceived as too outspoken, too opinionated.

Ironically, the same source of peace and contentment that Knepper had found in his personal life led to controversy and constant turmoil in his professional life.

"I'm not sure it should have," he said, "but it did for me. When I became a Christian in '78, I was completely unprepared for the sometimes heated animosity that I felt from people, from the media and from other players sometimes. Especially in the Bay Area, which is such a liberal, almost anti-Christian society.

"So, for me, it was real hard. Too many times, I allowed the difficulties of living my Christian life in a world, a baseball world, which is almost the opposite of Christian ethics and beliefs, to affect my enjoyment of the game and my ability to be a joyful Christian, a good witness to Jesus Christ in that game."

Of all the criticisms aimed at Knepper, perhaps the one that stung most was the quote attributed to him in 1980. "It was God's will," he was supposed to have said after giving up a game-winning home run.

Years later, he still bristled at that statement.

"That quote followed me around for years, and I never said it," said Knepper, the irritation showing in his voice. "That incident never even happened. In fact, I'm very much opposed to that type of theology, that everything that happened in my life was God's will.

"But that followed me around, and it made it hard everywhere I went. 'Oh, you're the guy that said, "It's God's will," ' and all that kind of stuff."

The Giants traded Knepper to Houston the following season. It was speculated that the focus on his religious beliefs had led to his departure. Knepper isn't sure. Whatever the reason, in Houston he was able to escape much of the controversy that had surrounded him in the Bay Area. That allowed him to concentrate on his pitching again, and over the next three years he switched from a power pitcher to a finesse pitcher.

By 1984, the transformation was complete. Knepper won fifteen games both that season and the next, and in 1986 he matched his career high with seventeen victories as the Astros won the National League West Division title. He pitched seven strong innings in Game 3 of the National League playoffs, but failed to hold a four-run lead.

Four days later, Knepper drew the starting assignment in Game 6 against the Mets. It would be the most important baseball game he ever pitched.

There were so many reasons Bob Knepper wanted to win that ball game. A chance to go to the World Series. Verification of his status as a winning pitcher. The boastfulness of the Mets. Loyalty to his teammates.

And one unspoken but very powerful incentive: the bias felt by so many Christians ballplayers.

"I'm sure I put a lot more pressure on myself because people had criticized a lot of Christian ballplayers for not having the killer instinct," said Knepper. "And so I put a lot of Christian ballplayers' reputations on my shoulders that game. I was going to go out and show—and this was probably more subconscious at that time—but I wanted to really go out and pitch and show that a Christian could be the guy in that key situation to have a great game.

"Which is really funny, because I believed then and I still believe now, whether I'm as competitive as I was before I was a Christian, or as competitive as a non-Christian, is really immaterial. That yardstick of measuring me does not pertain to my life. I'm not called to be as competitive as somebody else or as competitive as I was before.

"Even though I believe that, I do think I put a lot of responsibility on my shoulders to stand in the gap and represent Christian ballplayers as a whole. So, yeah, it was a very emotional game for me."

Previously, Knepper had never been a demonstrative pitcher on the mound. He was workmanlike, efficient, low-key. That afternoon, he stepped out of character. He was exaggerated in his antics. He pumped his fist in the air each time he retired a batter. He yelled encouragement to his fielders after defensive plays. He ran on and off the field between innings.

"I had always been pretty reserved in my mannerisms out on the mound," he said. "I never really showed much emotion. But Game 6 came along, and I said, 'Forget being reserved. You go out there and just let it all hang out.' For me, it was a big, emotional game to go out there and get us into Game 7."

It almost worked. For eight spectacular innings, Knepper pitched brilliantly. He dazzled the Mets with his assortment of off-speed pitches and breaking balls and his pinpoint control. The Astros staked him to a three-run lead, and he made it stand up going into the ninth inning.

The Astrodome was alive with excitement. The fans were on their feet cheering him on. The Houston players were poised for a celebration. Knepper appeared invincible.

Then came the cheap hit by Dykstra. A bleeder by Wilson. One out later, a double by Keith Hernandez. Just like that, Knepper was out of the game. Dave Smith came on, but he failed to hold the lead. A tie game. The Mets won in the sixteenth.

That was the end of the playoffs for the Astros, and the beginning of a long ordeal for Knepper as he struggled to come to grips with the crushing disappointment he felt.

He thought back to that game, and all the old emotions came back to him.

"In that ninth inning, when I just ran out of gas, or lost a little concentration or whatever happened, that was the lowest point in my career. Just the way that inning unfolded, I could look back and see an inch here and a fraction of an inch there, and that whole inning changes and we're in the seventh game.

"It was just a real major disappointment for us not to win that ball game. We had worked so hard, we had played so hard, and in the playoffs we had come through so many things that just seemed to be against us. And we felt the Mets had such a psychological thing against trying to hit Mike Scott, who would have pitched Game 7, that if we'd have won Game 6, we'd have won Game 7 and we'd be in the World Series."

Maybe if he had thrown a different pitch here, a better pitch there. Maybe if this ball or that one had been hit a little more one way or the other. What if this, what if that? That was what Bob Knepper thought about that winter.

Things were not the same in Houston after that dramatic 1986 season. Knepper slumped to a career-worst seventeen losses the next year. He rebounded to win fourteen games in 1988, but his achievement was overshadowed by a controversy surrounding his spring-training comments on Pam Postema, a female umpire.

Knepper praised Postema's work behind the plate, but added: "This is not an occupation a woman should be in. In God's society, woman was created in a role of submission to the husband. It's not that woman is inferior, but I don't believe women should be in a leadership role."

Knepper based his beliefs on the Bible. In the ensuing uproar, he answered his critics by reciting Scripture to support his views.

That same year, he spoke out against the cheating that went on in baseball, some of it by his own teammates. Pitchers were scuffing baseballs and batters were corking bats to gain an illegal advantage over opponents. Knepper did not approve of such practices, and found it increasingly difficult to remain silent on the subject.

"That was one of the reasons why my last couple of years with Houston were so hard for me personally," he said. "Because I allowed that to affect my relationship with ballplayers. I was player representative for the Astros, and it got to the point where it was just really hard for me to want to represent ballplayers that, well, for me they were cheating, scuffing balls or corking bats. There were only a couple. There weren't that many, but the rest of the team seemed to condone it or think it was okay, and that was real hard for me.

"Not meaning they had to be Christians, but to me it was just wrong to do something like that. And I think that caused a quiet separation between me and players on that ball club. Because I think it was pretty clear how I felt about it.

"It was me that caused the separation," he added quickly. "I felt that it was such a wrong thing to do that it alienated me from the team, in a quiet way. There were never any confrontations, never any arguments. We still got along just great, but there was a definite difference between me and some of the players doing that. It was just against everything I believed in, even as a non-Christian, for the game of baseball and life in general."

Knepper was asked if he was referring to Mike Scott, who had been the focus of the scuffing allegations during the 1986 playoffs.

"Well, I'm not talking about anybody in particular," he answered. "It doesn't do me any good, or anybody else any good, to come back now and try to start naming ballplayers who scuffed balls or corked bats.

"And it wasn't any one person in particular. It was just an overall attitude on the team and in the management that was really disheartening. When Billy Hatcher got caught one game corking his bat, we had a big team meeting about it, about how embarrassing it was to the team and how wrong it was. But about a month before, we had been warned how the umpires were going to be checking balls out there, so make sure everybody was clean out there.

"The hypocrisy was something that was just hard for me to look past and still enjoy the game. I allowed it to take my focus off the game of baseball, which was wrong on my part."

Knepper thought back to that 1986 championship series and the frequent complaints by the Mets over the alleged scuffballs thrown by the Astros' pitchers.

"The Mets made a big deal about it. And it was really funny, because one game that year I was hitting against them, and I can't think what pitcher it was, a right-handed relief pitcher, but he threw me a spitball. As a pitcher, I know very well what a spitball looks like.

"It just blew me away—you know, how they could be complaining and whining about some guys on our team scuffing balls, and they're throwing spitballs up there.

"But the '86 playoffs, that didn't bother me more than any other time. The whole thing bothered me. What people don't realize is, if I know my friend on the ball club is cheating, then what he is expecting me to do is lie for him. Because you've got reporters all the time coming up and asking, 'Is so-and-so cheating?'

"So you're stuck in the position of either having to lie for the guy or ratting on your team. And that was a position I didn't appreciate being put in."

What about throwing at batters? Knepper was asked. That was a common practice in baseball. Had he ever resorted to such tactics?

"No, I would never throw at somebody. I got aired out a couple of times by a manager for not throwing at people. I would get aired out in front of the whole team for not throwing at a particular player because he hit a couple of home runs off of me. That was kind of tough to go through.

"But there's no way in the world I would ever throw at a player. I don't care what the game meant. I don't care what the situation was, there's no game in baseball to me worth hurting somebody or maybe even killing somebody. There's no way I could justify that before God."

Knepper's tenure in Houston ended in July 1989, when he was given his release by the Astros. He returned to the Astrodome two days later to clear out his locker and pack his bags. He was still there when the game ended and the Houston players began filing back into the clubhouse.

He stood by the wall, next to the area where the postgame meal was laid out for the players.

"I was off to the side just watching the guys come in," Knepper remembered. "As they came by to get their food, most of them didn't even notice me, because as a ballplayer you've got a tendency to see somebody—a civilian, so to speak—in the locker room and you automatically just kind of ignore that person. Either they're somebody's friend or somebody who wants something or who knows what.

"And all of a sudden, I realized that's where I was. Guys would come in and they would look right by me. They wouldn't even notice me.

"I realized then how fast you're out of the game, and it goes right on like nothing ever happened. You know, you always want to think that the game is going to be less or that it's going to pause or hesitate or stumble when you leave it. But it doesn't. It just keeps right on going like you never were there."

It was getting late in the morning.

"I apologize if I've talked your ear off," said Knepper. "I'm a talker at times, I guess."

It was true that Knepper had talked a lot, but the time had slipped past unnoticed.

The conversation turned back to Game 6 of the playoffs. What if he had won that game, Knepper was asked. What if he had been able to hold the Mets scoreless one more inning, or if Dave Smith had shut down the New York rally in the ninth? Would it have changed anything? Would Bob Knepper's life have turned out differently?

It was a question he had asked himself many times over the years. And now, seven years later, Knepper finally had found the answer.

"I used to think, 'What if I had gone on and won that shutout, and that we go to the World Series? And let's say I win two or three games in the World Series.'

"It would have made no difference financially, because I was already under a long-term contract. That wouldn't have changed anything. And looking back right now, I'd still be here in Oregon. I'd still be selling my ranch.

"I might be able to look back with a more fond memory of that particular game, or that fall. But I don't see how it could change my life at all. Because right now in Wilbur, Oregon, where I live, it doesn't make a bit of difference to anybody whether I won that game or lost that game."

It sounds strange, he admitted, but he no longer even wishes he could change the outcome of that game. Looking back, it probably turned out for the best.

"I learned a lot from that game. I learned a lot about myself. I learned a lot about the value and the lasting value—or the lack of lasting value—that the game of baseball really has. And I'm not sure I'd give up that lesson for anything.

"It really helped put my life in perspective, to realize what's really important in life. Is it winning a game? Is it pleasing people who really don't care about me at all? The majority of the fans and the press, they don't really care about you as a person. All they care about is how you perform for them. So do I want to put that much emphasis on pleasing those people versus pleasing my God?"

It had been a long journey for Knepper since the winter after those playoffs, when he tortured himself by constantly replaying that game in his mind. Now, the game was over. It was in the past. He had made peace with himself, about a year or two ago, he said. "I think when I was out of baseball and got away from the game long enough, I could go back and re-examine my career unemotionally and just see things the way they were.

"By that time, I was able to just sit down and examine a lot of things about my life, where I just said, 'Hey, you gave it your best shot and came up just short.' You know, that's one of the lessons of life that baseball has showed me."

World Series rings. Championship trophies. Won-lost records. How important are they, anyway?

"There's a saying that if you live long enough," continued Knepper, "life will trash all your trophies. And that's true. I realized that if I had won that game, it wouldn't make any difference at this stage of my life. What's really important is not how many games I won or how good I pitched in '86 or '80 or whatever year. That's not important. That has no lasting value.

"I've learned that anything you do in baseball—all the records or all the games you've won—really has no lasting value. My relationship with Christ and my relationship with my family, that has lasting value.

"So I think as I worked through all that, I realized that game, it was just a game. I gave it my best shot. And as I got out of baseball, I was able to see things a little more focused, a little more clear, and not be involved so emotionally with it. It was just a matter of coming to the right conclusion."

8

BILLY HATCHER: THE HUNTER

Throughout his career in baseball, Billy Hatcher was known for his speed, not his power. He was a fast, exciting base runner and a fleet outfielder. He stole eighty-four bases one year in the minor leagues. In his first five full seasons in the majors, he averaged thirty-five steals a year. He was a singles and doubles hitter, best suited for the top of the batting order. The long ball wasn't his game.

But it was a home run he hit that made Hatcher famous. When all his stolen bases and sliding catches are forgotten, baseball fans will still remember that home run.

It was the most dramatic moment of the epic sixteen-inning struggle between the Houston Astros and New York Mets in the 1986 National League Championship Series.

The amazing thing is that Hatcher hit the ball into the stands not once but twice in the fourteenth inning of that game, when the Astros trailed the Mets by a run and appeared beaten. Hatcher's first drive off reliever Jesse Orosco was a shot that landed outside the left-field foul pole in the Astrodome. Undismayed, Hatcher hit another ball high into the left-field seats. The second time, the ball stayed fair.

At that moment, Hatcher was on top of the world. His home run tied the game in dramatic fashion. The cheering by the crowd was so loud it seemed the roof was going to blow off the Astrodome.

And Billy Hatcher, numb from excitement and overcome by the enormity of what he had just done, circled the bases as if in a dream.

"Really, running around the bases I couldn't feel anything because it was so loud in the Astrodome," he said. "It was like I was on a cloud and every time I picked my foot up to run around the bases, it was like I didn't come down."

But two innings later, Hatcher and the Astros came down with a crash. They lost that game in the sixteenth inning, and with it went their World Series hopes.

Afterward, the thing that Hatcher kept thinking about was the World Series ring that he had hoped to wear on his hand. Yogi Berra, the Houston coach who had played on fourteen pennant winners and managed two others, used to wear some of his World Series rings, and Billy always admired them.

"He would show me his rings," said Hatcher. "He would have them on, and he had one for every finger. I just said to myself, 'I want a ring.' I mean, after seeing Yogi and being around him and seeing what type of person he was and how much he loved baseball, I said, 'All I ever want is an opportunity—and I'm going to get that opportunity one day.'"

Someday, Hatcher told himself, he was going to have a ring just like those that Yogi wore.

Injuries were a part of baseball. After a decade in the major leagues, Billy Hatcher had endured his share of the minor ailments that put a ballplayer on the sidelines. Wrist, hamstring, ankle, groin—he had pulled, bruised or stretched them all.

Now, it was his right elbow. Playing for the Boston Red Sox late one season, Hatcher dislodged some bone chips in the elbow, and he faced the prospect of surgery when the schedule ended in a few weeks.

"I really don't know what's going to happen, because they're floating in there," he said at the time. "And sometimes I get to the point where I can't throw the ball or swing the bat. I'm hoping that they'll move out and I can finish playing."

The elbow had acted up in the past, said Hatcher, but it wasn't until a game at New York the week before that he had aggravated the problem.

"It's been bothering me off and on all year. I miss one game here. I miss another game there. The other night in Boston, I caught a ball and I hit the wall. I keep banging it up. The next night, I think it was the first game against the Yankees, I dove for a ball and I landed right on top of the elbow.

"I guess I might have moved the chips around in my arm. And the next night, my arm locked up when I went up there to swing the bat. It was very painful. After I got finished playing the game, I said, 'Something happened.' The next day, I couldn't even throw the ball."

Hatcher was thirty-two years old. He would turn thirty-three the day after the regular season ended. He knew he didn't have many years left in the game.

"I don't know how many more I can play. But I know I really don't want to play more than three more years. I've played baseball practically my entire life. And it's tough sometimes, being away from your family all the time."

Hatcher was sitting in a hotel room in Toronto, waiting to go to the ballpark for that night's game. He had been playing baseball professionally for thirteen years. That made for a lot of days and nights in hotel rooms, a lot of meals away from home, a lot of late-night flights and early-morning wake-up calls.

That wasn't so bad when he was single, but Hatcher was married now, and he had two children—Derrick, seven, and Chelsea, three. Derrick, like his dad, was a ballplayer.

"He just loves to play," said Hatcher. "He goes to the baseball games in Boston. He knows all the players on every team. I mean, he sits there. He's not like a seven-year-old who doesn't want to sit down, who wants to run up and down with the fans. He gets mad because he wants to sit there and he wants to watch the game. He just sits there and he watches.

"When he finishes watching, he wants to play. And he will play baseball every single day if I let him."

Now, Derrick was getting to the age where he needed his father's presence year-round, not just in the off-season.

"He needs me there," said Hatcher. "My family needs me there. I'm very content with everything I've done in baseball. It might happen sooner, but I would like to play maybe two more years."

Hatcher was still a productive ballplayer. Even with the elbow problems, he had batted a solid .287, scored seventy-one runs and driven in fifty-seven for the Red Sox. The tag "journeyman ballplayer" had been applied to him because he played for six teams in eleven seasons, but that term did not do him justice. Hatcher was a good player, and his record bore that out. He played more than eleven hundred games in the big leagues and got more than a thousand hits. He made his presence felt wherever he went.

And when the time came for Hatcher to give way to a younger player, he would do so, secure in the knowledge that he had made his mark in the game.

"Once I finish playing, I really don't care if people remember me as a baseball player or not," he said, "because I've done everything I wanted to do in baseball. My main goal when I started playing baseball, I wanted to play one day in the big leagues. I've done that. So, I'm satisfied. Everything else, I'm blessed.

"Once I finish, some other guy is going to step up in there and do what he has to do to play the game, and then he's going to be gone. So, once I'm gone, I'm gone."

It doesn't happen often, but sometimes a baseball team really clicks. All the parts fall into place, the players pull together and a true sense of unity and cooperation springs up in the clubhouse and on the field.

In 1986, the Houston Astros were one of those rare teams, and Hatcher was a part of the equation.

"The key was we had a great manager, Hal Lanier, and the team meshed," said Hatcher. "Everybody on that team knew their role. It was just amazing how it came together. There was never any bickering, because everybody knew their role.

"The guys on the bench knew when they were going to pinch-hit, when they were going to play. It was never, 'Why am I not in there today? Why this? Why that?' Everyone came together as a team."

The Astros were picked for fifth in most preseason polls, but they won their division. They were underdogs to the Mets in the National League playoffs, but they battled the New Yorkers on even terms through five tense games dominated by pitching, comebacks and close calls. Three of the games were decided by one run, one went into extra innings and another was won in the bottom of the ninth.

Billy Hatcher takes a curtain call after his dramatic home run tied the score in the bottom of the fourteenth inning of Game 6: "I couldn't feel anything because it was so loud in the Astrodome. It was like I was on a cloud." *Photo courtesy Houston Astros.*

True to form, Game 6 also went into extra innings. The two teams battled into the fourteenth, when New York finally broke the tie with a single run.

The Astros, already demoralized over having blown a ninth-inning lead, seemed to have run out of miracles. Their offense had been silent since the first, when they had scored all their runs. Inning after inning had gone by, and the Houston batters had failed to show any signs of life.

There was one out in the fourteenth when Hatcher batted against Jesse Orosco, a left-hander. The end seemed to be near. The Astrodome crowd, which earlier had been so raucous, was subdued. But Hatcher had not given up hope.

"Hal Lanier had told me before I got up there, 'If Billy [Doran] gets on, you're bunting him over,'" Hatcher recalled. "And then, I'm in the on-deck circle, and I'm rooting for Billy to get on. He struck out, I think, and Hal told me, 'Go for it.' He knew that I felt very good hitting against left-handed pitching. And Orosco threw a lot of fastballs, and I was a fastball hitter. So, I said to myself, 'I know he wants to get ahead of me.' They didn't want to walk me, because I was stealing a lot of bases then.

"So, I went up there looking for a fastball first pitch. He threw it, and he got it over the plate a little bit, but I turned on it too quick. I hit it foul, and it was out of the ballpark. That's when I said, 'Dang, I won't get that pitch again.'

"Then, I think I ran the count to three-and-two, or two-and-two, and he gave me another fastball. I hit it, and I was just hoping that it would stay fair this time. And it barely hit the net [the fair side of the foul pole in left field]."

It was the most memorable moment of a memorable series. That home run tied the score and brought the Astros and their crowd back to life. The suddenness of Hatcher's blow and the resulting shift in emotion only added to its impact. The din in the Astrodome was deafening as wave after wave of noise engulfed the playing field while Hatcher made his triumphant run around the bases. It was that noise and that electricity in the ballpark which Hatcher remembers most about the home run.

"I will never forget that when I hit the home run, I swung so hard the momentum knocked me back toward our dugout. Our first-base coach, he was hitting me on the butt before the ball went out because it was high. It was a high ball, and it just kept going up and up.

"And while I was running around the bases, it's not like you're thinking, 'I just hit a home run; it's tied up.' It was like, 'Now we're going to win this game!' It was like I could not even hear myself think running the bases, it was so loud.

"The reason I say it was so loud is that I had some family, and they were about a couple of blocks from the Astrodome, where I was living. Some of them didn't come to the game—they wanted to watch on television. And they said they could hear the people hollering from my apartment building. And it was a couple of blocks away! It was like the Dome was shaking, it was so loud."

Two innings later, in the top of the sixteenth, Houston fell behind again, this time by three runs. The Astros staged their last comeback in the bottom of the inning, putting two runners on base with one out. Once again, Hatcher came to the plate with a chance to tie the score. Another home run would pull Houston even. And Orosco was still on the mound.

Did he go to the plate looking to duplicate his earlier feat, Hatcher was asked.

"No, because it was one out and we had men on base. I knew I wasn't going to get another fastball to hit. I knew he was going to make me hit all sliders. I went up there looking for a slider first pitch. He gave me a slider first pitch, and I got a base hit."

Hatcher's single scored one run. Another run followed, but the game ended with the tying run on third and the winning run on first.

"We almost came back and got that one, too," said Hatcher. "Orosco threw Kevin Bass some nasty sliders to strike him out and end the game.

"It was very draining. After the game, about two days after the series was over, I went to New Orleans with my girlfriend at the time. I was there for maybe five or six days, and I didn't want to think about baseball. I don't even think I watched the World Series that year. I didn't want to have anything to do with baseball. I just wanted to relax.

"That whole series was so up and down, up and down, extra innings here, extra innings there, a pitch here, a catch there, that it took a lot out of everybody. It surprised me. I guess when you win a game like that, you go into another series and you get energy from that series. But as the losing team, you just want to forget about baseball for a while."

Billy Hatcher was a hunter. One year, he returned to his home state of Arizona in the off-season and applied for a license that would enable him to go deer hunting. He failed to get it, so he went out armed with a camera, not a rifle, in search of a deer.

When Hatcher found his prey, he snapped a picture of it. Suddenly, he heard some other hunters coming. The deer remained in place as the men drew nearer, so Hatcher did something unexpected: He picked up a rock and threw it toward the deer, startling it and sending it scurrying away to safety.

That was his deer, thought Hatcher, and he wanted to save it for himself. He kept the picture of that deer with him, and the next baseball season he pasted it in his locker. That way, he could look at that deer every day. It was a reminder of the prize that was out there, waiting to be claimed.

Hatcher returned to Houston in 1987 and experienced his most productive season, yet one marked by controversy and disappointment. He batted .296, scored ninety-six runs, stole fifty-three bases and hit eleven home runs, all personal bests. But the Astros slipped back to third place, with a losing record. Worse, Hatcher's individual achievements were tainted when a bat he was using one game splintered, revealing a cork center that had been added to it, in violation of baseball rules.

Hatcher drew a ten-day suspension for the incident, and he accepted the penalty without appeal. But he insisted he was innocent of any wrongdoing.

"It was just one incident where I did not have any bats," he explained. "We had just left Pittsburgh and I had broken two bats, and I was down to I think two bats. I used one of them in BP, and I needed another backup.

"Dave Smith used to swing the same model of bat that I used; you know, pitchers hit over there in the National League. I asked him if I could borrow one of his bats. He said, 'Yes, but make sure you get it out of the bat rack instead of the bat bag.'

"I went in there and saw one of the bats in the bat bag, and it had good grain and felt good in my hands, so I took it up there to hit with."

Was he embarrassed after getting caught with the corked bat?

"Well, I didn't know what had happened until they came and told me it was a corked bat. Then Dave told me they used to play games in the Astrodome where the pitchers hit home runs for beer and stuff. He said, 'That's why I wanted you to get one out of the bat rack instead of the bat bag.'

"I said, 'There's nothing I can do about it now.' If I was using a corked bat, if I knew the bat was corked, I wouldn't have been trying to bunt the two prior pitches that had been thrown to me. Then the pitcher threw a ball inside, it hit the bat and the bat exploded."

In August 1989, almost two years to the day after using the illegal bat, Hatcher was traded by the Astros to the Pirates. The following spring, he was traded again, this time to the Cincinnati Reds.

He got the news on April 3, while in the waiting room of a Houston hospital, where his wife was about to give birth to the couple's second child. Pittsburgh manager Jim Leyland called him on the phone to tell him of the trade, and all Hatcher could think to say was, "Okay."

Hours later, after Chelsea was born, Hatcher thought to himself, "That was two great events in one day!"

Hatcher opened that 1990 season with an eight-game hitting streak and stayed hot for two months as Cincinnati raced out to an insurmountable lead en route to the National League West Division title.

That fall, Hatcher got five hits in fifteen at-bats to help the Reds upset the Pirates in the National League playoffs. When the World Series opened, Hatcher was in left field as Cincinnati took on defending champion Oakland.

What happened next earned Hatcher a spot in the record books. In the first game of the Series, he walked his first time up, then hit two doubles and a single in successive at-bats. In Game 2, he opened with a double to right, and followed that with a double to left. That gave him five consecutive hits. On the bench, the Cincinnati players counted off his amazing streak. "Four in a row!" "Five in a row!" Hatcher bunted for a single his next time up to run the streak to six. Then he drove a triple over Jose Canseco's head in right field for his seventh consecutive hit, a World Series record.

Hatcher finished the Series with nine hits in twelve at-bats, a phenomenal .750 batting average and another record, as the underdog Reds pulled off a stunning four-game sweep of the A's.

"Going against the A's," said Hatcher, "we had a good scouting report on them, defensively and offensively, on what their pitchers try to do and how we're going to try to pitch to them.

"And I figured I was going to be hitting second. And my job hitting second was, [Barry] Larkin gets on first, hopefully he steals second or I get him to second, or hopefully he steals second and I get him to third. I try not to put any pressure on myself and try to make it as easy as possible.

"When you're underdogs like we were against the A's, just getting there is something special. And so, we said, 'Well, we're here, let's just do the best we can. Nobody is going to look back and say they just got killed. We're here—we're one of the two best teams right now in baseball.'

"So, you just take all the pressure off yourself, because they were expected to win. They were supposed to win. And so, myself, I was relaxed. We hadn't played against those guys, but just seeing them on television, they were awesome. They had their Cansecos, their [Dave] Stewarts, their [Mark] McGwires, Carney Lansford—I mean, those guys were a good team. But we knew we also had a good team. And the pressure was on them to win.

"In the first inning of the first game, Larkin made an out, I opened with a walk and Eric Davis hit a home run. You could sense right then and there that the crowd was very much into the game. And we knew with the pitching we had, if we were ahead in the sixth inning that as powerful as the A's were, with [Rob] Dibble, [Norm] Charlton and [Randy] Myers, we could take away some of their power. We had guys who threw the ball very, very hard. And so that was our game plan, to try to get to the sixth inning winning the ball game."

But seven consecutive hits? Had Hatcher ever managed such a feat before?

"Playing professional baseball, I've had times where I've had a five-for-five night and gotten two hits the next day. That's during the season, and you really don't think about it because it's a long season. Doing it in a World Series is special because you have everybody watching it, and everybody gets to see those feats."

In his career, Hatcher had played in fourteen postseason games. He had batted fifty-two times and gotten twenty-one hits, a batting average of .404. It was a telling statistic. Hatcher was at his best when the games counted the most.

He had a simple explanation for his postseason heroics.

"Once you make the playoffs," he said, "you don't have to worry about who you're battling next week, or what's the pitching matchup after you finish the series. You can concentrate totally on the pitchers they have at hand. You can start minimizing things about certain situations. You know you're going to face a right-hander [as a relief pitcher]. I eliminate the left-handers because I know in a key situation I'm not going to be able to hit off the left-hander anyway. So I know exactly which pitchers I'm going to be facing, or pretty close to which ones I'm going to be facing.

"So, I concentrate on them. I watch film on them. I watch and see how they're pitching, so it's like it gets locked into your mind. So, when you face them, you don't have to wait and take a pitch to see how hard they're throwing, to see their breaking balls break. You know they like to throw the slider, or they like to throw the curveball first pitch. It's like second nature. You know they're going to come at you with their best."

Hatcher was asked about his ring, and he held out his hand, where one could see the championship ring he now wore to commemorate his participation in that World Series. It was just like the ones Yogi Berra used to show him. Alone among the Astros who competed in the 1986 National League playoffs, Hatcher had later gotten to baseball's ultimate showdown. His ring was a testament to that.

"I will always wear this ring," he said. "I'll cherish it for the rest of my life. Just being in a World Series—a lot of guys who have played the game of baseball never got to play in a World Series. To play in a World Series, to win a World Series, to do as well as I did, that's something that can never be taken away from me."

By coincidence, the year he won his World Series ring was the year Hatcher had kept the picture of the deer posted in his locker. He never did find that deer again, but that fall, the hunter bagged the prize he wanted most.

9

MIKE SCOTT: THE PAYOFF PITCH

One image of the 1986 National League Championship Series stands out above all others. It was not Lenny Dykstra or Darryl Strawberry or any of the other Mets making a game-winning hit. It was not Nolan Ryan gamely throwing fastballs past the New York batters despite a bad knee, or Billy Hatcher driving the ball high into the left-field seats in the Astrodome. Nor was it Jesse Orosco leaping into the air in victory, nor Bob Knepper using his guile to hold off the Mets for eight heroic innings.

The real story of that playoff series was captured in a bucket of baseballs collected by the New York Mets during their loss in Game 4. There were seventeen balls in the bucket, and every one of them contained a scuff mark on it. This was the evidence gathered by the Mets to prove their allegations that Houston pitcher Mike Scott was illegally tampering with the ball before pitching it. This was the evidence presented to National League president Chub Feeney as proof of Scott's duplicity.

The Mets, unable to defeat Scott on the playing field, tried desperately to discredit him in the eyes of the public.

They interrupted play to ask the umpires to examine balls thrown by Scott. They gathered foul balls hit off Scott and sat in their dugout examining them for scuff marks. They complained to the newspaper writers and held up "scuff balls" to be recorded by the many cameramen in the New York clubhouse. Never mind that for all the scrutiny he underwent, Scott was never caught in the act of defacing a baseball, or that the umpires never found cause to reprimand him.

Scott and his alleged scuff ball became THE story of the playoffs.

So much attention was centered on the Houston pitcher and his tactics that during his 3–1 victory over the Mets in Game 4 in New York, the ABC cameras repeatedly focused on him to see what he was doing to the ball. If Scott rubbed the ball with sandpaper or cut it with some other object or smeared a foreign substance on it that day, it was never detected by the cameras.

"If you look at the playoff games, especially the one in New York," he said, "you will see the cameras zoom in on me constantly. I could go on stage with David Copperfield with as much as I was supposed to be doing to the ball. I must have been pretty good at it."

It had been two years since Scott had last pitched in a major-league baseball game. He had enjoyed three more good years with the Astros, capped off by his only twenty-win season in 1989. But the following year he hurt his shoulder and struggled through a losing season before undergoing arthroscopic surgery on the shoulder in December 1990. He returned in 1991, but after pitching only seven innings he was sidelined by more shoulder problems.

He was thirty-six years old and facing major surgery if he wanted to pitch again, so that summer Scott made the decision that all ballplayers dread. He called it quits, ending his thirteen-year career in the big leagues.

Now that he was out of the game, there could be no harm in admitting he had indeed doctored the baseball, as the Mets had so vociferously charged in 1986. If Scott had tampered with the baseball during his career, as had been said so often, surely he could confess to doing so now without any fear of repercussion.

Scott smiled at the suggestion. No, he said, he wasn't going to answer that question.

But if he had scuffed the ball, he was asked, would he ever admit it?

"No, I'll just keep it a mystery," he answered. "I wouldn't ever say one way or another."

He leaned back in his chair, the smile still on his face. "Let them keep guessing," he said.

Mike Scott was used to depending on his teammates in baseball. He threw the ball, they made the plays behind him. He shut down the opposing team, they scored the runs. That was the way it worked.

Even after his retirement from the game, he still counted on them for his well-being.

"Craig Reynolds and Terry Puhl, they're my brokers now," Scott said. "They're stockbrokers in Houston. They handle all my money."

Teamwork—that was what it was all about. Reynolds played shortstop for the Houston Astros when they won the National League West title in 1986. Puhl was a reserve outfielder and pinch hitter. Now, they played a higher-stakes game in the financial world, but they were still on Scott's team. His financial well-being was in their hands.

After leaving baseball, it wasn't the game Scott missed. It was his teammates.

"No, I don't miss baseball," he said. "My career ended at a good time for me. The Astros were rebuilding. The guys I played with were gone.

"We had a good group of guys there that pretty much played together for a long time. You don't see that much anymore. And it's going to get worse, with all the money involved now. Teams can't afford to pay everybody, so they're going to get scrambled around. But we had a nucleus of players that stayed together for five, six years, longer for some of the guys."

Scott still stayed in touch with many of his old Houston teammates. He recited some of the names. Billy Doran. Jim Deshaies. Alan Ashby.

"We still go on vacations with the Dorans. We're real close. Our girls pretty much grew up together. Alan Ashby is a good friend. He played a lot of golf with me. And Jim and Laura Deshaies, their kids and our kids get along real well."

Scott thought back to 1986, the year the Astros won the division championship.

"It's funny—we had pretty good players, but I think we won because we wanted to win the games. The only thing that mattered that day was winning the game. We didn't have the best talent, but we had a bunch of real good competitors. It didn't matter who got three hits or who pitched, we just wanted to win.

"You can just go around the team. Bill Doran and Alan Ashby, Phil Garner, Craig Reynolds—those are guys that are real calm. Well, I wouldn't say Billy or Phil are real calm, but those two guys, Alan and Craig, are just the most calm guys around. But, boy, the fire inside those guys to win games, you wouldn't believe. People wouldn't know it to meet them on the street."

Scott had that same relaxed, easygoing exterior. He was a friendly, pleasant man, and his glasses and thinning hair gave him a mild-mannered appearance. But his looks were deceiving once he had a baseball in his hand. On the field, he, too, was a competitor, as evidenced by his 124 big-league victories and 1,469 strikeouts.

"I've always been competitive," he said. "When I was a kid I'd go to the parks, and during basketball season we'd play basketball after school, during football season we played football and during baseball season we played baseball. I always played sports and liked to win and hated to lose. I'm not a bad loser, I just don't like to lose."

Scott now lived in Laguna Niguel, California, about one hour from Hawthorne, where he grew up. His house, in an upper-class neighborhood on a hillside overlooking the sprawling community, had been built in 1986, the year he signed his first big contract in baseball.

"We had lived in Arizona since I signed with the Mets," he said. "We moved out there because it was a great area to live, but you didn't need a down payment for a house. And I didn't have thirty or forty thousand dollars to put down on a house here at that time.

"So, when we had the money, we bought the house out here where we wanted to live but hadn't been able to afford to. But it was nothing really extravagant.

"I also joined the country club, which I always wanted to do. But they gave me a pretty good deal. That was a funny thing. *Sports Illustrated* came out to do an article on me. Ron Fimrite was the writer. He came out and said, 'Just do what you were going to do today, and I'll follow you around and we can talk.' So that day I was going to join the golf course and put up a deposit.

"It was a brand-new course, and they had the photographer there, and we took pictures of the golf course. It was in the magazine, so they gave me a pretty good deal to join the club. It worked out pretty good."

He played a lot of golf. Scott was not yet forty, and he had the time and the money to do what he wanted. Baseball had given him that independence.

Mike Scott, who dominated the Mets in Games 1 and 4 of the NL Championship Series, was the center of a controversy over his pitching tactics: "It didn't bother me. The bigger the hoopla, the better it was for me." *Photo courtesy Houston Astros.*

He was asked about his success in the game and how it had changed him.

"I don't think it did that much," he answered. "It makes you financially secure. In baseball, people see the big salaries. But not everyone gets rich. A lot of guys, the borderline players, they play five years, and they can't quit the game and have the luxury of retiring."

He was one of the lucky ones, Scott admitted. He had enjoyed big years, he made a lot of money and now he was set for life.

"I don't have to go out and do anything if I don't want to. But it took a while."

He laughed and added, "At least, I THINK I still have money. I haven't talked to Craig and Terry lately."

Mike Scott, at home with daughters Kimberlee and Kelsey and wife, Vicki, never would have attained stardom or been able to buy his dream house in Laguna Niguel, California, if it hadn't been for the split-finger fastball: "I'd probably be selling real estate or insurance. I'd probably be living in Arizona, still trying to get enough money for the down payment on a house out here." *Photo courtesy Vicki Scott.*

There was nothing magical about the split-finger fastball. "It's not a big secret pitch," said Scott.

He held out his large right hand and spread apart his index and middle fingers to demonstrate how to grip the ball when throwing the pitch.

"You don't have to have big hands to throw it. In fact, it's so simple that I try to help kids learn it. People ask me how to throw it, and I tell them, 'Just split your fingers and throw it.'

"The beauty of it is, if you split your fingers, you just can't throw it as hard as if your fingers are together. It just can't happen. So, you put it out there and throw it as hard as you can, and it's ten miles an hour slower. And sometimes it moves, and sometimes it doesn't.

"But when it doesn't, it's like a real good change-up, because your arm speed is the same. You're throwing it just the same, as hard as you can, but you can't throw it as fast with your fingers split on the ball."

Laguna Niguel is located off Interstate 5 in Orange County, California. Farther down the highway, about sixty miles from Scott's house, is San Diego, where he had gone in 1984 to learn the split-finger from Roger Craig.

His trip to San Diego that winter changed Scott's life. He learned to throw the split-finger fastball, and that was what made the house in Laguna Niguel and all its nice furnishings possible. Without the split-finger, there would have been no *Sports Illustrated* article and no celebrity membership at the local country club. Without the split-finger, Mike Scott might be selling real estate or insurance for a living.

"I went down there without having picked up a ball for probably two months," he recalled. "I just kind of got the basics and threw for about a week, enough to where I was good enough to know whether I could throw the pitch or not. And it was easy, real easy. It was real simple."

Easy? How could a pitch that had such a devastating effect on major-league hitters be so easy to throw?

"Well, for a couple of reasons," explained Scott. "One, I threw it a lot, because I canned my slider and my curveball. And to throw that pitch successfully, you have to have a feel for it, and you have to throw it a lot.

"Anybody that picks it up now, I'm sure they also have a pretty good breaking ball. So, they have a fastball, whatever breaking ball they have—curveball, maybe a slider—and then this pitch. Those guys say they have a split-finger fastball, but they throw it maybe in the fifth inning when they're leading five-to-nothing. But this pitch, you have to be able to throw it on three-and-one with the bases loaded and have confidence in it. And the only way you can do that is throw it a lot. That's what I did.

"I remember one game in '85, Alan Ashby was catching, and right in the middle of an inning he came out to talk to me. We had the signs— one finger was a fastball, two was a split-finger and three was a slider. He said to me, 'Why do we even have a sign for the slider? You never throw it. Why don't we just can it? You never need that thing.' He was right. There wasn't a situation where I'd rather throw my slider than a split-finger fastball, so we got rid of it. After that, it was just the two pitches.

"Most guys won't make that drastic of a change. But I was in a situation where I was almost forced to. And if you throw the split-finger on the side to a catcher, you don't see anything that's so spectacular.

But then you throw it to hitters and you see how they react to it, even when it does nothing.

"Most of the time, I threw it and it had just a little bit of down movement. Sometimes, they were straight. But like I said, they were off-speed, and the arm speed was the same. Once I started throwing it to hitters and watching their reactions, it was fun."

Had he seen Craig lately, Scott was asked.

"I see Roger here and there," he said. "He still lives down in San Diego. I might see him at the San Diego baseball school.

"Like I say, it's not a big secret pitch. But he took the time to show me how to throw it. He said, 'That's going to be a good pitch for you. You got it.' He gives you the confidence that you can throw it. He doesn't say, 'Well, it may work.' Every pitch, it's, 'That's a good pitch for you! That's going to work!'

"Basically, he convinced me it was going to be a good pitch for me." Scott smiled and added, "And it worked against their team a couple of times."

And what if he had not made that trip to San Diego and learned the split-finger fastball? How might he be spending his middle-age years?

"Who knows?" answered Scott. He looked around his spacious den, with the swimming pool out back and the hilltop view of the area leading out to Laguna Beach to the west. "I'd probably be selling real estate or insurance. I'd probably be living in Arizona, still trying to get enough money for the down payment on a house out here."

Mike Scott went from mediocrity to stardom overnight. One year, he was worried about losing his job. Two years later, he was an All-Star. He won twenty-nine games his first six seasons; he won eighty-six the next five.

Only one who has been down, as Scott was, can truly appreciate the enormity of his turnaround.

"I had never envisioned it," he said. "Making the All-Star team was something someone else did. There were no signs of that happening to me. I thought it would be nice, but . . . "

His voice tailed off as he remembered what it was like when he was in New York or Houston, just trying to hang on.

"I'd be walking around with Yogi Berra, one of our coaches in Houston, or Nolan Ryan or somebody like that, and people would come up to ask for their autograph. But after that year in '86, I went out to places in Houston and people would start to recognize me."

It couldn't have happened to a nicer guy, Scott's friends said of his transformation. He worked hard, he paid his dues and it was great to see him hit it big. He deserved everything he accomplished. And success had not changed him. He was still good old Scotty—friendly, unpretentious and good-natured.

But not everyone responded so favorably. With Scott's newfound success came charges of tampering with the ball and throwing illegal pitches. No one could get that good that quickly without cheating, charged his critics.

What people overlooked, Scott pointed out, was the unpredictability of the split-finger fastball. Not even Scott knew what it was going to do when he threw it at full speed. So, he chose his spots for it. If he got ahead in the count, say no balls, two strikes, he would throw the split-finger as hard as he could, knowing that he could afford to waste a pitch.

"The forkball is very erratic," he said. "You know, a lot of times on the highlights on the news, they'll show the one that just darts down. But that doesn't happen all the time. That's maybe when the count is oh-and-two and I'm trying to strike somebody out. I don't care where the ball goes, I just throw it as hard as I can. It's really not a very good control pitch.

"But every hitter, if he strikes out, he wants to see that ball. It just doesn't look right to him."

The hitters were asking for the ball a lot in 1986. That year, Scott led the National League in strikeouts, earned-run average and innings pitched.

He became almost unhittable in the final weeks of that season. So much of pitching is mental, he said, and that season he locked into an incredible groove.

"I don't know when it started, but after the All-Star break I really felt like every time I went out there we had a good chance to win. I just felt like something goofy would have to happen for us to lose. I didn't fear having a bad game.

"I made the All-Star team that year for the first time, but my record wasn't that good. I know at the beginning of the year I pitched well, but I didn't win very many games. I lost a lot of one-nothing, two-one games, and my record could have been a whole lot better.

"But toward September and into the playoffs, that's when I felt like I pitched the best. Usually at the end of the year you get a little tired. But when you're in a position to win, which we were, there's no time to get tired. You constantly get adrenaline, thinking, 'We've got to win this game, we've got to win this game.'

"Even when we got the big lead, we didn't let up. Strange things have happened. So, we still kept pushing and pushing until we did clinch it."

The tone for the 1986 National League Championship Series was set in the first inning of the first game. Gary Carter swung at and missed Scott's second pitch, and screamed at the umpire to check the ball. When umpire Doug Harvey found the ball clean and threw it back to Scott, the Astrodome exploded in noise. An angry Carter struck out on the next pitch and walked off, to the jeers of the fans. That was a portent of what was to come.

Scott remembered that moment with satisfaction.

"When the umpire threw the ball back to me, the crowd went nuts," he said. "I think it helped when Carter wanted the ball checked on that second pitch. It made me want to get him out a little bit more. I wanted to get him out, anyway. I wanted to get them all out. But that kind of heated things up and made it a little more interesting.

"I tell you, that talk about scuff balls really intensified late in the season when it became evident we were going to be playing the Mets. I don't know how many games we had left, but our pennant race was about over with. And they had won their division. That's when they started talking about it. And the New York press—if anybody can build something up, they can. So, that became the big issue of the series.

"It didn't bother me. The bigger the hoopla, the better it was for me. I think most players will tell you, 'Hey, just try to hit the ball.' When they started talking about what I was doing, it worked to my advantage. They were over there thinking, 'Well, he's doing this and he's doing that, and I can't hit that.' I think if you ask some of those guys, they would admit that now."

But for Scott, the most memorable moment in his 1–0 Game 1 victory came in the eighth inning, when he struck out Keith Hernandez with two runners on base.

"From start to finish of my career," said Scott, "when I was with the Mets and he was with St. Louis, and when I was with the Astros and he was with the Mets, Keith was the toughest out for me. He was one of the toughest outs in the league with the game on the line.

"And he hit me as good as anybody. He just seemed to guess with me. And he was the type of guy, if the game was five-nothing, I could get him out, because he lost interest. But if the game was one-nothing and he could make a difference, he was the toughest out in the league for me. Because he would bear down in that situation.

"He was the number one guy on that team I didn't want to face with the game on the line or guys in scoring position. And I ended up striking him out in that situation. That was the biggest moment of the game for me."

That first game in Houston was Scott's best performance. But it was his performance three days later, when he beat the Mets 3–1 in Game 4, that gained the most attention. Scott was back in New York, where he had started his career. And the talk of scuff balls was more intense than ever.

"It was an important game, because if we won we knew we were going back to Houston no matter what. And it was a different type of game for me. I was a day short on rest, and I wasn't throwing as hard. So, I threw a lot more balls down and away, curveballs away and fastballs up and in, and it worked.

"And I knew the Mets were going to be checking the balls. That didn't bother me. In fact, I probably got to throw more bad balls that day. The umpires got tired of throwing the balls out, so one would hit the ground and they would keep it in.

"The next day, they were screaming and yelling, and they had tubs full of baseballs and everything else. It must have been a slow news day, because there was sure a lot of press for this. It was a field day for them. It might be kind of fun to look at the papers and see all those stories again. I haven't seen them since we played there."

Would he ever tell if he had scuffed the ball, he was asked.

"Wait for my book," said Scott.

What about cheating in baseball? Was there much of it?

"Wasn't it Jay Howell who had pine tar on his mitt in the playoffs one year?" he replied. "It doesn't really give you an edge. It's surprising that that came up in the World Series, because it's no big deal.

"But there's guys who throw spitballs, there's guys who use pine tar on their bats, there's guys who steal signals. It's all part of the game. It's like, 'Let's see what we can do to win the game.' And if you get caught, you get caught.

"There's all kinds of things that go on. When I was with the Mets, we had a TV monitor in the bullpen. It was just zeroing in from center field. You could see every sign the catcher gave. We could stand out there, and if we knew it was a breaking ball, boom, we could give the hitter a sign.

"Some people want to put a big morals thing on it. It's just part of the game. It's not brain surgery. It's gamesmanship—people trying to win. It's a game. And you're trying to survive."

There was no pink slip for Mike Scott, as he once feared. He did not get cut from the team one spring and sent home to consider new career options. His passing from baseball was not just a one-line mention in the agate transactions, as it was for so many ballplayers.

Instead, he was given a hero's farewell by the Astros. A "Mike Scott Night" was staged in the Astrodome on the fifth anniversary of Scott's most memorable performance, his no-hitter against the Giants to clinch the 1986 West Division title.

The end for Scott had actually come months earlier, when his strong right shoulder finally gave out from the wear and tear of thousands of fastballs and split-finger pitches. He pitched only seven innings in 1991, and was touched for eleven hits and ten runs. Great Scott was finished, and he knew it.

"I pitched two games in '91 just to see if I could pitch. Afterward, I knew I couldn't. There was no point in it. We had a road trip to Chicago coming up, and I didn't know what to do. I knew I couldn't pitch, but I had signed a contract and I didn't want to just quit the team.

"And that day, the owner, John McMullen, called me up. He said, 'Mike, it's a waste of time. You shouldn't go out and pitch and get beat up like that. You should go ahead and retire.' That was a nice gesture. It ended on a good note."

Scott spent the next few months at home in Laguna Niguel, his first summer away from baseball and with his family in seventeen years. He was looking forward to retirement.

The timing was good. He got to leave baseball on his own terms, after five great seasons. He had taken a career that was headed nowhere and turned it into something spectacular. Like the split-finger, his life had taken a sudden and unexpected turn for the better.

Somewhere in his house, there was a real-estate license packed away. Scott did not know where, but it no longer mattered. He no longer had any use for it.

10

GARY CARTER: STILL THE KID

When the New York Mets were on the brink of elimination in the 1986 World Series, it was Gary Carter who staved off defeat.

He came to bat with two outs and no one on base in the bottom of the tenth inning, the Mets trailing the Red Sox by two runs in Game 6. Boston needed only one more out to win the championship.

Gary Carter could have been that final out. He could have hit the last fly ball or the last groundout, or swung and missed at the last strike of the World Series. He could have made the out that sent the Red Sox streaming onto the field in celebration.

The Mets appeared to be a beaten team when Carter stepped to the plate. Keith Hernandez, who made the second out of the inning, had already returned to the clubhouse in disgust, and he was drinking a beer in the manager's office. Kevin Mitchell, who would bat after Carter, was across the locker room making airline reservations on the telephone, his uniform already removed. The players in the dugout sat on the bench in silence.

But if others had lost hope, Carter hadn't. It wasn't his nature. He knew he wasn't going to make the last out of the World Series. He knew he was going to get on base, one way or another. The count went to two balls, one strike, then Carter lined a single to left field.

It wasn't a long home run or a run-scoring hit, but it was the start of one of the most incredible rallies in baseball history. Mitchell was hastily summoned from the clubhouse to pinch-hit, and he also singled. Ray Knight followed with another single to score Carter. Mitchell scored on a passed ball. Knight came home on the ground ball missed by Bill Buckner, and, incredibly, the Mets had won.

Two days later, New York beat Boston in the decisive seventh game to win the championship. In the seven games, Carter hit two homers and drove in nine runs, but it was that two-out single that will be most remembered.

After that World Series, Carter had one more big season in New York. Then age and the toll of almost two thousand games behind the plate began to catch up with him.

The Mets let him go after his batting average dropped below .200 in 1989, and Carter spent the next two years with the Giants and Dodgers. In 1992, he returned to Montreal to finish his career where it had begun eighteen years earlier.

He had not planned for that to be his final season, but as the year progressed Carter, a devout Christian, sensed he was being given divine guidance in deciding his future plans.

"God was giving me signs," he said. "In the book of Ecclesiastes, if you ever have a chance to read it, 3:1 talks about God's perfect timing and why things turn out for the best.

"About a week before I announced my retirement, I kept tossing and turning, trying to make my decision. My knees were going on me, and I knew I was going to have surgery on both knees at the end of the season. I thought if there was any hope to play again, I would go ahead and try to have the surgery done and rehab all winter long and get ready for the next season.

"And then God kept speaking to me and gave me some other scripture in Matthew 4:7—'Don't put the Lord God to the test.' Meaning, 'I've given you my signs, I've told you and it's time.'

"So, I went by His following, and that's why I finished off the way I did."

The way Carter finished off was to announce his retirement, and then in his final game, line a double to right-center field on his last at-bat to score the winning run.

"We won that game one-to-nothing," he said with pride. "It was my last at-bat in the major leagues. It was like a storybook. I accomplished everything I could imagine accomplishing in my career. I will always treasure everything. Now that it's over, I can do a lot of reminiscing. And I can think nothing but good thoughts."

The spring following his retirement as a player, Gary Carter went to work as an announcer and part-time instructor for the Florida Marlins. His hair was thinning and middle age was approaching, but he still had the ever-present smile and enthusiasm that had been his trademark throughout his baseball career.

"I still are 'the Kid,'" he said in intentionally fractured English.

Carter was seated on a stool in front of his locker in the Marlins' clubhouse at the team's spring-training complex in Melbourne, Florida. He pointed at the handwritten name "KID" on his catcher's mitt, bats and other equipment in the cubicle.

"See all my stuff there? I still write 'KID' on there."

Are you going to be "KID" the rest of your life? he was asked.

"Oh, I think so."

Carter got the nickname his first year in the big leagues, 1975, when he was an eager twenty-one-year-old kid brimming with energy.

"I've always been happy and enthusiastic," he explained. "It's been my personality. It's why I got tagged with the nickname 'KID.' And I've always played the game with boyish enthusiasm. It's really the way the game should be played.

"See you later, C.J.!" Carter yelled as Charles Johnson, one of the Marlins' young catchers, passed by. "We'll get you tomorrow if you can slide away from your outfielders' drills when we go one-one-one defense."

Johnson laughed and reminded Carter that he had the day off.

"We'll get you Friday, baby!" Carter shouted happily. "We'll get you Friday! Have a GREAT off-day!"

It always has been this way with Carter. Smiling, laughing, joking, chattering, spreading good cheer. But his sunny disposition and gregarious manner didn't endear him to everyone in baseball. Sometimes, he seemed too good to be true. Some of his teammates took digs at him in the newspapers. Some questioned his sincerity, and Pete Rose once suggested Carter was more interested in endorsements than winning.

Carter was unfazed when asked why some people had such negative reactions to him.

"I often wondered why they would think that way," he said. "But once they know me and all, they realize that there is no phoniness to it, that it's all real.

"And I developed a lot of friendships throughout my career. Especially when I at one time was supposedly the most hated player in the league because of the way I played and all. And then when I had a chance to move around and play on some other ball clubs, they would say the same thing, 'Gee, I didn't like you.' Then when they got to know me, they said, 'Gee, you're a great guy.' That's just the way it goes."

And why didn't they like Carter?

"It's the way I played. I smiled and enjoyed life. They said, 'Oh, this guy, he can't be real.'"

Outside the clubhouse, Carter stopped to autograph a picture handed him. A woman and her husband then asked if Carter could sign their baseball bat.

"I sure can," he said.

"Can we take a picture with you, also?"

"You bet." Carter stood between the couple, his arms around their shoulders, and smiled at the camera.

"Thank you, Gary," they said after the picture was taken.

"Thank YOU!" Carter responded enthusiastically.

A crowd gathered around him, and soon Carter was writing his autograph on pictures, caps, scorecards and almost anything else offered to him. The only thing he wouldn't sign was a baseball card.

"I don't sign the cards," he explained, "because I have a commitment with the Leukemia Society that if someone makes a donation in my mom's name for twenty-five dollars, then I'll sign the card for them. I've raised about two-point-five million dollars for the Society already."

Carter's fund-raising efforts for the Leukemia Society are a tribute to his mother, Inge, who was diagnosed with the disease on her thirty-seventh birthday. She died six months later. Gary, who was only twelve at the time, learned of her death after returning home from a Little League game.

"I was always a churchgoing kid with my family until my mom passed away," he said. "At that time, I didn't understand why a loving God as we know Him would take someone away like my mom."

Carter said that his mother's death "turned me off God for a while and on to sports." In a way, sports was what saved him.

"I could have gone down the wrong path very easily. But I didn't because sports was so much a part of my life. I'm very grateful for that."

Carter was the all-American boy in high school in Fullerton, California. He was captain of the football, basketball and baseball teams. He was the quarterback of the football team and received a scholarship offer to play at UCLA. But when he tore ligaments in his right knee playing football his last year in high school, he decided to concentrate on baseball.

He signed with the Montreal Expos for a $42,500 bonus when he got out of high school in June 1972 and went off to play Rookie League ball. His teammates there remember him less for his play on the field than for his exaggerated hustle. He not only did the best calisthenics on the team, he always did them in the front row in order to be noticed. "How am I doing?" he would ask his manager and coaches.

Carter went to spring training with the Expos the next year, and it was there he became a born-again Christian.

"My roommate in my very first big-league spring-training camp was John Boccabella. And John Boccabella was the guy that led me to the Lord. I felt like there was something missing in my life, and I realized what I was missing was the peacefulness that Christ gives to you. I turned my life over to Him and made Him my personal savior. And if I died today, I'd be a happy camper and know where I'd be going to. And I'd be able to live an eternal life.

"It wasn't always easy being a Christian in baseball," he continued, "especially when you take a stance like I did. I got criticized for it, but it's a part of the game, and you take the good with the bad. But I felt that it was a part of my life, and I wasn't afraid to take that stance and say that Christ was a part of my life.

"Players now have taken more of a stance. Early on, back when I accepted Christ, there weren't very many who would come forward and talk about their faith. And there were some bad times that went with that.

"But, hey, for the most part I was very grateful to have lived my life the way I did. There's always going to be some criticism, and there's always going to be personality conflicts. You're not always going to be loved or liked by everybody. It's just an acceptance, you know. I've always been the kind of guy that's wanted everybody to like me. But that's not always the case."

It didn't help when Carter made it to the big leagues to stay in 1975 and was proclaimed the "catcher of the future" in Montreal. Or that Gene Mauch, the Montreal manager, was quoted as saying the Expos would never win without Carter behind the plate.

Despite the buildup, Carter began his career in Montreal as an outfielder and backup to incumbent catcher Barry Foote. Carter still has the scars to remind him of the two years he spent in the outfield.

"I broke my thumb once and opened my head once." He pointed to a scar on his forehead. "I was playing left field, and Dwight Evans hit a line drive at me. Carl Yastrzemski was on first base. This was in Winter Haven, where there's a short warning track with a brick wall.

"I went back on the ball thinking I could catch it, and it ticked off my glove and BOOM, I hit that wall! I came off the wall and I knew I was hurt, because there was blood everywhere. I picked the ball up and tried to throw it, and I made the play, but I knew I was hurt."

He rubbed his head where he had cut it open. "Like I said, I was dangerous out there. I cracked a couple of ribs robbing Dave Cash of a home run one time. I think it was '76. There was all kinds of things that happened to me. I got hurt so bad they thought it would be best if I put the catching gear back on and protected myself."

Carter moved behind the plate on a full-time basis and became a star in 1977, hitting thirty-one homers and driving in eighty-four runs. He was a rare commodity in baseball—a catcher who could hit for power and drive in runs.

He was a seven-time All-Star in ten years in Montreal, and in 1982 he became one of the game's highest-paid players, signing an eight-year contract worth $1.87 million a season. But when the talented Expos failed to win a title, Carter became the focal point for the team's perennial disappointments. He knew then it was time for a change.

"There was too much finger-pointing going on," he said. "And [owner] Charles Bronfman was very adamant about the contract I had signed before the '82 season. He made the comment that 'I will regret the signing of Gary Carter for the rest of my life.'

Gary Carter was the man who kept the Mets alive with his two-out hit in the tenth inning of Game 6 of the World Series: "I went up there, and I really had confidence that I was going to be able to come through. And to me that was rewarding in itself, that I didn't make the last out." *Photo courtesy New York Mets.*

"I think because of the way the salary structure was back then and the fact I was one of the highest-paid players and all, he really wanted me to move on. They felt like I just threw their whole salary structure out of whack, and they could get some quality players for the same amount of money. So, they sent me on my way."

Where the Expos sent him was New York, in a blockbuster deal on December 10, 1984. The Expos got four young players, including infielder Hubie Brooks. The Mets got Carter, and with him a world championship.

New York was Gary Carter's kind of town.

"When I went there," he began, "it was the best thing that could have happened to me at the time. Meaning that I was in Montreal for ten years and I was really not the recognizable person that I became when I went to New York.

"And they brought me there sort of as the last piece of the puzzle to not only handle the pitching staff but to give them something offensively as well. Fortunately, I was able to come through with big years the first three years there.

"Especially '85, when I had my most home runs in a season with thirty-two and drove in a hundred runs. Then in '86, I tied the team record for most RBIs with a hundred and five, which was later broken by Darryl Strawberry. But at the time, Rusty Staub was the only guy that had done it."

There was no need to double-check the numbers. When it comes to reciting his statistics and records, Carter is as accurate as he is thorough.

"And I became the first Met to ever have back-to-back hundred-RBI seasons," he continued, "and I came in third in the balloting for MVP in the league. It hurt me because I had injured my thumb and was on the disabled list for fifteen days.

"But I just look back at those first couple of years—those were tremendous years for me. So, getting my feet settled into New York was great for me, and I felt it really was a turning point in my career. The only downside to it was when I started hurting physically. They also started to bury me there.

"So, it's just a matter of you have to take the good with the bad sometimes. But when you're on a high and you're playing well and all, it's the best place in the world to play. You bet. If you're winning and all, it's the best place, no question. No question."

And the Mets, as well as Carter, were on a high back then. They made a run at the pennant in 1985, finishing three games behind the Cardinals. In 1986, everything fell into place, and New York won 108 games to win the National League East title in a rout.

"I tell you what: We had a real special team that year because we had a great mixture," Carter recalled. "We had some good veteran players, we had some good young players. For the most part, it was just a team that really stayed together, played together and pulled for one another. And there really was no dissension, not really any jealousies or anything.

"It was just really a special team. There was one game we ran out of players and we were playing in Cincinnati. It was an important game for us, somewhere in the middle part of the year. I ended up playing third base that game just because we had run out of players.

"We also had a fight and there was a couple of guys that were kicked out. So [pitchers] Jesse Orosco and Roger McDowell took turns pitching and playing right field. Depending on what situation we were in, Jesse was in right field when Roger was pitching to right-handers, and then Jesse would pitch against the left-handers and Roger would go to right field.

"It was just a neat thing, and it seemed like every time we took the field we really felt like we were going to win the ball game. We weren't a cocky ball club, which everybody said we were. We were just a very confident ball club."

That confidence was put to the test in the National League Championship Series against Houston. It was a series dominated by dramatic comebacks, tense extra-inning games, brilliant pitching performances and, most of all, the specter of Mike Scott. The Houston right-hander not only beat New York twice, he so dominated the Mets he was the focus of their attention even when he wasn't pitching.

They spent much of their time complaining about Scott's tactics and dragging out scuffed baseballs to prove their charges that the Houston pitcher was indeed cheating. Carter was perhaps the most outspoken of Scott's accusers, but his constant complaints only accentuated his poor performance at the plate in that series. He managed just four hits in twenty-seven at-bats and drove in only two runs, hardly the kind of performance worthy of a player of his stature.

"It was a frustrating experience," Carter admitted. "I didn't hit a lick. I was like one-for-twenty-two or something until I got that game-winning hit off Charlie Kerfeld in Game 5 to win it for us. And then I got two hits in Game 6, but I didn't hit very well in that series. I hit .148 or something like that."

Carter frowned briefly, then quickly smiled and added, "But I got some timely hits."

And does Carter still stand by his charges that Mike Scott illegally scuffed the ball?

"Well, the allegations were there," Carter said coyly. "But whether or not they were true, I'll tell you this, the man could pitch. But how do you go from one hundred thirty-five strikeouts to three hundred six the next year? He had to have been doing something.

"But let me tell you this: In the playoffs he was unhittable. And that's what we were facing in Game 6 when Knepper had a three-hit shutout going into the ninth inning, and they were up three–nothing. We realized if we were going to do it, if we were going to win it, we were going to have to win it then, and not wait until the next day to try and beat Mike Scott at home. Because he just had a way.

"We gathered about a dozen balls when he pitched at Shea and beat us. And I mean to tell you, there were some balls that looked pretty nasty. We sent them to the league office and they said, 'Nah!' They didn't fine him or anything, and they found nothing really wrong.

"Whatever he did, I credit him, but I mean to tell you, his balls were unhittable. UN-hittable! However he got it done, God bless him. If he got away with it, God bless him. But if he wants to tell you that he cheated, fine. I'm not going to say any more than that."

How could Scott get away with cheating given the scrutiny he was under during the playoffs? Carter couldn't say, but he insisted the pitcher was doing something to the ball, that he had to have something with him when he went to the mound.

"There was times when umpires would go out there and check him, and he would have it wherever and somehow or another he was able to take it off. And he would go back in at the end of the inning and put another one on.

"Doug Harvey, he was asked the question and again they never charged him with it. He got away with it. So, if he got away with it, God bless him, you know. And again, I don't know if he will ever, ever admit to it. But I'll tell you what, whatever he did or however he did it, it was awesome. Because he was unhittable. And I don't think there's any human being alive that can throw the way he did and make the ball do what he made it do."

What Carter will concede now is that all the talk about Scott proved to be counterproductive.

"We were so taken by the way that he was throwing that we were already defeated before we got to him. He was just throwing the heck out of the ball.

"The first game, he struck out thirteen, and he got me three times. And I thought it was an accomplishment when I made contact and grounded out to third. I was glad I didn't get the 'sombrero.' I got the hat trick, but I didn't get the sombrero. The golden sombrero is when you strike out four times. That's a tough night when you get struck out four times. I only got the sombrero one time in my career. It was off Andy Messersmith at Dodger Stadium.

"Anyway, Scott was awesome. He threw a five-hit shutout at us there and then the next game he allowed three hits and won that. He was the league championship MVP and he was well-deserving of it. He was, like I said, unhittable. He really was."

And what does he think of Mike Scott now? Carter flashed the familiar smile.

"I think's he's a great guy. Now that I've got to know him a little more at some of these golf tournaments and stuff like that, he's a real likable guy. You know, I don't think anyone will ever accuse him anymore, and I don't think he'll come out and tell anybody about it, either. Whatever is done is over with."

Look at a history of the World Series. The first thing you will notice, Gary Carter pointed out, is all the great players who never played in one.

"Like Ernie Banks, to name one," he said. "And there was others that never had a world championship ring. Carl Yastrzemski and guys like that played in a World Series but never got a championship ring. I was fortunate to say I got one.

"For me, it was just a thrill to finally play in one after twelve years. And to have won it in the manner that we did was a bigger thrill, coming back in Game 6 the way we did."

Carter smiled at the thought of it. Game 6 might have been his finest moment. The Mets, trailing by two runs, were down to their last out when the Kid came to bat in the tenth inning. It was a moment he will never forget.

"When I came up, the thing that went through my mind was, 'Two outs in the bottom of the tenth and we're down five–three and I could make the last out of the game.' Alls I kept thinking about was during my childhood I kept imagining what it was like to be up in the World Series. I used to play games out there in the alleyway, bottom of the ninth, bases loaded, two outs and I'm the guy up—I'm not going to make the last out.

"I went up there, and I really had confidence that I was going to be able to come through. And to me that was rewarding in itself, that I didn't make the last out."

Calvin Schiraldi was pitching for Boston. Carter had caught him the year before, when he was with the Mets. He knew Schiraldi couldn't beat him in that situation.

"I knew him well enough that I knew what was in his gut. I just felt strongly that I was going to come through whichever way it was, whether it was get hit by a pitch or coming through with a hit or walking. Whatever it was, I was not going to make the last out. I just felt strongly about that."

Carter worked the count to two balls, one strike before lining Schiraldi's fourth pitch into left field for a single. The game, and the World Series, turned around on that one hit. It was followed by two more singles. There was the wild pitch. Then Bill Buckner missed the ground ball, and the Mets had won.

"It was like we were stunned," remembered Carter. "Because they were on the top step ready to celebrate. I heard that Oil Can Boyd had already gone into the clubhouse and had popped the cork on one of the champagne bottles. That's how confident they were that the Series was over.

"And it would have been their first championship since 1919, or 1918. Yeah, 1918. So, there was a lot of things riding on that. And everybody remembers the ball through Bill Buckner's legs. Not the fact that the guy had over twenty-seven hundred hits in his career, but the fact that ball went through his legs.

"I felt the guy was a great player. He was a gamer. The guy played his heart out all the time, and you had to admire him for even going out on the bad ankle he had. He had a tremendous career. And what Boston fans will remember him most for was that ball through his legs.

"And you know what? Even if he had caught it, I think Mookie would have been safe. The only thing was, he probably would have held

Ray Knight at third base. But when the ball went through his legs, there was no hope. The ball went out into right field and there was nobody there to pick it up.

"So, I felt sorry for him," Carter continued. "I really felt bad. Because he played his heart out and he was struggling big time. And I gotta kind of blame John McNamara for maybe not putting Dave Stapleton in there for defense, late inning like that."

But Buckner was on the field, not Stapleton. He missed the ground ball, and the Mets won the game.

"And then we were a team of destiny," said Carter. "And we knew that Game 7, it didn't matter. We fell down, the first few innings we were down three–nothing, until we broke it open I think in the fifth or sixth inning.

"I still remember in Game 6, when I came to the plate and got the hit to left field, just for a split second they flashed on the board, 'Congratulations, Boston Red Sox, World Champions.' They had to eat their words on that."

It was just like the imaginary games he played as a kid back in the neighborhood, when he dreamed of batting with two outs in the last inning of the World Series. Back then, he always got the hit, also.

The sun was shining outside. It was springtime in Florida. A new baseball season was about to begin. What could be better?

"Okay, baby, have a great off-day!" Gary Carter shouted to a couple of players as he prepared to leave the ballpark. One of the players yelled something back.

"Yes, sir, yes, sir, be there for that!" answered Carter. "Be there or BE SQUARE!"

He was a lucky man, he said. He was no longer playing baseball, but the radio job with the Marlins was the next best thing.

"I don't have to move my family anymore. And they're really at that prime age where I need to be home. My oldest is fourteen, my other daughter is twelve, then my son is eight. I really feel strongly it's time to spend more time at home. Even though we do sixty-nine games on the road, which is really half the time, we do only forty-one games at home, and the other forty games I don't even have to go to. I stay at home.

"It's like out of that span I'm going to get back two months of that time that otherwise I would lose. And I felt that those two months were time that I was wasting on the bench when I was waiting to play. That's the toughest part. When I was a regular player in the game, it was great. When I stopped being a regular player, that was the tough part, going to the ballpark knowing that I was going to sit on the bench and watch the game.

"Now, at least I'll be talking about the game. I'll be active in the booth, and I'll also have a chance to throw some batting practice and all when the team's on the road. I can go out early with the guys and throw with them and take a little BP."

Yes, said Carter, the time had come to hang it up, and he had known it.

"There really wasn't anything for me to accomplish. I got to the two-thousand-game plateau. I got to twelve hundred RBIs. I've had the three hundred home runs, I've had the thousand-plus RBIs, the thousand runs scored, the two thousand hits. I added on to my National League record for games caught and total chances and putouts and all that stuff. I've played in a World Series, been MVP of the All-Star Game twice, played in eleven All-Star Games, hit .300 in All-Star competition, two home runs in the World Series in one game, nine RBIs in the World Series, won a world championship, was on three league-championship teams. I accomplished everything I could ever have imagined accomplishing. There was just no more incentive for me.

"So, I figured I would get into a new line of business as far as being a broadcaster goes. And I can help out here a little bit. I'm always going to be involved in the game. I love the game too much not to be.

"But now I feel that I can enjoy my life the way it should be. And if one day I go to Cooperstown, it will be a great day. And if I don't, I'm not going to lose any sleep over it. If it was meant to be, it was meant to be."

It was Carter who broached the subject of the Baseball Hall of Fame, but when asked to elaborate on his chances of induction and what it would mean to him, he preferred to consider a different type of immortality.

"You know, the way I look at it is if what I've done in my career is not good enough to get me there, then so be it. But as long as I'm part of 'God's Hall of Fame,' that's all that matters. I'll share a little poem with you that has always meant something to me in my career. It came from

John Wooden's book *They Call Me Coach*. The author of it is anonymous, so I don't know who it is, but it goes something like this:

> To have your name inscribed up there is greater yet by far
> Than all the Halls of Fame down here and every man-made star.
> This crowd on earth, they soon forget the heroes of the past;
> They cheer like mad until you fall and that's how long you last.
> I tell you, friend, I would not trade my name, however small,
> If written there beyond the stars in that celestial hall
> For any famous name on earth or glory that they share;
> I'd rather be an unknown here and have my name up there.

He recited the entire passage from memory. There is a similar message about God's Hall of Fame printed on the back of a custom-made baseball card Carter produced of himself. On the front is a picture of Carter in his Montreal uniform. On the back, where normally a ballplayer's statistics would be shown, Carter has included his favorite books of the Bible, his favorite Bible verse (John 14:6) and an inspirational message about his salvation.

It is only fitting that Carter would use a baseball card to convey his beliefs. He has been an avid collector of baseball cards since his boyhood days, and he has a collection worthy of a superstar.

"I've got over a hundred thousand, I'm sure," he said. "But I have no desire to sell them or anything. I'm going to just hand them down to my kids."

Carter reached into his bag and pulled out a box of 1993 cards he had purchased just that day.

"I got this one for a set for my son. But I have my own sets, too.

"I mean, I go back to 1953," he added proudly. "I've got every card in every set!"

He was no longer a twenty-one-year-old rookie or the young boy playing ball in the neighborhood and dreaming of the World Series. But one thing hadn't changed. Gary Carter was still a kid at heart.

11

RAY KNIGHT: THE RIGHT MAN FOR THE JOB

Sometimes, when he is having trouble sleeping because of his on-going problem with kidney stones, Ray Knight will get out of bed at three o'clock in the morning and go to the trophy room in his house in Athens, Georgia.

There, he might open the trophy case that covers an entire wall of the room and take out the bat he used to hit the winning home run in Game 7 of the 1986 World Series. Holding it in his hands in the quiet darkness, he will remember the inside fastball that Boston's Calvin Schiraldi threw him with a count of two balls, one strike leading off the seventh inning. He can still recall everything about that moment. The feeling of anticipation and excitement when he drove the ball deep to left-center field, knowing he had hit it hard enough but not being sure if it would be long enough. The elation that came with seeing the ball clear the fence. The joy he felt as he almost floated around the bases.

Next, he might pull out the home-run ball and hold it in his hands once more. Or he might take down the glove he used throughout that World Series, just to feel the familiar leather.

"I never used that glove again," Knight tells visitors to the trophy room.

And always on these sleepless nights, he gets out the videotape of that World Series and sits in front of the television to watch the replay of Game 6.

He has seen that game dozens of times, but the reaction is the same every time.

"I can't look at that tape without getting chills," he will confide. "Remembering how it was. And almost having the exact same feelings. When the camera is on me, I can remember exactly what I was feeling."

He watches as the Red Sox score two runs in the top of the tenth inning, putting themselves within three outs of the world championship. He remembers running off the field and going up and down the dugout yelling encouragement to his teammates, telling them not to give up.

"You just get on, man," he yelled at Wally Backman, the leadoff hitter that inning. "If it means taking the first pitch, get on any way you can. If you get on, we'll win this ballgame!"

He still recalls saying those things, knowing that if Backman got on, the next batter, Keith Hernandez, could hit a home run, and the game would be tied.

On the television screen, Backman flies out to left field. Hernandez flies out to center. The Mets are one out from defeat. The New York players are shown in the dugout, discouraged and subdued. Knight remembers being there, holding his batting helmet and his bat, feeling sad for the first time and then looking up to see the scoreboard flash the message, "Congratulations, Boston Red Sox, World Champions."

"It ticked me off," he will tell you. "I just felt . . . I can't explain it—I saw that and it was a mixture of sadness and madness at the same time. Not just because it was flashed up there, but because of the fact that it was a concession."

The pain from the kidney stones is forgotten as Knight watches Carter gets his hit to left field. The camera is on Kevin Mitchell, the next batter, but Knight can see himself standing in the on-deck circle, excited by the possibility he might get to bat after all. Mitchell fouls off the first pitch from Boston's Calvin Schiraldi. Strike one. Off-camera, Knight has turned his gaze to the stands, where his wife, Nancy Lopez, is seated.

It is a scene he has described many times over the years: "I look up and Nancy has her head in her hands, crying and just boohooing and looking at me. And I put my hand up and said, 'Don't worry about me, I'm fine.'"

Knight laughs every time he tells the story. "She was so concerned about me being in that pressure situation, and I was not affected at all. I mean, I was just glad, and my adrenaline was pumping so much and I'm really under control but excited that I might get a chance to hit. And I knew if I got a chance to hit, then we were going to have a chance to win, because I was the winning run."

The sounds from the television are growing more animated as Mitchell hits a one-strike pitch into center for another single. The voice of announcer Vin Scully can be heard exclaiming, "Suddenly, the tying runs are aboard and Ray Knight will be the batter!"

Knight leans forward in his chair, his heart racing as he relives that moment. He remembers walking from the on-deck circle to the batter's box, thinking only about getting a good pitch to hit. "I knew Schiraldi, and I knew he couldn't get his breaking ball over. I knew that he was basically a one-pitch pitcher. And I was just going to look for a pitch that looked fat and drive it."

Schiraldi throws a fastball on the outside part of the plate for strike one. A roll of toilet paper sails out of the stands and lands in front of the backstop.

The next pitch is a sinkerball, down and in. Knight swings and hits a dribbler down the third-base line. It rolls foul, and Scully's voice is saying, "So, Knight comes back to hit with the count no balls and two strikes."

Knight can be seen walking back to the plate, stepping back in the box and checking his bat. Schiraldi nervously blows on his hands to warm them.

Watching from his TV room, Knight knows what will happen next, but he could not be any more confident of the outcome now than he was that night, at that exact moment when the World Series hung in the balance.

"Even with two strikes, all I did was look for the ball out over the plate. I knew he couldn't get me out inside. I knew he couldn't strike me out inside. I knew I could get the bat on the ball. I just knew he couldn't throw the ball by me.

"And so I stepped out of the batter's box, and my only thought was, 'I have to protect the outside part of the plate and not let him throw me a "bitch pitch" out there.' So, I just thought right-center field and thought about the ball on the outside part of the plate."

Knight is out of his chair now, watching himself swing at an inside fastball from Schiraldi and hit the ball over second base for a single.

"Here comes Carter to score, and the tying run is at third in Kevin Mitchell!" Scully is saying excitedly on the TV.

Now, Boston manager John McNamara is going to the mound to pull Schiraldi, and NBC cuts to a commercial. The room is illuminated only by the flickering images on the screen while Knight reflects on that at-bat and that swing.

"He tried to bust me in with a fastball, and I was able to fight the ball off for a base hit but with the right approach. I knew in my mind he didn't have enough fastball to throw it by me on the inside part of the plate. That's knowing yourself as a hitter and knowing the pitcher."

The game resumes, with Bob Stanley on the mound for Boston and Mookie Wilson batting for New York. The count goes to two balls, two strikes, then one of Stanley's pitches can be seen shooting past catcher Rich Gedman. Mitchell runs in from third to score the tying run, and in the background, there is Knight on second base, arms waving in the air as he leaps in celebration.

"Can you believe this ball game at Shea?" asks Scully.

"Oh, brother!" answers his broadcast partner, Joe Garagiola.

Another pitch, another foul ball, and Scully points out that Boston's Marty Barrett had Knight picked off second base if only Stanley had turned and thrown the ball to him.

"If it had been a good throw, I would have been out," Knight will admit. "But I'd rather be out at second than out at home on a base hit, so I just kept getting a bigger and bigger lead."

And suddenly, the scene on the television is that of a ground ball rolling through Bill Buckner's legs at first base, and Knight, with third-base coach Buddy Harrelson alongside him, happily running down the third-base line, waving his arms, grasping his head in joy and disbelief, jumping onto home plate with the winning run and being mobbed by his celebrating teammates.

"I'm running hard to third," Knight can remember, "but I'm resigned that we were going back to play defense. And all of a sudden I heard Buddy yell something. I don't know what he yelled, just 'Ay-yi-yi-yi!' and I touched third and looked over my shoulder and saw the ball bounding into right field. And the rest of that time, it was like I was on a carpet. I was just floating home."

Ray Knight resurrected his career in 1986 and was named the MVP in the World Series: "Every time there was a crucial situation, two outs in the ninth or whatever, it seemed I was the person who happened to be up at the plate, and most of the time I came through. It was just my year to have the opportunity to perform." *Photo courtesy New York Mets.*

Watching that moment once more, alone in a quiet house in the middle of a sleepless night, Knight can still feel all the crazy emotions he felt back then. He has tried to describe those feelings, but his words cannot adequately capture them.

"Just a tremendous explosion of emotion," he will tell you. "Just complete numbness. Unbelievability. Chills and feelings that I'd never felt before. People talk about dying and coming back to life. I don't know what that feeling is like, but whatever feeling I had that night is something I never had again, even when I hit the home run in Game 7. I mean, I had a burst of elation, but the feeling I had scoring the winning run that night was just indescribable."

The replay of that moment is shown again on the television set. Knight sees himself slumped on the dugout bench, overcome with exhaustion and emotion, as teammates and coaches come by to embrace him. His uniform is covered with dirt and his hair is disheveled.

He sits back in his chair at his home, and he watches and remembers. It no longer matters that he is unable to sleep. If he didn't know better, he would think all this was a dream, anyway.

Fame is fleeting in baseball. Four months after being named the Most Valuable Player in the 1986 World Series, Ray Knight left the New York Mets in a contract dispute and signed with the Baltimore Orioles.

The issue was not money. The Mets offered him $800,000, while the Orioles gave him only $475,000 plus incentives. But Knight wanted a two-year deal. The Mets would not sign him for more than one year.

It did not matter that Knight hit the decisive home run in the World Series. Or that he scored the winning run in the dramatic tenth-inning rally in Game 6 against Boston. Or that his sacrifice fly capped a ninth-inning rally against Houston, enabling the Mets to win the memorable sixth game of the National League Championship Series. Or that his .298 batting average during the regular season was eighth-best in the National League. Or that he always seemed to deliver the big hit when the Mets needed it the most and was praised by his teammates for his leadership, his inspiration and his enthusiasm.

The Mets' front office was unwavering in its negotiations with Knight.

"I had made up my mind with Nancy that I was only going to play two more years," Knight explained. "I didn't want to move again. I loved New York in '86. I loved being there. I loved playing there. I loved my teammates. I thought we were a real special group. I did not want to leave.

"But they were just unyielding and unbending on a two-year contract. It was never a money decision. Never. It was a one-on-one, man-to-man decision of me not feeling like they wanted me back.

"I looked Frank Cashen [Mets general manager] in the eye that day that we negotiated, and I didn't see any remorse or any feelings of concern for Ray Knight being a New York Met. All I saw was, 'Here it is, it's a business deal. This is what we're offering. If you don't like it, go ahead.' And I didn't like it, so I took a hike."

After the negotiations broke down, and Knight was casting about for another team, he received a call from Mets manager Davey Johnson. He told Knight he wished there was some way he could stay with the team. Knight replied that because of the way the contract talks had been handled, and the things Cashen had said, that was not possible. He didn't feel wanted in New York.

"Well, I certainly want you and need you on this ball club," insisted Johnson.

But there was no turning back. Knight signed with Baltimore, and played there for one season. The next year, he went to Detroit, where he ended his playing career in 1988. After retiring from the game, he spent much of his time caddying for his wife, Nancy, on the women's golf tour. He also went to work for the ESPN sports network as a baseball analyst and broadcaster.

Knight's television job occasionally took him to New York to broadcast games from Shea Stadium, and there he would spend time visiting with his former manager. Even after Johnson was fired as Mets manager in 1990, the two men stayed in contact with one another.

Knight had chances to return to baseball during this time, but his family considerations kept him from doing so. Nancy was a famous golfer, one of the most successful and popular athletes in the country, and the demands of her sport kept her on the road much of the time. The couple had three daughters, and Knight had a son by a previous marriage. It would be too great a strain on the family if Nancy were on the golf tour and Ray were with a baseball team.

Knight decided the only way he would go back to baseball would be as manager of a major-league team. It was something he had wanted to do since he was a young man. In 1992, he interviewed for four such jobs. The response was always the same: You are managerial material, but you can't go from the TV booth to the dugout as a manager; you need to get back into uniform before you can take over a ball club.

In May 1993, Knight was still working with ESPN when he called Johnson at his fishing camp in Ocala, Florida. The two men talked about managing, and Knight asked for advice on interviewing for a job.

"Look," said Johnson, "just be yourself. Tell them what you think, what you expect and what you want. And don't compromise your feelings, because when you do get the right job, they'll understand what you expect. And if you get anything less than that, then you're able to have a beef about it."

The next day, a Monday, Knight was at ESPN, and he turned on the television set to hear that Johnson had been hired to replace Tony Perez as Cincinnati manager.

"Holy moly!" said Knight. "This is really crazy. We were talking about it just last night."

Thirty minutes later, the telephone rang for Knight. It was Jim Bowden, the general manager at Cincinnati. He offered Knight the job as Reds hitting coach. And he wanted an answer in three to four hours.

Suddenly, Knight was excited about the prospects of returning to baseball; of going back to Cincinnati, where he had begun his career, and being reunited with Johnson. But first, he knew he would have to work it out with his family.

"There's no way I can let you know in two or three hours," Knight told Bowden. "And there's no way I can report on Tuesday. If I take the job, I'll have to go home and get everything right with my family."

Knight talked it over with Nancy, and they realized this really was his one free shot at going back to baseball without disrupting his family. He would be working from late May until early October—essentially the summer months, when the children were out of school and could join him in Cincinnati. That would give him the opportunity to see how he liked being in the dugout, plus enable him to get some valuable experience if he should seek a managerial job in the future.

There was one other consideration. Knight would have the chance to work for Davey Johnson, the man he called "one of my top two or three friends—someone I just have great respect and love for."

That afternoon, Knight called Bowden and accepted the job.

Three months later, Ray Knight was in a hotel room in Los Angeles getting ready to leave for the ballpark later that afternoon.

He apologized for pushing back an interview that had been scheduled for that morning, but the ball club's flight from Cincinnati had not arrived until late the night before. By the time he had checked into his room, it was early morning, so he had chosen to sleep in until noon.

It was one of the inconveniences of major-league baseball and the constant travel, but Knight was enjoying himself nonetheless.

"I've had a great time," he was saying. "I've enjoyed everything about being back. I love putting on the uniform and, really, I still feel the same way I've always felt, that's it's a privilege and an honor to be a part of a major-league organization.

"I try to instill that in the players. I think they've begun to take a lot for granted. I see that. And the game has changed. But I think with the right type of approach, the proper way to play the game and the proper way to approach the game can be reinstilled. It's been a challenge to me."

It was a different type of feeling from playing, Knight added. When you played, you could make a contribution to the team every day, if not with your hitting or fielding or base running, then by exuding a positive attitude in the clubhouse and on the field or by being an upbeat person. In coaching, you influenced the team in more subtle ways.

"I really immerse myself in each of the players and try to do something positive each day," he explained. "As a result, you get a lot of gratification working with a young hitter, or even a veteran hitter who has struggled.

"You sit down and look at the videotape of him hitting, and you learn and converse with him, and then you see that he grasps what you're saying. And he goes out in batting practice and there's some application, and that night he gets a couple of hits. And all of a sudden, he takes off for ten or twelve days and is right on the ball, and you can see the confidence.

"That's a great feeling—and not unlike the contribution of getting a big base hit. You feel good having guys show confidence in you and start coming to you and asking for your advice and your help. It's rewarding."

He also enjoyed working with Johnson. The two of them went back a long way. They met in 1978, when Knight was a young infielder with the Reds and was being groomed as Pete Rose's successor at third base, and Johnson was playing his last year in the big leagues with the Phillies and Cubs.

"I talked to him a little bit then, just a player-to-player relationship, not anything deeper than that," said Knight. "He told me he always liked the way I played and he watched me."

The two men followed each other's careers from a distance over the next few years. Knight was an All-Star performer for the Reds, but in 1981 he was traded to Houston. There, he turned in two more solid seasons, making the All-Star team one year and batting over .300 the other. It was while he was in Houston that he also married Nancy Lopez, who already had established herself as a Hall of Fame golfer. Johnson, meanwhile, had begun managing in the minor leagues, and in 1984 he was hired by the Mets.

"As soon as he became manager of the Mets," said Knight, "he tried to acquire me because he liked what I brought to a ball cub, the way I went about my business professionally.

"And then finally, in '84, I was riddled with injuries with the Astros. Basically, I had missed about the first half of the season with all kinds of injuries, from vertigo to kidney stones to leg pulls to a torn rotator cuff. I was just maybe fifty percent of myself, and Davey insisted that Cashen acquire me.

"I went over there and really wasn't healthy. I hit .280 for them in '84, and we finished a game or so behind the Cubs. In '84, I had a couple of operations, one on my elbow and one on my shoulder. And I just didn't feel right physically.

"A lot of people gave up on me, because obviously I wasn't playing very well. But Davey knew my heart, and we became close because he saw me go through the operations and really work hard to come back, and never complain and just continue to accept whatever role they thrust at me.

"Howard Johnson had come over, and I'd gone from being an everyday player to platooning with him. But I kept telling Davey that one-on-one I was going to win the job—as soon as I got right, I was going to win the job."

Those were tough times, admitted Knight. He was booed so much in New York, Nancy suggested he start wearing cotton in his ears at Shea Stadium. Knight was making $600,000 but he wasn't producing, and the New York fans didn't let him forget it.

"The fans don't know anything except that you're making a lot of money and you're going out there and going oh-for-four every day," he said. "And maybe making errors and not looking real crisp.

"So the fans are tough. They were brutal on me in '84 and '85. They'd look at my record and obviously see that I had been a solid everyday major-league player, and now I was just a shell of that. And they booed.

"But it never bothered me, because I know that's a part of it. And a long time ago, when I was nineteen or twenty, I decided to put all that stuff behind me and not worry about the distraction of what people thought or what people wrote. I knew I was only going to be as good as I was strong mentally. I'd seen a lot of players with outstanding talent, far greater than me, that succumbed to the pressures mentally of fans and organizations and scouts. I just was not going to let the mental aspect beat me.

"So, I was strong enough mentally to overcome anything that they threw at me. And it was real rough in '84 and '85. I had negative press and was booed almost every time I stepped on the field."

He recalled an incident at Shea Stadium that illustrated his plight.

"I got four hits one night against Gene Walter with the Padres, and there's like fifty thousand fans there. They booed me when the game started, but when I got my second hit, they started cheering. My third hit, they were cheering. By my fourth hit, I had the crowd.

"The next night I start, and there's another big crowd. I'm still only hitting like .230, and as soon as my name is announced I was booed. I can't believe it—are there fifty thousand NEW people here?"

Knight laughed so hard, he had to pause to catch his breath.

"I said, 'Lord have mercy, what a turnover. Of those fifty thousand people the night before, NONE of them came back!'"

Was baseball still fun during those troubled seasons, he was asked, when he was struggling with so many illnesses and injuries and subjected to so much criticism?

"Yeah, baseball was always fun for me. I like the pressure. But it was hard, because I was injured so much in those two years. It was just a struggle physically.

"I had led the Astros in hitting two years in a row, and I'm hitting .300 when all of a sudden I'm hammered with the kidney stone. And then I came back too quickly, in four or five days, and I pulled a muscle. Right out of the hospital. One thing just led to another.

"I go into the hospital in New York with the vertigo, and I'm there for eight days. So, in a matter of a month, I'm in the hospital twice for fifteen different days, and I never went on the disabled list. As soon as I came out of the hospital, I went right back to playing. I was something like two-for-thirty-five, the worst slump I'd ever been in in my life.

"You know, looking back, the thing I probably would change in my career would have been not to play every day, no matter what. I played with twenty-eight stitches in my chin, never missed a game. I played with twenty stitches in my mouth, lip and nose, and I played after getting beaned. I played with a broken finger, with a pulled thigh muscle that now has big holes in it because I would just take a shot and play. I took twelve cortisone shots one year with my shoulder. I ended up having to get two operations on that. I played '83 the whole year and hit .305 with a torn Achilles tendon.

"I just loved to play. And really, the repercussions of '84 led over to '85. But I didn't lose my joy for the game. I was frustrated that I wasn't able to do what I was capable of doing, but I still loved putting on the uniform."

Knight stopped to check the time. It was three o'clock. He would have to be leaving for the ballpark soon.

The Reds were in Los Angeles for a three-game series. They would not be back the rest of the season. That meant this might be Knight's last appearance in Dodger Stadium in a major-league uniform.

Whatever happened, it had been an enjoyable year, as had almost all of his years in baseball.

"Nineteen seventy-nine was great because that was the first big year I had in Cincinnati," he said. "I went to Houston in '83 and '84 and really enjoyed that. And I certainly enjoyed Baltimore in '87. I didn't really enjoy Detroit my last year because I knew it was my last year, and I was sad.

"That was the only time I was really sad going to the ballpark. Because I would go to the ballpark knowing that might be my last time—you know, going to Anaheim or Comiskey Park or whatever.

"But '86, that was extra-special. That was the most gratifying year."

He remembered the hard work and the long hours he put in prior to spring training, trying to work himself back into playing shape. He remembered going to spring training and hearing how the Mets were trying to get rid of him. He recalled the disparaging remarks and the whispers that he was washed up.

"I was basically buried by the fans and the media as a player. It was my most gratifying year simply because I had to fight back from oblivion, really. And I didn't really have anybody that believed in me at that time.

"Hojo [Howard Johnson] was there and Kevin Mitchell was there and they had Tim Teufel who could play third, and they had Gregg Jefferies coming and Dave Magadan coming. There were five guys who could play third, so everybody was looking at one of those five and not looking at me. And I was just bound and determined to show them that I was going to be the third baseman.

"When I got healthy, I could go out and play again the way I had always played. And I didn't think in my mind that any of them could play any better than me—certainly not winning-type baseball better than me. And after the first week, Davey saw it, too, and he let me go out and prove it.

"I came back and had a great year. That was the year I drove in I think seventy-six runs on like four hundred thirty, four hundred forty at-bats [officially, 486]. And to top it off with the World Series made it just a tremendous, self-satisfying year."

He had been approached about writing a book on that season, said Knight. That was how big of a year it had been for him, but he had decided against it.

"Shoot, Gary was doing one, Keith was doing one, Davey had just done one, Doc was going to do one, Straw was going to do one eventually, Dykstra was doing a book. So I said, 'Heck, there's no reason for me to do a book if all these people are writing books.' So, I just turned it down.

"But it was gratifying to read all their books and think about the respect that I had on the ball club, and all the key hits I got that year. Every time there was a crucial situation, two outs in the ninth or whatever, it seemed I was the person who happened to be up at the plate, and most of the time I came through.

"You can't ever perform and be a great player unless you're thrust into those crucial situations. And that year, a lot of times that we needed something to happen, it was me up at the plate. So, it was just my year to have the opportunity to perform, and fortunately I came through most of the time."

There were so many highlights, so many heroics that season. The two-out, two-strike hit in Game 6 to fend off almost certain defeat in the World Series. The home run in Game 7. But none was more special to Knight than the fly ball he hit in the ninth inning of Game 6 of the National League Championship Series. That fly ball tied the score and enabled the Mets to win in extra innings, with Knight again playing a decisive role by driving in the go-ahead run in the sixteenth and final inning.

"That's the greatest game I ever played in," he said. "You know, people talk about Game 6 and Game 7 of the World Series, but without that sixth game against Houston, we don't go to the World Series. And that's the epitome, to get to the World Series. Once you're there, every-thing else is icing on the cake."

It was difficult to talk about that epic game in the Astrodome with-out getting swept up in the sheer enormity of it, added Knight.

"It was so . . . you know, sixteen innings, four hours plus, and you're hanging on every DOGGONE pitch. I mean, you're fighting for your life. And we didn't want to go to the next day, because we would have to face Mike Scott."

Knight grinned. "Not that we were afraid of him, but we just gave him credit where credit was due. He was just one heck of a pitcher."

He began reciting the dramatic moments and the many emotional ups and downs endured by both teams.

"We're down three-to-nothing going into the ninth, and there was a feeling of, I don't think it's frustration, but anxiety. And probably scared, too, thinking, 'Man, if we don't do something here, we're gone. This is it.' It becomes a real pressure-packed deal.

"Then we tie it up and go into extra innings. And it was just emo-tionally wretching. Your guts were just in knots. Not from being scared, but from just the magnitude of that situation. We go ahead and then Hatcher hit his home run. And then I get the base hit that drove Darryl in to put us ahead in the sixteenth.

"After that game, after Jesse struck out Kevin Bass to end it, and I was interviewed by Johnny Bench on radio, I could hardly talk. It was like I was about to cry, because I was emotionally spent. I had concen-trated so hard for so long. Every ground ball, every pitch, every at-bat was critical for sixteen stinking innings.

"We flew back to New York on the charter—Nancy was there with me—and I bet I didn't say two words. I slumped down on my seat, and I was so physically DRAINED. I've never been more exhausted in my life, and it was from the mental exertion. They said some of the guys trashed the plane in the back. It must have been the guys who didn't play. Because the guys that played, we couldn't have trashed anything, we were just so tired and exhausted."

Knight was asked about Mike Scott, who had been the focal point of the Mets' repeated allegations about scuff balls. Had the Houston pitcher really tampered with the baseball?

Knight's reply was in sharp contrast to the harsh accusations made by the Mets during that playoff series.

"I was one of the people that actually said that he probably scuffed the baseball. We had balls that had evidence of scuffing on them. But, you know, since then and thinking about all that, I think that really created a negative approach in our dugout. You start focusing on something else other than just the baseball and you make somebody better than what they are.

"I'd rather just talk about Mike and not the thought that he may have scuffed the baseball. Because he was a heck of a pitcher. And I don't know for sure that he did. All I know is the split-finger he threw, it looked like a fastball, and it just disappeared. The bottom fell out of it. It was just unhittable when he threw it right.

"He was the best pitcher in the game, I think. I faced Roger Clemens in the World Series, and he certainly wasn't as tough as Mike Scott was in 1986. Roger was at least hittable. He had a great fastball and a nice, tough, tight slider, but I still knew I could hit him. But with Mike Scott, when he was right, you were just HOPING that you could hit him."

But when all was said and done, it had been Knight who was the biggest hero of the postseason—not Mike Scott or Roger Clemens or any of the Mets who penned their own books that year. Knight was the one who got the big hits in the World Series as well as the decisive National League playoff game. He was the one who had the World Series MVP trophy displayed in his home.

At the time, he had joked he might not be able to display the trophy because of all the awards and mementos Nancy had won in her golf career. But he had found space for it.

"I've won some MVP awards from the Reds and the Astros, and Player of the Week awards, the Fred Hutchinson Award and the comeback player award," said Knight. "I have quite a few awards there, but nothing compared to Nancy. She's won forty-seven tournaments and probably has hundreds of trophies that we don't even have displayed. And it's a big trophy case. It covers a whole wall in one of our rooms.

"But I told her, 'Honey, this is going right in the middle.' And she was real excited about it. So, it's in the center of the trophy case. Right middle shelf, right smack dab in the center, surrounded by all of her trophies.

"So, if you were to come to my house, all you'd have to do is just look in the middle of the trophy case, and there it is."

12

MOOKIE WILSON: THE BALL WON IT FOR US

The ground ball rolled between Bill Buckner's legs and came to rest in the outfield. It might have gone unnoticed in the ensuing celebration at Shea Stadium had not Ed Montague, the National League umpire stationed down the right-field line, thought to pick it up.

Montague stuck the ball in his pocket and left the field. Later, he was in the umpires' dressing quarters at the stadium when Arthur Richman, the publicist for the Mets, stopped by to visit.

"Here, Arthur," said Montague, handing the ball to Richman. "I want you to have it."

The umpire took out a pen and placed a dot on the baseball to identify it as the "Buckner ball." Richman thanked him and headed to the Mets clubhouse. There, he asked Mookie Wilson to autograph the ball.

"Sure, Arthur," said Wilson. He took the ball and wrote on it: "To Arthur, the ball won it for us. Mookie Wilson 10/25/86."

Six years later, the ball was sold at an auction in New York. The winning bid, not counting the 10 percent commission to the auction house, was $85,000. That was the same amount of money Wilson earned for the entire 1982 baseball season, when he had his best year with a .279 batting average, ninety runs scored and fifty-eight stolen bases.

Mookie Wilson is not much of a sentimentalist. The 1986 World Series was the highlight of his baseball career, but today one can look around his house in Eastover, South Carolina, and see few souvenirs of those games.

"I have a couple of bats I had made special for that Series," he says. "And pretty much, that's about it. I don't have a whole lot from that. Maybe a pair of shoes or something of that nature. But you have two or three pairs, anyway, so if one pair is wet you put on the other pair. And it was wet during that Series.

"But other than that, I don't have a whole lot. A ball autographed by all the guys—that's about it."

Too bad he didn't keep the ball he hit past Buckner to win Game 6, it was suggested to Wilson. An $85,000 souvenir would be worth hanging on to.

Wilson dismissed the notion. "No, I've never been a collector of baseballs and any memorabilia of that nature. I just haven't been.

"And if I had kept it," he added, "I never would have known the value of it anyway because I probably would have put it on the shelf somewhere and never known. I was more than happy to sign it for Arthur at that point in time."

Besides, Wilson pointed out, when Richman sold the ball he donated most of the proceeds to various charities and other organizations. Some of the money went to the indigent fund of the Association of Professional Baseball Players of America, which helps ex-players and their families with financial difficulties. Richman also made donations to a fund for umpire Steve Palermo, who suffered a spinal injury when he was shot interceding in a robbery, and to the Krieger-Kennedy Institute at Johns Hopkins Hospital for research on adrenoleukodystrophy, in memory of umpire John Hirschbeck's son.

"That makes me feel good, that he didn't just keep the ball for himself or put the money in his pocket," said Wilson. "That really makes me feel good."

Mookie turned his attention back to some other figures he had been studying. He was preparing to take an exam for his securities license, which would qualify him to do financial management. He had joined the Mets as a part-time coach and public spokesman, but in the off-season he had another pursuit. And this one dealt with dividends, P/E ratios and interest rates, not batting averages, on-base percentages and runs batted in.

"I'm probably going to start my own business," he said. "But, no matter what I do, once I get my license I can always do financial management. That's something I can do out of my home.

"It's always been something I've been interested in doing, and I'm about to accomplish that in the very near future. In the next couple of weeks, as a matter of fact."

The more he talked about it, the more excited Wilson sounded.

"I won't actually be managing people's money. That's not something I particularly want to do. I'm more interested in helping people set up their financial future, more or less. There probably will be some investments involved, but I won't be doing that directly. I will probably just act as an advisor, and in that capacity be talking about helping people set up retirement funds and that type of thing.

"You know, you've got to go in to help people who do not make quote, unquote, big bucks—people who think that they got to have several millions of thousands of dollars to make a financial investment. There's a couple of things I can help them with—mutual funds, annuities, that type of thing."

Wilson lived in a small community outside of Columbia, South Carolina, where he had played baseball for the University of South Carolina. His home was on Hayward Wilson Road, which was appropriate, since Mookie's given name is William Hayward Wilson.

"That's something that happened strictly by accident," he said. "That was the name of the street when I got here."

He had returned to his native South Carolina in 1988, the winter before the Mets traded him to Toronto, where he played the last two years of his baseball career.

Wilson has two daughters and a son, Preston, who had just completed a season in the New York Mets' minor-league system.

Preston, one of the top prospects in the organization, had a chance to become the second member of the family to wear a Mets uniform. But he wasn't quite following in the old man's footsteps. Mookie played the outfield his entire career; Preston plays third base. Mookie was a singles and doubles hitter who relied on his speed on the base

Mookie Wilson hits his memorable ground ball off Bob Stanley (46) as Ray Knight (22) leads off second base, next to shortstop Spike Owen (5): "It's just the circumstances that made it such a big deal. Hey, it happens all the time." *National Baseball Library* photo.

paths; Preston hits for more power. Mookie was five-feet-ten and 170 pounds; Preston is six-feet-two and 187 pounds.

Mookie laughed when asked if his son was a young Mookie Wilson on the field.

"I think the only similarity that we have is the enthusiasm for the game. Talent-wise, there is no comparison. He's much bigger, much stronger. I think he's more refined at his age than I was.

"The enthusiasm for the game is the part that is the same. His love for the game is tremendous. And I think you have to have that in order to play baseball."

It was not easy to find Mookie at home. And when you did catch him there, he frequently was on his way somewhere else.

"I'm on the go a lot," he said. "I do a lot of traveling, but it's limited to in the state right now. I do a lot of speaking engagements at schools, churches, that type of thing. Community service is basically what it is."

He enjoys speaking to young people, explained Wilson. And he knows he has much he can share with them.

"Basically, I try to give them part of my experience of living in a small town and going to a city like New York or Toronto and having to deal with the everyday pressures. That type of thing. Just try to relate what I've seen during my travels in my playing days.

"And I try to help kids to believe in themselves and not good-luck charms or anything of that nature. You know, that they're going to be the people that determine who they're going to be or what they're going to do. It's not going to be anyone else, regardless of what someone tells you. And I tell them to make sure they get an education and stay away from drugs."

The story Mookie Wilson relates to his audiences begins with a young boy growing up on a farm in rural South Carolina. He was one of twelve children of Jim Wilson, a sharecropper who worked the land in exchange for a portion of the corn, watermelons, soybeans and cotton he grew—and a place to live. Mookie said there was always food on the table and hand-me-down clothes to wear, but he can also tell you his house had no indoor plumbing or hot water.

"Was I poor? That's an understatement," he says.

He remembers working in the fields with his father from sunup to sundown in the summer and fall, and often having to start school after the school year was already under way.

"There were seven boys and five girls in my family, and my parents set us straight. My father never forced us to do anything—to play ball, not even to go to school. But he would say, 'Be the best at what you do, digging a ditch or whatever.' And I want to be the best."

The name "Mookie" was given to him as a child. "It was just kind of a pet expression that my mother used. There really isn't anything to it."

Mookie played baseball with his brothers and sisters, and when he got good enough he got to compete in weekend games in the nearby town of Ehrhardt, which had a population of fewer than one thousand.

"That was the big leagues to us," he recalls. "It was where everybody went to see you play baseball on Sunday."

As a senior in high school, Mookie led Bamberg-Ehrhardt to the state championship in baseball. He played two years of ball at nearby

Spartanburg Junior College, then turned down the offer from the Dodgers to pursue a college degree at the University of South Carolina. It wasn't until after he had helped the Gamecocks to a second-place finish in the College World Series his senior year that Mookie signed with the Mets and began his pro career.

He had little money in the minor leagues, so Wilson looked for ways to cut his expenses. When he was married to his wife, Rosa, while playing for Jackson, Mississippi, in the Texas League in 1982, Mookie decided it would be more economical for the couple to have their wedding at the ballpark.

"I figured we could hold the ceremony in the ballpark and get out of paying some bills," he said.

Mookie was shocked at the resulting publicity the home-plate ceremony generated.

"I didn't think about things like that. I'm not that way."

When Mookie talks about determination and self-discipline, he speaks from experience. He was named the International League's Rookie of the Year after scoring eighty-four runs and stealing forty-nine bases for the Mets' Triple A Tidewater, Virginia, farm club in 1979, but still he did not receive a promotion to the big leagues. His response was to teach himself to become a switch-hitter the following season. A natural right-hander, he learned to bat left-handed in order to take advantage of his speed getting down to first base.

"There were some ballplayers who said, 'Why would you want to do that now and take a chance on staying another year in Triple A?' I figured it wouldn't hurt me to take advantage of my speed. I'd already shown I could hit right-handed, and what did I have to lose? If it didn't work in two months, I could always go back to the way I was. It was sort of a 'betcha-can't-do-it' thing, and that was a challenge to me."

It was a gamble, but it paid off. Mookie led the league with one hundred fifty hits and stole fifty bases. By the end of the 1980 season, he was in the big leagues to stay.

Mookie can also speak of what it is like for a small-town boy to make it in New York. He can recall a nervous young man arriving in the big city and proclaiming, "I'm very anxious to play in New York, but I'm not anxious to live in New York. At the end of the season, I like to spend time back home. I see enough concrete during the year."

He can relate the thrill of taking over as the Mets' starting center fielder in 1981 and adding some excitement to a struggling ball club.

He can tell of a young player in a hurry, outrunning fly balls in the out-field, stealing bases and swinging at any pitch that came near the plate. He can talk of an aggressive hitter so eager to swing at the ball that he rarely drew a base on balls, who was so adept at hitting bad pitches he could boast, "There isn't a pitcher around who can pitch around me."

Mookie Wilson hit the jackpot in 1983 when he signed his first big contract, a five-year deal worth $2.5 million.

But Mookie can also talk of overcoming adversity while in New York. Twice, he underwent surgery on his right shoulder, and in the spring of 1986 he was sidelined with an eye injury after being struck in the face by a throw during a base-running drill.

He can tell of the frustration of going from being a star to playing a part-time role his last five years with the Mets, sharing time in the out-field with Lenny Dykstra. Wilson chafed under the setup, but the irony of the situation was that by the time the Mets finally got around to trading him to the Toronto Blue Jays in August 1989, Dykstra was also gone from the team.

"You can complain too much," Mookie said at the time of his trade.

Finally, he can tell of playing in one World Series and four League Championship Series during his twelve years in the major leagues, and then coming home to his native South Carolina at the end of his play-ing days, finishing one career but beginning another.

People still recognize Mookie Wilson and stop him on the street to talk baseball.

"Oh, yeah, all the time," he said. "I do be recognized, and it's a good feeling that people do recognize you from your days of playing and remember some of the things that you did. And they always want to talk baseball—sometimes too much, but for the most part it's fun."

And always, the people want to talk about the ground ball.

"All the time. As a matter of fact, that's the first thing they mention." He laughed just thinking about it. "Everything else comes after that. They must find out about that first."

So, Mookie takes them back to that Saturday night, to the bottom of the tenth inning at Shea Stadium, when the Red Sox held a two-run lead and the Mets were one out from losing the World Series.

Mookie Wilson, now a special instructor and speaker for the Mets, is still remembered for the ground ball he hit in the Mets' come-from-behind victory in Game 6 of the World Series: "That's the first thing they mention. Everything else comes after that. They must find out about that first." *Photo courtesy New York Mets.*

"At that point, to be honest with you, it was just like, most everyone thought that our chances were pretty slim. It was quiet on the bench. That surprised me. It was like we were accepting what was happening. We had some guys already going in the clubhouse to undress."

Then came the hits by Gary Carter, Kevin Mitchell and Ray Knight. Suddenly, it was a one-run game with runners on first and third. The next batter was Mookie Wilson.

"By the time it got to me, things were totally out of hand," he recalled. "One guy gets on, another guy gets on, another guy gets on, and all of a sudden you say, 'We have a chance.' No one knew what was happening.

"When I get to home plate, we were down by a run and I'm just up there to, for lack of a better term, save face. I just don't want to embarrass myself. I'm up there to try to make contact."

On the mound was Bob Stanley, who had just come on in relief for the Red Sox. Wilson knew what to expect from the Boston pitcher.

"Basically, he threw running cut fastballs inside and sinkers away. That's pretty much what he was throwing. Nothing tricky. Stanley wasn't really a tricky pitcher. He was pretty basic. You know, just keep the ball down and away, in tight and that type of thing.

"I hit against him in an exhibition game, and he got me out with balls low and away. So I was looking for the ball low and away. The first pitch was up and away, a ball, but I swung."

Wilson fouled off the pitch for strike one.

"'No big deal,' I said to myself. 'Just cool down and relax.'"

Stanley's next two pitches were high for balls. That made the count two-and-one. Then came a sinker, low and away. "His type of pitch. I fouled it off."

One more strike and the game would be over. Wilson couldn't afford a mistake. He fouled off another pitch, then another. He guessed Stanley would try to throw the next pitch outside, so he moved up to protect the plate. Thinking back on it, Wilson believes Stanley detected that shift and changed his tactics because of it.

"The count was in his favor, so he could take a chance. He tried to tie me up inside."

The next pitch came inside, catching Wilson by surprise and forcing him to jump out of the way. But the pitch also fooled catcher Rich Gedman, who missed the ball, letting it roll to the backstop.

"I don't know if it was a cross-up between the pitcher and the catcher," said Mookie. "The ball was inside, and it probably was still moving inside. It might have been tailing inside more than the catcher expected. It was very difficult for me to say what the ball did. I've seen the films and it wasn't that badly thrown of a ball. The only thing I can think of is that the ball moved more than the catcher expected or it was the wrong pitch."

Once the ball got past the catcher, Wilson looked down to third base, where he saw Mitchell hesitate.

"I started yelling, 'Let's go, Mitch!' I wanted to run down there and pull him home. I was on the spot up there."

Finally, Mitchell ran home with the tying run. Just like that, the outlook changed for Mookie Wilson.

"I can't lose now. I stepped to the plate, we were losing; I'm still at the plate, now the score is tied. We're in a much better situation now than we were when I got there. So, I had nothing to lose now. The rest of it was just a freak accident."

Wilson hit a pop foul on the next pitch, then lined a ball into the stands for yet another foul. It was the sixth pitch he had fouled off against Stanley. Finally, on the tenth pitch of his at-bat, Mookie hit his famous ground ball down the first-base line.

"When I hit it, my first thought was I had a chance to beat Buckner to the bag. That's my very first thought."

But Bill Buckner never caught the ball. Instead, it rolled past him while Ray Knight scored the game-winning run, and Mookie Wilson became a World Series hero.

And what if Buckner had fielded that grounder? Would he have been able to make the putout at first base? Or would Wilson have beaten out that ball for a base hit?

"It would have been close," said Mookie. "It would have been very close. I thought I had a chance."

He laughed. "But we'll never know now."

In the years following that World Series, Mookie Wilson and Bill Buckner occasionally ran into each other. When they did, they seldom mentioned the ground ball.

"We don't really talk about it," said Mookie. "We did the first couple of times—making jokes about it, actually. If the subject comes up, it's nothing that we avoid talking about or anything of that nature.

"But we don't make a long discussion of it. We've been in baseball too long. We know those things happen. It's just the situation, the circumstances that made it such a big deal. We have spoken about it, but not at any length because, hey, it happens all the time."

Instead, Wilson and Buckner will talk about such things as baseball in general and how it has changed since they first came up. Just two old ballplayers talking about the game they love.

"People want to know if Buckner and I get along," Mookie said. "Some people have the impression we're at each other's throats because of that play. I guess it's a natural thing to wonder about, but I tell them, 'We were friends before, and we were friends after.'"

13

BILL BUCKNER:

LEAVING BOSTON

A new house. A new town. A new life. Bill Buckner was looking forward to it.

"Where I'm living now, we're really out in the sticks," he said. "This is a different world."

He was on a farm outside Meridian, Idaho, about four miles west of Boise. Meridian had a population of seventeen thousand. Buckner played before bigger crowds almost every night in Fenway Park. The Red Sox drew that many people on a BAD night. Seventeen thousand people was nothing.

Buckner liked it that way. This was the Old West. Wide-open spaces. Mountains. Blue skies.

"I'm kind of a mountain man. I was born a hundred years too late. That's what my wife says. I should have been a cowboy.

"But I get a little bit of that now. I have a cattle ranch, also. I do a lot of riding, helping with the ranch—the roundup, stuff like that."

It was a Thursday morning in December. Buckner was getting ready to go out and look at some land. In addition to his farm and his ranch, he had bought another farm, where he planned a real-estate development.

"I'm doing another subdivision close by the town I'm living. Building some houses. Looking to build some more.

"This is different than anything I've done before. It's new. It's the first time I've ever really done anything besides baseball."

He had come to the right place. The Boise area was booming. The population of Meridian had almost doubled just since 1990.

"Yeah," said Buckner, "it's growing like weeds."

The real-estate business was what prompted him to leave his home in Boston, he said. He had lived in New England for nine years, since his trade to the Red Sox in 1984. He had enjoyed Boston. So had his wife, Jody, and their two girls, Brittany and Christen. That was why they stayed, even after Buckner retired as a ballplayer in 1990.

But Buck had owned a thousand-acre cattle ranch in Star, Idaho, a few miles west of Meridian, for several years. His brother, Bob, ran the ranch. Then Buck started buying and developing land in the area. This was where he did his business.

"Everything I have going is out here," he said. "Trying to do a real-estate development over the phone, the cattle ranch, my family all lives out here—it didn't make any sense to stay in Boston."

Some people thought it was the fans who drove him out. Not true, said Buckner. They might like to think that, but that wasn't the case, no matter what was written or said back in Boston.

"No, that had nothing to do with it. Most of the people are very nice."

But some of the fans, well . . .

There was one night the past summer, in July 1993. Buckner was in Pawtucket, Rhode Island, the home of the Red Sox Triple A minor-league affiliate. He was working as a roving batting instructor in the Toronto Blue Jays' farm system.

Buckner was walking out of the ballpark, carrying his travel bag, when a boy asked for his autograph. So Buck stopped to sign his name. He was good about that sort of thing. A kid wants your autograph, you take the time to give it to him. Twenty years in baseball, and he had scribbled out his name thousands of times.

But this time was different. Buck reached out to take the boy's pen, and he heard someone call out: "Don't give him a ball. He'd just drop it anyway."

Buck didn't say anything. He just went ahead and signed the boy's baseball card. Then he took his bag over to his truck and put it inside.

But he got to thinking about the comment, and the more he thought about it the madder it made him.

So, Buckner turned around and went back to find the person who'd made the wisecrack. It was an eighteen-year-old kid. It didn't matter. Eighteen, thirty, fifty, seventy-five. Buckner didn't care how old he was. He was fed up.

For seven years, he had been hearing about the ground ball that rolled between his legs in the World Series. For seven years, people had taunted him about it. For seven years, people had asked him about it. They wouldn't let it die. He had been a patient man. He had explained what happened. He had tried to be good-natured about it. He had taken his lumps over it. He never ducked responsibility.

But not a week went by that someone didn't say something about the ground ball. Reporters asked him about it. Acquaintances brought it up. Fans ridiculed him. It was more than a man could take. He was sick of it. Seven years was too much.

Buckner grabbed his tormentor by the shirt collar and lifted him up.

"You better watch what you say," he said.

Some bystanders quickly separated the two, and there was nothing more to the incident. No harm was done. No charges were filed. That was that.

Or was it? Afterward, there were stories in the newspapers and on television reporting the confrontation. Buckner told the media he was tired of it. He was leaving. He didn't want to hear about the error anymore. It was time to move on.

But, on the other hand, it was just one loudmouth fan. Just one ill-mannered teenager. You can't judge a whole city by one jerk. . . .

"Yeah, that stuff was blown out of proportion," said Buckner.

Outside, the mountains were outlined against the blue sky. The wide-open spaces stretched to the horizon. The Boise River ran through town. It was a far cry from Boston and the Charles River.

"That was nothing," he continued. "Just a rude kid that needed a little spanking. He was very rude. He needed to work on his manners a little bit."

But why that kid out of the thousands of tormentors? What was it about that taunt that caused Buckner to lose his cool after enduring so much abuse over the years? What had caused such a strong reaction this particular time?

Buckner shrugged.

"Everyone has a bad day," he said.
One bad day. No one is perfect.

He hadn't had time to unpack all of his belongings. The Buckners had arrived in their new home just a few weeks earlier. There were still boxes and cartons stacked up and waiting to be opened.

Somewhere in those boxes were most of Bill Buckner's baseball mementos, the souvenirs and trophies gathered over twenty-three years in professional baseball.

"Yeah, I've still got them boxed up. I've got a couple of things out; not too many. I've got my silver bats hanging up. Most of the pictures and everything else, the trophies, are packed away in boxes.

"Hopefully, they'll get out here one of these days when I get in the right place."

He had his silver bat from 1980, the year he won his batting championship. Buck batted .324 for the Chicago Cubs that season to lead all National League hitters.

There was an interesting story behind that batting title. On the next-to-last day of the season, Buckner got three hits in five at-bats to take a five-point lead over Keith Hernandez of St. Louis in the batting race.

The next day, Cubs manager Joe Amalfitano gave Buckner the option of sitting out the final game to protect his lead. Or Buck could have chosen to drop down to the bottom of the order to bat as few times as possible.

Buck thought about it a while, and after batting practice went to his manager's office.

"If I'm going to do this," he told Amalfitano, "I want to do it right. I'll hit third."

The move almost backfired. Buckner went hitless in four times up that afternoon. That gave Hernandez, who was playing later in the day, the opening he needed. All Buck could do was sit in the clubhouse and sweat it out while waiting for the results from the Cardinals game.

He was so nervous he cut himself five times while shaving after the game. Finally, he got word that Hernandez went only one-for-four to finish with a .321 average. Buckner won the title by three points.

"I was pretty nervous," he recalled. "That's what I remember most about that day: a lot of anxiety. Obviously, you play every game to win, but playing on a last-place team at that point in time, I was thinking about the batting title. That's something that you don't get a chance to do very often.

"There was a lot of anxiety—you know, the thought that, 'Hey, you need one hit to guarantee your win.' You put a lot of pressure on each at-bat. Too much anxiety.

"I kind of slipped into that," he added. "I got real hot right at the end of the season. I wasn't expecting to win. The last few days of the season, I got real hot, and everybody else kind of slipped down. So, I didn't have that much time to think about it, for a period of weeks or whatever.

"It was more fun than anything else, although there was a lot of anxiety on the last day."

So, why had he risked it all by playing that last game? He could have sat out and protected his lead. Other players had done it; Buckner could have played it safe, too. But he didn't. Not Billy Buck. That wasn't the way he did things.

"Well, it's a one-hundred-sixty-two-game schedule. That's just the way it is. I believe it'd be unfair—it's not fair to the guy in second place. I'd expect him to play.

"And I just felt like I wanted to play as many games as I could. I might end up with two thousand nine hundred ninety-nine hits, and that one at-bat I didn't get could have made the difference.

"I didn't want to cheat myself. I just felt that that was what I needed to do."

He was asked about some of his other mementos. What about his 1986 World Series ring? Hadn't that been sold at an auction just a month earlier?

"Well, I don't know where that came from," said Buckner. "They said my World Series ring, but I have that."

The 1986 World Series ring? It was reported to have been auctioned by Leland's for $33,000. But the ring was somewhere in Buckner's house?

"Yep."

But what about the hand-signed letter of authenticity that went with that ring, the note to a private collector that read: "Hope you enjoy my 1986 World Series ring. The nightmare of 1986 is over! Your pal, Bill Buckner."

"I don't know where all that comes from," said Buckner. "I've got the ring right here."

You never wrote that inscription?

"Nope."

That being the case, it must be very upsetting to read such stories and hear such reports.

"Oh, a lot of stuff bothers me about some of that related stuff," said Buckner. "I've seen so much of it, I just laugh it off. That's all you can do."

Well, there had been mix-ups before. Leland's also sold the ball that rolled through Buckner's legs. The winning bid was $85,000, plus another 10 percent commission to the auction house for a total of $93,500. That was back in 1992.

But after the auction, Buckner claimed that he had the World Series ball, the one that Mookie Wilson hit.

"Yeah, that was kind of a joke," he said.

So, you never actually had that baseball?

"No, not really. I was just playing around."

But $93,500 for a baseball—any baseball—was it worth it?

Buckner laughed. "I don't know. It's kind of a waste of money to me. But I guess you can spend your money any way you want to."

It did seem a little crazy.

"Yeah, when you think about people going without food to eat, and then to pay so much for a negative thing, not a positive thing. I think it's ridiculous. The whole thing has gotten stupid, if you think about it—the negative aspect of sports. If it was the home run that won the World Series, that I could see. Someone could be proud to have something like that.

"I mean, they make Mookie Wilson out to be some kind of hero or something, when he really didn't do that much."

Take the ball Hank Aaron hit for his record 715th home run. Bill Buckner was playing left field for the Dodgers the day Aaron hit that historic home run in Atlanta. Buckner almost climbed the left-field fence in pursuit of that ball.

"Yeah, I wanted to get the ball."

Instead, the ball was caught by Tom House, one of the bullpen pitchers.

"But if no one had been out there," said Buckner, "I would have jumped over the fence and got the ball."

Bill Buckner, a controversial figure in the 1986 World Series, still considers it one of the highlights of a distinguished career: "A lot of guys don't get a chance to play in the World Series. It was a thrill for me. That's the way I look at it." *Photo courtesy Boston Red Sox.*

Now, that would have been a baseball souvenir worth having. But a baseball that resulted in an error?

And now this, Bill Buckner's World Series ring supposedly sold at auction. And with it the inscription, "The nightmare of 1986 is over!" Was that really how he felt about that World Series? Was it a nightmare that Buckner would like to end?

"No. I feel like, hey, I'd do it again if I got the opportunity. A lot of guys don't get a chance to play in the World Series. It was a thrill for me. That's the way I look at it.

"Yeah, I would do it all over again. I'm sure the Red Sox would, too."

It was ironic that Bill Buckner would own a cattle ranch. Cattle meant beef. And Buckner rarely ate beef.

"I may be the only cattle rancher in America who doesn't eat red meat," he said.

Instead, he and his wife followed what he called a "health-food diet." Buckner was forty-four years old and as trim and fit as he was in his playing days. No wonder he had been able to play ball for more than two decades.

"I took care of myself," he said. "I ate right, and I did a lot of training. It was a combination of those two things, along with the desire to be good no matter what."

He still took care of himself. He was an active man, on his feet a lot. He spent a lot of time outdoors. He even went jogging on occasion. The ankle that had caused him so much pain over the years was a little sore, but nothing serious. It wasn't like the old days.

Buckner barely noticed it anymore.

"I'm kind of pleasantly surprised," he said. "I think I kind of have a little freak of nature. I think it kind of fused together a little bit to where . . . "

How could he explain it? Bones that didn't mesh properly, four operations to fix the ankle, swollen joints, stretched tendons . . .

"Before, it was bad, but it wasn't bad enough. It was still moving around. Now, the bones are kind of stuck together. They don't rub together as much, and they don't get irritated.

"Just as long as I don't get crazy," he laughed.

He could still do pretty much anything he wanted to do. Tennis, golf, hiking, all that stuff. If he didn't overdo it, the ankle was fine.

"I go hiking in the mountains all the time. I'm not actively involved in sports, so that's the key. All the pounding and whatever that's done. It's taken a lot of pressure off it."

Maybe that was the problem all along. He shouldn't have been playing baseball on that ankle. He shouldn't have dragged himself out on the field day after day on an ankle with the bones grinding against one another. Not after a tendon was removed, not after the staph infection, not after all the bone fragments that moved around in the ankle. Not after hundreds of games and countless hours of practice on the damaged joint.

It must have been tough playing in such incredible pain all those years, all those games.

"Well, I think it would have been for a lot of people. I don't think too many people could have done it. But it was just a love for the game and a burning desire to be successful. And I'm very self-motivated.

"So, it wasn't difficult because I enjoyed doing it. It was difficult in the sense I had to spend a lot of time getting ready to play every day— and in the off-season, trying to repair the ankle. I probably did a lot more work than the average person had to do.

"But I'd do it all over again. It was a great life. To be able to play more than twenty years even under healthy conditions would have been an accomplishment. Like I said, I don't think too many people could have been able to do what I did. I pretty much played on one leg for fifteen, sixteen years."

And what did that encompass? What did he go through just to get ready to play baseball every day during the season?

"Well, a lot of weight training." Buck laughed. "A lot of ice. Mainly, ice and whirlpool."

He was asked about the ankle injury that had caused him so much suffering over the years. Did he remember the play when he was hurt?

"Yeah, it seems like it was yesterday."

April 18, 1975. Dodgers versus Giants at Dodger Stadium in Los Angeles. John Montefusco was pitching for the Giants. Marc Hill was the catcher. Davey Lopes of the Dodgers had been working with Buckner on a new way to slide into a base, barely touching the ground. Buckner tried to steal second base.

"I remember sliding into the base," he said. "At the time, stealing was just coming into baseball, and I was having some success stealing bases. I was trying to learn to slide a little quicker into the bag, and I slid a little bit too late."

He caught his left foot on the base, and his ankle was twisted beneath him as it absorbed most of his weight. The force of his momentum then flipped Buckner over the bag. When he landed, the pain in his ankle was so great, he began crawling away. He made it all the way into the outfield before help arrived.

Buckner should have been sidelined for several weeks while the injury healed. But three days later, he hobbled to the plate as a pinch hitter with runners on first and third in the seventh inning of a tie game. Buck crossed up everyone in the ballpark by laying down a bunt. He beat it out for a base hit to score the winning run. It was classic Buckner.

He won the ball game for the Dodgers, but his ankle never recovered. For the rest of his career, Bill Buckner was a one-legged ballplayer.

"That really wasn't the biggest problem, when I hurt the ankle," he continued. "The biggest problem was when I had surgery, I got a real bad staph infection. That really complicated matters."

That surgery, the second on his ankle following the injury, took place in October 1976. Four months later, the Dodgers shipped Buckner to the Chicago Cubs.

Did the Dodgers give up on him too quickly?

"No, not really. I was an outfielder, and I was going to have to move to first base. They already had Steve Garvey at first. So, it was the right move for them and for me at the time because Garvey was going to be playing first."

Still, it was hard not to imagine what might have been. What if he hadn't tried to steal that base that day in Los Angeles? What if he hadn't hurt his ankle? What if he had played on two good legs his entire career?

Buckner figured he would have stolen fifty bases a year and won more than just one batting title. He figures he would have gotten three thousand hits in his career.

"I also don't think I would have been traded by the Dodgers. I'd probably have stayed in Los Angeles, so it cost me a few championships and a chance to play my entire career in good weather."

But he had a great career anyway. Twenty-two years in the big leagues. Two World Series. He won a batting championship. He led the league in doubles one year and tied for the lead another year. He played hurt. Billy Buck was a heckuva ballplayer.

"You know, I obviously wasn't the greatest player who ever played. But I don't think too many people could have done what I did with the conditions I played under. I dedicated myself—I don't think I could have gotten much more out of what I had to work with. I don't think a lot of players can say that."

What about the Hall of Fame? Buckner got 2,715 hits in his twenty-two years in the big leagues. He had sixty-one more hits than Ted Williams, the greatest Red Sox hitter ever. Only three players—Pete Rose, Al Oliver and Vada Pinson—finished with more hits and failed to make the Hall of Fame after becoming eligible. Buckner drove in 1,208 runs, the equivalent of twelve 100-RBI seasons. He hit 174 homers and 498 doubles. He stole 183 bases, even on a bad leg. His career batting average was a solid .289.

Those could be Hall of Fame numbers. There are players in Cooperstown who did less. Buckner becomes eligible for the Hall in 1996. He deserves consideration. Sure, it's a long shot, but he has a chance.

Was it something he had thought about?

"Well, I haven't really. Certainly when it comes my time, I'm going to be looking at the paper. You know, just to even get consideration would be a feather in my cap.

"I think I'm going to come up a little bit short. But I think what matters is what you think about yourself. And I think that I got as much out of it as I possibly could. I guess you could say I'm in my own Hall of Fame."

How often had Bill Buckner been reminded about "the error"? A thousand times? Ten thousand? Once a week? Twice a week?

How many times did a man have to hear about one mistake?

"It was okay for the time being," he said. "That was a big Series and a great Series. But they keep beating a dead horse. It kind of gets old after a while."

He didn't say what "it" was. There was no need to. "It" was the play that followed Buckner around. "It" was what people remembered him for.

He missed a ground ball. There was nothing unusual about that. Hundreds of ground balls roll past ballplayers every season. But it was Bill Buckner's misfortune to miss a ground ball at the end of one of the most incredible games in World Series history.

Buckner might not have been able to make the putout even if he had fielded the ball. He claimed afterward neither he nor pitcher Bob Stanley could have gotten to first ahead of Mookie Wilson.

The Red Sox might have lost the game anyway. No one knows. They still could have won the World Series. There was another game to play. A lot of people don't remember that. All they know is that the ball rolled through Buckner's legs.

Buckner was tired of hearing about it. He wouldn't talk about the play anymore.

"There's nothing more to say" was all he would say.

He was asked about the fans in Boston.

"They're tough," he said. "They're like New York. If you're going good, they're great. If you're not, then it gets a little tough.

"But they know their baseball pretty good and they come out to the ballpark. That's the bottom line. You have to get them out there. And they support the team. It's a great place to play when things are going good. Tough when it's going bad."

That was part of the problem. The Red Sox weren't just another team. They were part of the culture. Boston was a great baseball city. It had tradition. Baseball really meant something there. The fans cared about the game and they cared about the Red Sox. And the Red Sox hadn't won a World Series since 1918. Red Sox fans had been waiting a long time for another title. They had it within their grasp in 1986, only to see it slip away.

Maybe Buckner could have missed a ground ball for another team in the World Series, and it wouldn't have mattered as much. But he missed one for the Red Sox in that World Series and in that game. Red Sox fans couldn't forget that.

Buckner hadn't known much about the Red Sox past when he arrived in Boston. But he knew all about it by the time he left.

"I played with the Dodgers. I started out with a successful organization. They were always in first or second place. The losing thing really didn't enter my mind.

Bill Buckner walks off the field after his infamous error that ended Game 6: "As a player, I had to be under a microscope. And it's not a good thing sometimes." *AP/Wide World Photo.*

"You know, Boston has had some great teams and some great players over the years. They just haven't made that final step. In one sense, I think the fans should feel fortunate to have that opportunity to see a lot of great players and great teams. On the other hand, now I can understand a little bit the frustration. If they'd just win that one championship, then that would kind of clear things up."

He paused for a moment before adding, "Maybe they wouldn't have anything to talk about then."

You had to wonder what it was about baseball that made the fans take it so seriously. It was just a game. But people lived and died with baseball. They flocked to the stadiums by the thousands. They watched on television. They pored over the box scores. They became an extension of the game.

"It's hard for me to fathom that people put that much of their life into it," said Buckner. "But it's not for me to decide what infatuates them or what occupies their time. It's a free country and you can do whatever you want with your time and your energy and your ideas.

"It's just hard for me to fathom that people really put their whole lives into watching baseball games and being fans. That's hard to realize. But, on the other hand, if that's what they like to do, then more power to them."

It was something Buckner had thought about a lot. It was a strange phenomenon.

"The whole idea of professional sports is kind of crazy, really, if you think about it. But if you get all the rewards and the money, I guess you have to take—if people are going to pay all that money to watch you play, obviously you're going to have pretty big fans. And if they're big fans, they're going to do some crazy things and say some crazy things. I really think the whole idea of professional sports is pretty crazy."

Because of all the money involved?

"Yeah. And being paid to go out there and play a kid's game. To play it when you're forty years old. That's kind of crazy.

"That whole scheme of things to me is hard to fathom. So I can understand if there are people who will pay all that much money to watch games. Some of these people go to every home game—they'll really be into it and get involved. And they react both ways, positive and negative.

"As a player, I had to be under a microscope. And it's not a good thing sometimes. You know, now that I'm out of it, I just try to think of the positive things. I mean, it's still a great way of making a living. I wouldn't even think twice about doing it again. I would do it in a minute.

"But you have to have a thick skin at times."

No one knew that better than Buckner. He played 2,517 games in the big leagues. He played in two World Series and one All-Star Game. A lot of good things happened to Bill Buckner. But people still remember him for one missed ground ball.

He can't watch the World Series without hearing about it. Every year, it comes up. Every year, he is reminded of it.

"Yeah, it makes me mad. That's part of the reason . . . "

Buckner stopped himself before completing the sentence. What was he about to say? That was part of the reason for leaving Boston?

" . . . I mean, it's nice being out here," he continued. "No one talks about it. In Boston, you spent most of the time talking about it. Somebody does at least a couple of times a week. I've been out here two months, and this is the first time I've heard it mentioned."

He was twenty-two hundred miles from Boston, where he played five years on a bad ankle. He was two thousand miles from Shea Stadium, where Mookie Wilson hit a ground ball to him. Maybe that was far enough. Nineteen eighty-six was in the past. Bill Buckner wanted to put it behind him.

14

DAVE STAPLETON:

I KNEW I SHOULD HAVE BEEN IN THERE

Dave Stapleton was ready. He had started loosening up in the sixth inning. He did some stretching exercises. He sprinted up and down the runway that led from the dugout to the visitors' clubhouse at Shea Stadium. He went inside and swung a bat. He threw a ball to warm up his arm. He rode an exercise bicycle to get his legs loose. He was ready.

But the call never came. Stapleton never got off the bench in Game 6 of the 1986 World Series. Bill Buckner stayed at first base.

The Red Sox scored two runs in the top of the tenth inning, and the players waited to see what manager John McNamara would do. Boston had won seven postseason games that year, and in every one of them Stapleton had taken over as a late-inning replacement for the crippled Buckner. Stapleton was the better defensive player. Buckner was injured. It was the obvious move. The Red Sox needed only one more victory for the World Series title. There was no need to tamper with success, no reason to change a winning formula.

But this time, Buckner stayed in the game. Stapleton remained in the dugout. With two outs, the Mets tied the score. There was a runner on second base. Mookie Wilson hit a grounder down the first-base line. It should have been the third out. The game should have gone into extra innings. Instead, the ball rolled through Buckner's legs. The Red Sox lost the game, and eventually the World Series.

Dave Stapleton never played in another major-league game. But he should have played in that one. He would have fielded that ground ball. He would have gotten the out. Stapleton knew it. The other ballplayers knew it. Maybe deep down, even the manager knew it.

But Stapleton never got the chance. His career ended one ground ball too early.

It was past nine o'clock on a summer evening, and Dave Stapleton was still working the phones at his home in Loxley, Alabama. He was a home builder, and business was good. At times, it was almost too good.

"Sometimes, it seems like everybody and his brother is calling me," he said in a weary voice. "And I'm trying to make calls, too, building these houses. That's part of it every night. My wife says I'm on the phone too much. Hold on a second, there's the phone ringing again."

Stapleton had gotten into the building business in December 1987, his first year out of baseball. He was in a partnership when he started, but two years later he went out on his own. It was a struggle for a while, but he had turned the corner.

He returned from his phone call.

"Just in the last, I'd say, about twelve months, it's taken off," he continued. "I got real busy last year about June, July, August, somewhere in there, and it's been crazy since then.

"We're in a good market down here, though. The part of Alabama I'm in, southern Alabama, we've got a lot of water area—Mobile Bay, the Gulf Coast area. There is a lot of activity down here. We're in a building boom, I wouldn't be afraid to call it. We're in a very good situation as far as building. Yeah, right now I've got more than I can handle. I'm turning down work."

His supper was in the other room, still uneaten. No time for that now. There were still phone calls to make. But Stapleton wasn't complaining. It was better to have too much work than too little.

"I don't mean it's going to always be like that, but I've got myself established now. I try to build a real quality home. Everything I take up I try to do first class. When I played ball, I tried to do it the best I could do. Anything I do, I do the same thing.

"That takes a while to establish. When you get out in the real world and you start your own business, no matter if you've got a name and people know you, you've still got to establish yourself in that field. It takes several years to do that. Like I said, it's just in the last year that all that hard work is paying off."

Stapleton's voice tailed off into a yawn. It had been a long day. He worked from five-thirty in the morning until six in the evening almost every day. The evenings were spent on the telephone. And always, there was paperwork that had to be done.

"It's some long hours. You do what you have to do. Right now, there's a lot going on, and it takes more hours. So, you take advantage of it while the going is good."

Timing is everything. Stapleton knows that from playing baseball. After that final season with the Red Sox in 1986, he went to training camp with the Seattle Mariners the following spring. The first week in camp, he pulled a quadricep muscle in his leg. He was further slowed by tendinitis in his Achilles tendon. The injuries bothered him, but they didn't stop Stapleton from going out every day and playing.

He hit the ball well that spring. "I got something like twenty-seven at-bats and got eleven hits," he recalled. "I hit something like .380 that spring. I thought I had the team made. I felt like I was back to my old ways. I was swinging the bat real well."

Stapleton was so certain he would make the ball club, he had his parents drive his vehicle from Alabama to the Mariners' training camp in Arizona the last week of camp.

"I thought I was going to take it back to Seattle with me," he said. "I had them drive it all the way out there. That's how confident I was I had the team made."

On the last day of camp, the Mariners gave Stapleton the bad news. He wasn't going north with the team. He was given his release instead.

That was the end of his baseball career. Twelve years in professional baseball, seven of them in the major leagues, and it was over just like that.

He was in shock. He wasn't ready for it to end.

"It was difficult. Sure, it was difficult." Stapleton paused to think about the abrupt departure from the game he loved and the slow realization that it was time to start planning for the rest of his life, outside of baseball.

"It was weird. I felt like I was still going to catch on with somebody. I guess part of it was my own fault. I never called one person. I never called any of the general managers or managers I knew in the game.

"I probably should have. At the time, I had pulled that muscle, and I was still trying to play on it. I couldn't run and move like I was capable of. That hurt me as much as anything. When I got through with spring training, I said I'll just take a couple of weeks off now and give myself time to heal up."

It had seemed the sensible thing to do. In retrospect, it might not have been the right decision. But it doesn't do any good to think about it now. It's all in the past now.

"It's hard to catch on when you go to spring training and you get cut the last day. Everybody has got their ball club set at that time. So, it really makes it difficult to try to catch on with anybody."

Stapleton would like to have had at least one more season. One more chance to show what kind of ballplayer he was.

"It was weird," he continued. "Seattle called me back in June and asked me to play with one of their minor-league clubs. Try to start back over again. But my wife was pregnant and was due for a baby in a week or two, and I told them, 'It's just not a good time.' I turned down the chance to come back.

"It was with a Double-A team. They told me it may be only temporary. If somebody on the major-league team was hurt, they were going to look at me again. It was temporary. It might be only two or three weeks. It didn't sound that wonderful to me at the time, so I turned it down. That was my last opportunity."

How do you feel about it now? he was asked. Any regrets now?

"About that?" Stapleton mulled it over for a moment. "You always have some regrets. I still wish I was playing ball. In my heart, and I really mean this sincerely, I still feel like I can play right now. I'm still in pretty good physical condition. I haven't gained that much weight. I've still got quick hands, and I still think I can hit and still think I can field."

Dave Stapleton played in all seven of Boston's victories in the 1986 postseason, but manager John McNamara kept Bill Buckner on the field at the crucial moment in Game 6 of the World Series: "He wanted him to be out on the field when everything was won. But we didn't get that opportunity." *Photo courtesy Boston Red Sox.*

The fatigue left him. He no longer sounded like an overworked businessman closing in on forty years of age.

"I don't have any doubt in my mind I can play, but it would take three or four months of hard work, of conditioning, to get in the kind of physical condition you need to get in to play. Right now, I've got a business going, and I would have to forget the business for that length of time. It's just kind of hard to do that when there's no guarantees that you will make it—not when you've got something established like a business and you're trying to make it work."

That's just the way it was. Stapleton knew that, and he accepted it.

"It's just time to settle down and stay home and do what I've gotta do," he added. "And not chase my dreams anymore, even though I'd like to."

At a desk nearby, there was a stack of paperwork waiting for him. He could not put it off much longer. The various forms and documents had to be filled out tonight. That was the way it was in this business.

"I spend so many hours at work now," he said, stifling another yawn, "then come home and do paperwork. I've got barrels of it right now that I need to do. I hate to do it. Hate it with a passion. But that's just all part of it."

Bill Buckner and Dave Stapleton. Fame and obscurity. Their baseball careers became intertwined in 1984. Stapleton started that season as Boston's regular first baseman. His future with the ball club looked bright. He had been runner-up for the American League's Rookie of the Year award four years earlier, and he had played every infield position plus left and right field for the Red Sox. He batted over .300 one year. He had hit thirty-four homers over the previous three seasons. He could be counted on for sixty-five runs batted in a year.

But in Boston's home opener in 1984, Stapleton tore some ligaments in his left knee. He underwent surgery to repair the damage and was out for the remainder of the season. The Red Sox, in need of a replacement, sent pitcher Dennis Eckersley and infielder Mike Brumley to the Cubs in exchange for Buckner. Eckersley later became the dominant relief pitcher in baseball. Buckner revived his career in Boston. Stapleton wasted away on the Boston bench. Buckner and Stapleton. The star and his understudy.

It was not a pleasant experience for Stapleton.

"Basically, I went from being an everyday starter to someone who hardly could even get on the field those last two years. For me, it had more to do with the manager than Buckner. The manager we had then, John McNamara, was more or less the type of manager that played one person every day. If you were in the lineup, you were there to stay. Your bench was nonexistent.

"And that hurt me a lot, not getting a chance. Because I was well. I was fine after '84. I could still play. My knee was in fine enough shape that I could still play ball and hit and everything."

Stapleton began to recite the statistics. Even now, years later, the numbers were burned into his memory.

"I got sixty-eight at-bats in '85 and thirty-nine at-bats in '86. You can't walk up to the plate after sitting on the bench two, three weeks at a time and go up there and hit line drives. I don't care what kind of ability you have. It just ain't that easy. It's hard enough to play every day and hit them.

"All of that hurt. I guess if I had any resentment, it's toward the way McNamara used me back then. I don't think he gave me any kind of chance at all, and that basically hurt me with other clubs, too. They'd see I wasn't playing and wonder what was wrong with me. I had players come up to me all the time, and even managers, and ask, 'How come you ain't playing? What's your problem?' 'I ain't got no problem,' I would tell them. 'I just ain't getting a chance.' That's just the way it goes."

Playing baseball had always been fun for Stapleton. But sitting on the bench wasn't. Still, he worked his tail off every day. He did everything the ball club asked of him. He never complained. He was "a good soldier"—a team player. He warmed up pitchers in the bullpen. He put on the catching gear and worked behind the plate in simulated games, when a pitcher recovering from an injury had to regain his sharpness by throwing in game conditions under the hot afternoon sun in an empty stadium.

"It wasn't something I enjoyed," said Stapleton, "but I'd have done anything to get in the ballgame, just to get the chance to play. Because that was what was fun. It wasn't no fun sitting. It was only fun when you were out on the field."

It appeared that Stapleton's hard work and patience had paid off in 1986, when the Red Sox won the division title and Buckner came up lame for the playoffs. Buckner stayed in the lineup, but in the American League Championship Series against California, whenever the Red Sox led in the late innings, McNamara called on Stapleton to take over at first base. The same pattern followed in the World Series—until Game 6, when the Red Sox were on the brink of the title.

That night, Stapleton sat in the dugout, waiting for the call that never came. McNamara changed his game plan. Stapleton watched from the bench as disaster unfolded. It was an experience he will never forget.

"I was already loose," he recalled. "I was sitting there with my glove. I was ready to go in. I had already done everything that I had done in every other game that I went into in that situation. I had already done my sprints. Loosened my arm up."

McNamara never said anything to Stapleton. Managers don't justify their decisions to players. It didn't matter. In this case, no explanation was necessary.

"That particular game," Stapleton began, choosing his words carefully, "if the truth was known—and I don't know if anybody would admit it, but most people know it—all they were trying to do was leave Buckner out there so he could be on the field to celebrate when we won the game. But my contention always was you don't get to celebrate until you win it. Everybody could celebrate when you win—even running out from the dugout. You've got to win it first.

"Not to say we would have won it. The game would have been tied if the ball was caught. So, we still would have gone into extra innings. But at least we would have got that chance.

"Like I said, McNamara was too confident the game was going to be won. And he wanted Buckner—because he had been there all year, whether he was hurt or healthy, he had been a good soldier—he wanted him to be out on the field when everything was won. But we didn't get that opportunity."

After the game, Stapleton kept quiet. He didn't criticize his manager or second-guess his decision. He didn't complain to his teammates. He was a good soldier, too. But he knew a mistake had been made. It was no secret among the players. Boston players, New York players, writers, fans—everyone saw what had happened.

A trace of anger crept into Stapleton's voice. "I think everybody knew it. Our manager knew it. He wouldn't admit it to this day, but he damn well knows that he messed up. And he very well could have cost us the World Series that year.

"I don't blame any of the players. I don't blame Buckner. Anybody can make an error. But he wasn't . . . "

Stapleton stopped to search for the right words. He didn't want his thoughts misinterpreted. "If you watch him going over for the ball, you can tell he's in a half limp just getting over trying to get to the ball. He just shouldn't have been out there is the way I feel."

Bill Buckner. A tremendous ballplayer, a courageous ballplayer—but the wrong man in the wrong place that night.

"Buckner was a good ballplayer," said Stapleton, "but Buckner was hurt. He was in a lot of pain at that time, and he couldn't move properly, I didn't think. He was a gung-ho type guy. He would have played if he had to walk out there with a crutch. He was that type of guy. He would go out there on crutches if you let him. And basically, that's what I feel like happened. I think McNamara let him."

When Stapleton returned to his home in Alabama after that World Series was over, he received dozens of letters from fans telling him he should have been in the ball game. People stopped him in stores or restaurants and said the same thing. Fans from Boston, friends from Alabama, they all told Stapleton the same thing. He should have been in the game. They couldn't believe the manager didn't put him in.

But did it really matter who was playing first base? Buckner later claimed that even if he had fielded the ball, he wouldn't have gotten Mookie Wilson out at first. The pitcher, Bob Stanley, was slow breaking to the bag, said Buckner, and Wilson was a fast runner. Buckner's conscience was clear. The play couldn't have been made anyway. He could have kept Ray Knight from scoring all the way from second base, but the Mets still would have been at bat. They still might have won the game on the next batter.

This scenario was presented to Stapleton. What did he think about Buckner's explanation? Was the importance of the error exaggerated if Wilson was going to beat both Buckner and Stanley to the base?

"I never noticed that," said Stapleton. "I don't have any idea, because I guess I felt like if I'd been there and fielded the ball, I'd have probably charged the ball to start with. I'd have taken an angle and come in and probably just touched the bag myself and not had to worry about that.

"I didn't play like most first basemen. If anybody would look back on my stats, they would see I didn't have a lot of assists. Me, I see more first basemen that are content to catch the ball and always let the pitcher cover and just flip it to them. It looks like to me they like to lead the league in assists—those little flips to the first-base bag. I always felt like that was just one more chance for somebody to drop the ball.

"So, I was always the type of player if there was any possible way I could come and get the ball, I came and got it and touched the bag myself. I didn't let the pitcher take it and make the play."

A lot of it had to do with Stapleton's background as an infielder, he explained. He had played second base, third base and even shortstop. He was used to charging the ball.

"You're more aggressive and you feel more confident being a middle infielder, playing second, playing short. You're more confident with your fielding ability, that you can charge those balls and get them on the move. I think that had a lot to do with my fielding."

And what about Game 7? Did the crushing disappointment of letting victory slip away from them in that fateful tenth inning carry over to the following game for the Red Sox?

"Yes, it did. I didn't think our chances were good after that. I thought our chances were better when we jumped out ahead three-to-nothing in the next game. I said, 'Well, maybe.' But Bruce Hurst had to pitch on not enough days' rest. He pitched brilliantly in all the other games he pitched, but he just finally ran out of gas, basically.

"There again, some of the moves that were made after Hurst left, I would disagree with. But that's the manager's choice, bringing in who he wants to bring in in those situations. So, he has to live with that as far as I'm concerned. It may not bother him. Maybe he felt like he'd done everything he could in his power. Maybe he thinks he'd done everything that was right. I don't know. I'm sure he would second-guess himself some. I believe he would."

Again, it was back to McNamara. Stapleton was asked how he rated as a manager. He pulled no punches with his reply.

"I thought he was probably the worst manager I ever played for, from the minor leagues on up."

If that was the case, how did McNamara ever become manager of a major-league baseball team?

"I don't know," answered Stapleton. "I don't know. He did well at Cincinnati. I don't know if it was because of his players or what. But as far as his managing ability, I never thought anything of it.

"All he was doing was riding the horses, is what I thought. He put the guys out there and put the same names in the lineup every day, and there wasn't no managing to it. Take a pitcher out if he was starting and was in trouble and put a reliever in. I think anybody could have done what he did that year as far as managing goes. No, I didn't think anything of his managing ability."

Another question about McNamara was asked. Stapleton let it pass. He preferred not to discuss the manager anymore.

"I don't have many good things to say about John McNamara. I hate to just sit here and beat on somebody, because it's just all in the past. I've got my own opinions of him as a person and as a manager, and some of those things I probably best keep to myself. Things that I saw and watched, not only in the game but away from the game. Some in the dugout and some not in the dugout.

"Like I said, I've got my own opinions about that, but I'm not going to sit here and talk about those things. I don't think that's proper."

The conversation turned back to the ground ball missed by Buckner. Had Stapleton watched it on replays?

"I've seen it on TV plenty of times," he said. "It seems like they've shown it every year in the World Series."

Does it bring back any special memories when he sees it?

"Aw, there ain't much memories to it now. All that's pretty much in the past. That's probably more—I don't know whether it's sad or what it is. Like I said, it seems like to me more or less now I'm saying, 'Well, they're still beating that dead horse.' I probably say that every year now. That's all history."

He yawned again. "I think my name was even mentioned—I don't know if it was this year, it was the year before. It surprised me. Tim McCarver [the network broadcaster and former major-league catcher] was talking about it during the Series, about how they didn't bring me into the ball game and left Buckner out there to celebrate. He even mentioned that on TV in the Series.

"And I said, 'Well, there's somebody else that saw that besides the players that we were playing with.' I mean, McCarver was a player also, so he realized what went on and what happened. He saw what happened that year, and he even brought that up that particular night on TV."

It was one of the most talked-about plays in World Series history, and by not being on the field Dave Stapleton was a part of it. It must be nice to be linked, at least indirectly, to such a memorable event, it was suggested to him.

"Well, it's no thrill, really. I don't really feel linked to it, because I wasn't a part of it. Indirectly, I guess you could say, but that play doesn't mean anything more to me. That's in the past.

"I have my feelings about what happened then, but beyond that, it doesn't bother me one way or the other now. You can't turn back those hands of time."

Dave Stapleton has three children. Two boys, one girl.

"Yeah, they play ball, too," he said. "I'm coaching them in the summertime, too. Besides building, that takes up the rest of my time during the summer."

Once, when the younger boy was four or five years old, Stapleton showed him how to shoot a layup in basketball. But the boy couldn't do it, because he kept jumping off the wrong foot. Stapleton watched him as he went outside to work on shooting the layup. He did it over and over, maybe thirty, forty times, before he finally figured out how to jump off the correct foot.

"He was not going to quit until he did it right," recalled Stapleton. "He's not satisfied to do anything unless he does it good. He's a real determined little youngster."

It was the same way with Stapleton when he was growing up. He laughed when he thought about it.

"Yeah, that's what my folks say, anyway. I was very determined, and I wanted to play ball all the time. And that's the way he is. He can go out there and stay all day at practice. When you get done with two hours of practice, he says, 'Throw me some more!' 'Hit me some more!' 'Let me hit some more!' It's nonstop. My tongue's dragging, I'm ready to go home, and he's still going."

He still enjoyed playing ball himself, he said. Baseball, softball, it didn't matter, just as long as it involved a bat, a ball and a diamond.

"I still get a kick every time I go out and play ball. Softball, whatever it is. I love it. I love it with a passion. And I don't like it when I can't do it to the best of my ability. And right now, even playing softball, I don't have time to work out like I'd like to, to be the best I can be at that particular sport.

"Softball, you might think you could walk out and hit it. Well, you get some pretty good competition with that now. Especially down South. They take it serious. And like I said, I don't have the time to go out and hit. My legs aren't in the kind of condition they need to be. You go out there and you play all day long, and after about two or three games, my legs are like spaghetti."

He laughed at the thought of it. "I could still go out and play two or three games, even now. So I'm not in terrible shape. I'm just not in the kind of condition I was ten years ago."

Stapleton could still get in that kind of shape, though. Just give him enough time, and he could do it. He proved that in the summer of 1992, when he was one of the former players invited to join a team put together by former Red Sox pitcher Bill "Spaceman" Lee.

The team was called the New England Gray Sox, and it boasted an impressive lineup. Stapleton ticked off the names on the roster. There was George Foster, a feared slugger for Cincinnati's "Big Red Machine" of the 1970s who once hit fifty-two home runs in a single season. Some of the other players included Ozzie Virgil, Mike Stenhouse, Mario Guerrero, Bill Almon and even Bill Buckner. Among the pitchers were Lee, Bob Stanley, Pedro Borbon, Ferguson Jenkins, Roger Moret and Tug McGraw.

"We had some pretty good name players," said Stapleton. "We had a pretty decent ball club. It'd surprise you. We had a five-game tour of New England. I went back and worked out for about a month and got in semifair shape, went back and played some ball.

"We had a good time. We rode the buses and stuff together and toured New England. It was fun. We played against what was supposed to be collegiate all-star type players, and a few former minor-league players and one former major leaguer, Len Whitehouse, a pitcher who played with the Twins.

"Those young players—those college players—they got a little bit of a taste of what it was like. They got their lunch most of the time." He laughed. "The only game that was close was the last one. I think we beat them one run. Most of the games were eight- and ten-run games. We pretty much dominated the kids.

"We still had good pitching. Those guys, they might not throw as hard as they used to, but they still know what to do with the ball. They still could place it, and they still could make it do tricks."

Stapleton played second and third base for the Gray Sox. He discovered he could still field the ball and throw with his old crispness. Most of all, he found out he could still hit.

"I hit the ball good. I hit the heck out of the ball. I was the only one in the group that hit a home run, as a matter of fact. I felt pretty good about that. Foster, he can still hit it a ton. And Ozzie Virgil can still hit the ball well.

"But I hit the ball well, and played well in the infield. George Foster, he said to me, 'Man, you ought to try out for one of these expansion clubs.' I took that as a compliment. I felt good when he said that."

Stapleton thought about going back and trying to play some more. But that would have meant putting the business aside and spending three or four months getting himself back into playing shape. He knew he didn't have the time or financial resources to do that. He couldn't afford to take that gamble.

"If I had been one of those players who had made enough money that I was financially stable enough that I didn't have to.work and could take off a few months, I believe I would have done it. I would have already done it.

"I would have already got in shape, and I would have been in spring training. I would have called everyone I could have called, and went back and showed somebody I could still play. But I didn't have that luxury—I don't have that luxury."

So, Dave Stapleton builds houses instead. But he can still play ball. He could always play the game. All he ever needed was a chance.

15

CALVIN SCHIRALDI: NO RELIEF

I wouldn't wish anything that happened to me on my worst enemy.

—CALVIN SCHIRALDI

The tough part of being the bullpen "closer," Calvin Schiraldi once said, is dealing with failure. The closer is the man who comes in to close out the game and save a victory for the starting pitcher. One mistake often means failure. And failure means you not only let down yourself, but also your team and your fellow pitcher.

"I don't like being in the position where I can throw one pitch and lose the game," Schiraldi said. "I take things personally a little more than I should, especially in relief. If I give up a starter's win, it can linger a little too long."

In 1986, when he was thrust into this role, Schiraldi did not fail often. He was the untested rookie who came up at midseason and took over as the ace of the Boston bullpen. Lou Gorman, the Red Sox general manager, called him "a savior." Schiraldi saved nine games and won four in the last two months of the season. He pitched fifty-one innings and allowed just eight earned runs, which figured out to an impressive 1.41 earned-run average. When injury and ineffectiveness hampered the Boston relief corps late in the season, Schiraldi WAS the Red Sox bullpen. The Red Sox could not have won the division title without him.

But when Schiraldi failed, he did so spectacularly.

It happened in Game 4 of the American League playoffs, which ended with Schiraldi crying in the dugout, a towel draped over his head.

It happened in Game 6 of the World Series, when Schiraldi needed only one more out to finish off the Mets but instead surrendered three consecutive singles.

And it happened again in Game 7 of the World Series, when Schiraldi gave up a home run, two singles and a wild pitch to the first three batters he faced to blow open a tie game.

A relief pitcher has to put a bad game behind him, they say. He can't dwell on a bad pitch, or a costly hit. But those were no ordinary games. They were not routine pitches or typical hits. It was not easy to forget about them, especially when so many others wanted to remember them.

There was no way to pinpoint when Calvin Schiraldi's right arm finally gave out on him. It was not a simple matter of throwing one pitch too many, or tearing a ligament one day or waking up one morning with a sore arm. He did not "blow out" the arm. It simply wore out, gradually, from years of throwing fastballs and change-ups and curves.

"Let's see," Schiraldi said with a sigh when asked what happened to his pitching arm. "I was just—there was never any one pitch. It was like an accumulation over the years. And then my arm just kind of went dead."

It was after the 1991 season, Schiraldi's last in professional baseball. He had pitched briefly that year for the Texas Rangers, his fifth team in an eight-year career of disappointments, mediocrity and unrealized dreams.

He developed arm problems, so he spent the following season in rehabilitation in order to pitch again. He rested the arm, he underwent physical therapy and he worked out.

And then, in February 1993, Schiraldi tried to make his comeback.

"I thought I had it back," he said, "and I went to throw for a scout. And there was nothing there. I had been throwing pretty well up until that point.

"But the day I threw for him, there was just nothing there. And the next day, I couldn't lift my arm up. So, I said to heck with it."

He was only thirty years old, but it was not that difficult to leave the game. Baseball had ceased being fun, Schiraldi admitted. In the major leagues, it was no longer a game, it was a job.

"The people who say that it's not are full of it," he said.

But when did baseball become that way? When did it lose its appeal, its youthfulness? Did it cease being a game once he stopped playing for the joy of it and became a professional, selling his services for a paycheck?

No, said Schiraldi, it was just something that happened. It was a gradual process, like hurting his arm. Somewhere along the way, the fun went out of the game.

"There's not a specific time. But it's a job. I mean, you're talking you're at home for two weeks, you go on the road for two weeks. You're never settled. You get through with a game at midnight, you fly four hours and get in at four o'clock and then get up and go to the ballpark. I mean, you're away from your family all the time."

That does not mean he was ready to quit. "You have to earn a living," pointed out Schiraldi, who made as much as $600,000 in one season. "And there's not too many jobs that pay that well."

But once he got hurt, he had no choice. His sore arm made the decision for him.

So, in the summer of 1993, with another baseball season under way, Calvin Schiraldi went back to school at the University of Texas, where ten years earlier he had pitched the baseball team to the national collegiate championship. He resumed work on his degree, in kinesiology, the study of muscular movements.

"I want to coach," he explained.

How much longer did he have before graduating, he was asked.

"I really don't know," said Schiraldi. "I'm going to go until they tell me to stop."

Calvin Schiraldi arrived on the campus of the University of Texas in the fall of 1980, and became a member of one of the most talented college baseball teams in history.

Roger Clemens, the future Cy Young winner and Most Valuable Player in Boston, was one of Schiraldi's teammates. Billy Bates, who played for Cincinnati's 1990 World Champions, was on that team. So was Mike Brumley, who later played for the Red Sox, Cubs, Padres and Astros. Bruce Ruffin went on to pitch for the Phillies and Rockies. Pitcher Mike Capel, Jeff Hearron and Jose Tolentino also made it to the major leagues. Kirk Killingsworth made it as far as Triple-A.

Schiraldi, who led Austin's Westlake High School to the state championship in baseball, had turned down a chance to sign with the Chicago White Sox in order to play for the Longhorns. He knew he wasn't ready for the pros.

He had gotten sick his senior year in high school, and had lost the zip on his fastball.

"I had strep throat," he said. "I couldn't eat for two weeks. My mouth swoll up. I lost like thirty-five pounds, and I lost my fastball. I didn't get it back until my junior year in college."

Even without his fastball, Schiraldi was good enough to win thirteen games as a sophomore at Texas. And then, his junior year, his fastball reappeared just as suddenly as it had left him.

"It was whenever the fall [season] was over with," he said. "I came back for the spring, and there it was."

That season, Schiraldi was the best pitcher in college baseball. He won fourteen games and lost only two, allowing fewer than two runs a game. On a pitching staff that featured three other future major leaguers, Schiraldi was the ace. He won four more games in the College World Series to lead Texas to the 1983 national championship and earn for himself the Most Valuable Player award of the CWS. Baseball America named him the "College Pitcher of the Year."

The New York Mets selected Schiraldi as the 27th overall pick in the player draft that year.

Schiraldi began his pro career at Double-A Jackson, Mississippi, in the Texas League, but he struggled to get hitters out and was demoted to Class A. His second year, he returned to Jackson and won the Texas League's Most Valuable Player award by compiling a dazzling 14–3 won-lost record and 2.88 ERA. That performance earned him a promotion to Triple A the second half, and finally to the big leagues at the tail end of the season.

"I remember my first game was the second game of a doubleheader after Dwight [Gooden] had pitched the first game," said Schiraldi. "It was pretty nerve-racking."

The Mets thought enough of Schiraldi to give him an early-season recall in 1985, but he fractured the small toe on his right foot when he was hit by a line drive. He was placed on the disabled list, and after his return pitched ineffectively and was sent back to the minors.

"I think I came back too soon and got all screwed up. I started to throw differently and just never really got comfortable again. Then I got sent down, and I still didn't pitch that great when I went back to Tidewater."

That winter, the Mets traded Schiraldi, along with three other prospects, to the Red Sox for left-hander Bob Ojeda. Schiraldi continued to struggle with Boston in the spring of 1986. He developed bicep tendinitis in his throwing arm, threw poorly and was sent back to the minor leagues again.

It was then that the Red Sox decided to make a reliever out of Schiraldi. He resisted the move at first, but then quickly made the adjustment. At Pawtucket, Boston's top farm club, he began pitching out of the bullpen and enjoying success. Soon, he was being used as the closer, and he thrived in the role. Halfway through the year, he was leading the International League in saves, with twelve.

"I'd never done it before," said Schiraldi. "I'd always wondered what it was like. So, it was kind of exciting for that fact. And then I started to throw well, which helped.

"It's great when you're doing well, which I was doing at Pawtucket. And we were winning. Pawtucket hadn't won in a while, and we were winning. That made it feel pretty good."

The season was at its midway point when Boston, desperate for bullpen help, summoned Schiraldi to replace reliever Steve Crawford, who had been placed on the fifteen-day disabled list. Schiraldi thought he would be with the team for just two weeks, until Crawford returned. It turned out to be a much longer stay than he anticipated.

Schiraldi joined the Red Sox without fanfare on a West Coast road trip, and was employed as a middle or long reliever.

"Steamer [Stanley] was the closer," he said. "Steamer and Joe Sambito. That kind of helped my situation, just going in there like that, because I was pitching three innings at a time and doing fairly well.

"I mean, I wasn't pitching in any games that we won. We'd get behind four or five runs and then I'd pitch. That helped my confidence, because I was throwing well."

Schiraldi threw so well that he gave up just one run in fourteen and two-thirds innings over five games. And then, one night in Boston, the Red Sox had a two-run lead in the ninth inning when the Royals put two runners on base with nobody out. Manager John McNamara called on Schiraldi, and he got Boston out of the jam by throwing third strikes past the first two batters he faced and retiring the next one on a groundout. It was his first save.

A week later, Schiraldi posted two more saves in two nights at Detroit. From that point on, he was the Red Sox closer.

The key to Schiraldi's success was simple: He threw his ninety-plus-mile-an-hour fastball past the hitters. The fastball was moving better than it had in years, and he was throwing it for strikes.

"It got life to it," he said. "I don't know how to explain it. It just went where I wanted it. It just felt nice and easy to throw, like I wasn't really making an effort at it."

Schiraldi seemed to thrive in his new role. In one stretch, he got five saves and one win in six appearances. He got his ninth and final save on September 21, nailing down former Texas teammate Roger Clemens' twenty-fourth victory of the season. A week later, the Red Sox clinched the East Division title.

Schiraldi, like Clemens, was riding high. He was a hero in Boston, one of the bright young stars on a title winner. But for all his success, Schiraldi seemed to have one flaw as a reliever: He continued to brood over his failures.

Asked now how he liked the pressure of the stopper's role, he said, "I liked it when I did well. But when I did bad, I took more things to heart than just blowing games off. I mean, if you lose, I took it to heart. Or, if I blew a save for a starter, I took it to heart. That's probably what hurt me the most."

Bill Buckner missed the ground ball in the World Series. Bob Stanley threw the wild pitch. But did anyone endure as many agonizing near misses or as much heartbreak that postseason as Calvin Schiraldi?

It started in the American League Championship Series, which Schiraldi says was even more tense than the World Series.

"To me, the league playoffs are more important than the World Series. If you lose the championship series, basically nobody remembers you. The World Series, at least you're there. And there's a lot of people who haven't been there. I don't really know how to explain it, but to me the championship series is really the big series."

It was in Game 4 of the American League playoffs that Schiraldi was first thrown onto the hot seat. The Red Sox trailed two games to one and needed a victory to even the series. Schiraldi, taking over for Clemens, struck out one batter and was on the verge of getting out of a bases-loaded, two-out jam in the ninth inning when he threw two fastballs past Brian Downing. One more strike, one more fastball, and the game would be over. But Schiraldi didn't throw the fastball. Instead, he threw a curveball, and it hit Downing on the leg, forcing in the tying run. The Angels went on to win the game in extra innings.

"I just made a stupid pitch," Schiraldi recalled.

By not throwing the fastball?

"Yeah."

Did the catcher call for the breaking ball?

"No, I shook him off. I mean, I don't know what I was thinking. It was stupidity."

Maybe it was a good idea to try to cross him up, it was suggested. Wasn't Downing looking for the fastball?

"Yeah, but you don't want to get beat with your second pitch—your second, third or fourth pitch. If you're going to get beat, get beat with your best one."

That was the game that ended with Schiraldi in tears. It was the low point of his season.

"It was pretty brutal," he said. "Fortunately for me, my wife was there. That made things a little easier. But, if things hadn't turned out the way they did, I don't know what would have happened."

Relievers don't often get a second chance. But Schiraldi got one that weekend. The next day, the Red Sox staged their dramatic ninth-inning rally to prevent the Angels from closing out the series.

"I didn't get to see much of it, because I was warming up," he said. "That was probably some of the best times in the bullpen that I can remember. The fans were screaming at us, they were all in the bullpen, the police were in the bullpen, and then we take the lead and they all have to get up and clear out. That was pretty fun. We were screaming back at the fans."

That game also went into extra innings, and when the Red Sox took the lead in the eleventh, Schiraldi was called on again to nail down the victory. The fans mockingly cheered him when he entered the game, but Schiraldi, throwing only fastballs, struck out the first two batters and, fittingly, retired Downing on a pop-up to end it.

"It tended to make up for the night before," he said.

Three days later, the Red Sox beat the Angels in Game 7 to win the pennant. Schiraldi closed out the game in style by striking out five batters in the final two innings.

The World Series was next, and it was like a giant carnival.

"It's more of a spectacle," said Schiraldi. "You go out, and you can't get anything done because you're talking to people the whole time. You're talking to reporters, and they're everywhere. You kind of lose sight of the game.

"I mean, there's no room on the field before a game or before practices. It's just hard to get things done. It's hard to concentrate on baseball."

And then came the big moment. Game 6, bottom of the tenth inning, the Red Sox leading by two runs, Schiraldi on the mound. He got the first two batters out, and Boston was just one out from the championship. He thought he had the game under control.

"Yeah, I did, because we had a two-run lead. And I don't really know what happened."

The next batter was Gary Carter. Schiraldi, still throwing fastballs, fell behind in the count, two balls and one strike.

"So, I tried to groove one to him," Schiraldi recalled, "because I knew if he hit it out of the ballpark we still had a one-run lead. And he got a base hit to left, I think off a two-and-oh pitch or something."

That brought up Kevin Mitchell, who fouled off Schiraldi's first pitch for a strike. "Then I kind of hung a slider a little bit and he got a base hit to center."

It wasn't the fastball that Mitchell hit, but Schiraldi had no qualms about his pitch selection on that occasion. He and Mitchell had been teammates and friends in the minor leagues, and they often talked about what they would do if they ever faced each other in a game.

"I used to talk to Kevin all the time," said Schiraldi. "I really liked Mitch. When we were at Tidewater, I told him I'd throw him sliders every time, until he proved to me he could hit it. That's what guys were getting him out on at Triple A.

"Yeah, he couldn't hit that pitch. You could tell him it was coming back then and he couldn't hit it."

And what happened this time?

"I guess he figured out I was going to throw it and he waited on it."

Did Mitchell get lucky, or had he learned to hit the pitch?

"He definitely learned to hit it," said Schiraldi, "because he's knocking the crap out of it now."

Schiraldi still had one more chance to finish off the Mets, when he faced Ray Knight. He came close, getting ahead of him oh-and-two. Schiraldi was one strike away from glory. And then . . .

"I made an oh-two pitch to Ray which I thought was a great pitch. He just fought it off and blooped it over the second baseman's head."

Three straight hits, all of them singles, none of them particularly hard hit. Schiraldi threw sixteen pitches that inning, and twelve of them were in the strike zone. He made good pitches. He had lost neither his control nor his poise. But he couldn't get the third out. That would be the stigma he would carry with him from that World Series.

Two days later, Schiraldi was back on the mound, with the score tied in the seventh inning of the decisive seventh game. Again, Knight was the batter. This time, he hit a fastball over the left-field fence for a tie-breaking home run. A downcast Schiraldi gave up two more hits and threw a wild pitch before retiring a batter. Then he was out of the game, and the Mets were on their way to a three-run victory and the championship. The World Series was lost in that terrible inning, but Schiraldi said he does not recall those events. Like a shell-shocked combat veteran, he has blocked them from his memory.

"I don't remember much about Game 7," he said. "I remember the home run, and that's about all I remember, when Ray hit the home run."

Were you throwing well? he was asked.

"I don't remember," he answered.

And what happened on the home run?

"I just remember I grooved the fastball."

What about that off-season? Was it difficult recovering from all that had happened to him in the World Series?

Schiraldi thought for a long time before answering.

Calvin Schiraldi, right, who became Boston's star relief pitcher in 1986, celebrates with fellow Texans Spike Owen (left) and Roger Clemens after the Red Sox clinched the American League East title: "I liked it when I did well. But when I did bad . . . I took it to heart. That's probably what hurt me the most." *Photo by Dick Johnson.*

"Not really," he said finally. "I don't think it was really that difficult. I think the thing that helped it out was that parade they had for us in Boston. That was pretty nice. That was pretty special."

Calvin Schiraldi was never the same pitcher after that World Series. He pitched five more years in the big leagues, but he managed only twelve more saves, he lost thirty-three games while winning just twenty-six and he allowed more than four earned runs per game.

He had always been a winner before, dating back to his boyhood days. As a teenager, he led his Babe Ruth League team to the Texas state championship. His high school team won the state title. His college team at Texas won the national championship. His first year in pro ball, he helped the Mets' Lynchburg farm team win the Carolina League title. A year later, he pitched Jackson to the Texas League championship. In 1985, he was a member of Tidewater's International League pennant winner. He played a key role in Boston's winning the 1986 American League pennant.

But after that 1986 World Series, things changed. Schiraldi didn't win. His teams didn't win.

The decline in his fortunes began immediately, when his ERA ballooned to 4.41 and his saves total dropped to six in 1987. The memory of his World Series misfortunes was fresh on people's minds that season, and he was the target of much abuse.

But "not in Boston," he pointed out. "Leastwise, not early. I got more shit going on the road than at home.

"Just people flapping their yaps," he added.

As for the writers, well, they weren't Schiraldi's favorite people in the first place.

"To me, I don't like reporters," he said. "Because reporters think they're experts. They've never played the game and they don't know anything about how people feel, and they try to dig, they dig too deep to try and get stories that cause controversy. They're more interested in basically causing trouble than writing about the game.

"They're looking at who's squabbling with who and everything like that. That just irritates the heck out of me. I've never been a big fan of reporters.

"That's probably the reason why they never talked to me, because my answers were basically yes-and-no answers."

Schiraldi's once-promising career with the Red Sox was short-lived. At the end of the 1987 season, he was traded, along with pitcher Al Nipper, to the Chicago Cubs for relief star Lee Smith.

Schiraldi had mixed emotions about the deal.

"I didn't want to leave, because I really liked the area that I was at, and the guys on the team. But I didn't particularly care for relieving anymore. I wanted to start, and that's what the Cubs were going to let me do."

His return to a starting role didn't produce the results either Schiraldi or the Cubs had anticipated. He posted only a 9–13 won-lost record in 1988, and the Cubs struggled through a losing season.

The next year, Schiraldi returned to the bullpen and posted another losing record, but, nonetheless, it was an enjoyable summer. Chicago was "the greatest town in the world," he said, and the Cubs were experiencing the thrill of a pennant race. Then, in a cruel twist, Schiraldi was traded to San Diego on August 31, just as the Cubs were closing in on the division title.

Calvin Schiraldi was the losing pitcher in the last two games of the 1986 World Series: "I don't remember much about Game 7. I remember the home run, that's about all . . . when Ray [Knight] hit the home run." *Photo courtesy Boston Red Sox.*

"That really sucked, I thought," he said. "You know it happens, but I wanted to see what Chicago would do with a championship team. And I knew I wouldn't be around to see them clinch and all that."

The next season was spent in San Diego, pitching out of the bullpen, with mediocre results. The Padres released him the following spring, and he was picked up by first the Houston Astros and then his other home-state team, the Texas Rangers. Except for a brief stint with the Rangers, Schiraldi pitched in the minor leagues for those two organizations in 1991. Then came the dead arm and the end of his career the next year.

"I would liked to have gotten the chance to start on a regular basis," Schiraldi said, looking back over his career. "Like with the Cubs, I started in '88, then in '89 they moved me back to the bullpen. Then I got traded to San Diego and I have three starts and throw really well, and the next year they got me back in the bullpen. That's the only thing about the game that I don't understand.

"That's the only regret I have. I never really got a chance to start continuously. I had one year and that was it."

But what if things had turned out differently in that World Series? What if Schiraldi had gotten that last out to win Game 6? What if he had stemmed the tide in Game 7 and the Red Sox had rallied to win? Would his career have turned out differently?

"I don't even think about it," said Schiraldi. "I never thought about that."

What did happen is more important to him than what might have happened.

"I look at it as a growing experience for myself personally," he said of the World Series. "For my life. I mean, I got through that, and I figured if I can get through that I can get through just about anything."

So, he was tested and he passed the test?

"Yeah. I grew up."

Does he think of the World Series very often?

"No."

But there were some aspects of that postseason that still anger Schiraldi. He recalled when he lost Game 4 of the playoffs and the picture on the television screen was of his wife, Deborah, crying in the stands.

"They had the camera right in her face," he said. "They were pretty brutal about that. There was an article in the paper about it. When somebody's husband was pitching or at the plate or whatever, they'd kind of shove people around to get a picture of the wife.

"If something goes wrong, which happened to me, they don't have to be on TV. That just kind of pissed me off. I mean, I'm real negative toward the media. That didn't help matters."

Schiraldi used to wear his World Series ring, he said, but now it was on display in his home, along with some of his other baseball mementos.

A big man at six-feet-five with dark good looks, Schiraldi had a comfortable house in Austin, about thirty minutes from where he grew up. He and Deborah had two children, a girl and a boy. Their daughter, Samantha, was three years old. Their son, Lukas, was only two months.

"Lukas is spelled L-u-k-a-s," noted Schiraldi.

And is the boy going to be a baseball player someday, his dad was asked. Schiraldi shook his head.

"I'm going to try to get him into golf," he answered.

16

BOB STANLEY: THE JIMMY FUND

It's human nature to say, "This can't happen to us." But from all those visits, I should have known that cancer can happen to anyone.

—Bob Stanley

Birthdays can be traumatic events in the Bob Stanley household.

October 25, 1986, was the day Bob's wife, Joan, turned thirty-three years of age. It also was the day the Red Sox lost Game 6 of the 1986 World Series.

That was the game the Red Sox led by two runs with two outs in the bottom of the tenth inning. That was the game Bob Stanley was called on to save after three consecutive hits chased Boston reliever Calvin Schiraldi from the mound while cutting the Red Sox lead to one run and putting the tying and winning runs on base.

That was the night that Joan Stanley sat in the stands at Shea Stadium and watched her husband hurrying out of the bullpen and onto the playing field with a world championship on the line. So many bad things had happened to Bob Stanley in his career, and so much criticism and anger had been directed at him. So many times, he had been in the wrong place at the wrong time. "God, please, not tonight," Joan prayed as she looked toward the heavens.

Bob also offered up some prayers that evening, standing on the mound trying to realize a boyhood dream. "Please, God, help me to be a World Series hero."

That night, the Stanleys' prayers went unanswered. Bob threw a wild pitch—some say a passed ball—that allowed the tying run to score. Mookie Wilson hit a ground ball through Bill Buckner's legs to drive home the winning run for the Mets. The Red Sox lost that game, and two nights later, the World Series.

Bob Stanley was no hero in New England that fall. Worse, he, along with the ill-fated Buckner and the dazed Schiraldi, received the brunt of the criticism for Boston's stunning loss.

Not long after that World Series ended, the Stanley's three young children were playing outside the family's house in Wenham, Massachusetts, when a yellow car stopped in front of the driveway. A man got out of the car, walked over and picked up the bicycle belonging to five-year-old Kyle Stanley.

"Take that!" the man shouted as he raised the bicycle over his head and threw it to the ground. He then got back in his car and drove off.

Bob Stanley pitched three more seasons for the Red Sox, but never with the success he had enjoyed early in his career. In 1987, he worked as a starter and lost fifteen games, won only four and gave up more than five runs per game. He returned to the bullpen the next two years and was a solid if not spectacular reliever, saving nine games, winning eleven and losing six.

It was after the 1989 season that Stanley called it quits following thirteen years in the big leagues, all of them with the Red Sox. For all the ups and downs, and all the harsh words directed at him, Stanley had compiled an impressive record in a Boston uniform. He won 115 games and saved 132. He pitched 1,707 $\frac{2}{3}$ innings in 637 games, working primarily as a reliever. Perhaps someday, when they look back on his accomplishments, the Boston fans will appreciate Stanley for his years of tireless effort, for his durability and, most of all, for his devotion to the club.

That winter, the Stanleys had more important things on their minds than Bob's legacy with the Red Sox. They had three children—two girls and one boy: Kristin, Kyle and Kerry. "Three Ks," Bob liked to say. "That's the only way I'm going to strike out the side." It was a pitcher's joke. "K" is the scoring symbol for a strikeout. Three Ks in a row was a pitcher's dream—and, for Bob, a father's pride.

Kyle was the middle child. He was a typically healthy and active eight-year-old who liked to play sports. In baseball, he was a pitcher, just like his dad. He was a youngster who rarely complained, but starting in November of 1989, he began waking up in the middle of the night, crying from intense headaches.

Bob began to notice other problems Kyle was experiencing in the following weeks. He checked his son and saw that his right eye appeared to be drooping.

Kyle was examined by doctors, and they believed he was suffering from migraine headaches. That seemed to make sense, because Bob had a similar problem when he was Kyle's age. But as a precaution, further tests were recommended.

On January 19, 1990, there was another birthday in the Stanley family: Kyle was turning nine. But this would be no time for celebration.

It was on that day the Stanleys were told by doctors at Children's Hospital in Boston that Kyle had cancer. There was a tumor the size of a man's fist in the sinus area behind his right eye. That was the cause of the headaches.

That year, the Stanleys prayed for something more important than a World Series game. They prayed for the recovery of their son.

The doctors said Kyle faced a year of chemotherapy and radiation. The treatments began immediately, and Kyle spent six of the next nine weeks in the hospital. Either Bob or Joan, or both of them, sat at his bedside around the clock.

The irony was that during his days as a baseball player Bob Stanley had walked these same hospital corridors and spent many hours in these same rooms visiting other children with cancer. Those goodwill visits were made on behalf of the Jimmy Fund, the prime fund-raising arm of the Dana-Farber Cancer Institute and its Children's Cancer Research Foundation. Bob would meet with young cancer patients, sign autographs, participate in fund-raisers, give freely of his time on behalf of the Jimmy Fund—whatever was asked of him. Joan also chipped in, once putting out a cookbook that raised $18,000 in donations.

"We really worked hard with the Jimmy Fund," Bob said later. "But you never know what can happen. You never know. Cancer can hit any-body, no matter how nice you are or who you know."

One day, Bob arrived at the hospital to visit Kyle, and he was recog-nized by a man in the parking lot. The man walked over and reached out to shake Stanley's hand.

"Thanks for all you've done for the Jimmy Fund, Bob. My son has cancer, and he's here at the clinic."

"Mine, too," said Bob. "I'm with you now, friend."

The Jimmy Fund, like so much else in Boston, has deep ties to base-ball and the Red Sox. The fund dates back to 1948, when the city had two baseball teams, the Red Sox in the American League and the Braves in the National League.

The fund was named after a twelve-year-old cancer patient under the treatment of Dr. Sidney Farber. It had been just one year earlier, in 1947, that Dr. Farber and a small group of scientists had achieved the first remission in childhood leukemia through the use of chemo-therapy. Dr. Farber became known as "the father of modern chemotherapy," and in conjunction with the Variety Club of New England, he established the Children's Cancer Research Foundation in Boston.

On behalf of the foundation, Dr. Farber made an appeal for dona-tions in order to buy a television set that would allow his young patient, identified only as Jimmy, to watch his favorite team, the Braves. The request was aired from Jimmy's bedside on the national radio show *Truth or Consequences*. Among those who participated were several mem-bers of the Braves, including star pitcher Warren Spahn.

The response was so great that enough money was raised not only to buy Jimmy his television set, but also to begin construction on a center devoted to the research and treatment of cancer. Jimmy was further rewarded when the Braves, who adopted the Jimmy Fund as their offi-cial charity, went on to win the National League pennant that year.

Five years later, in 1953, the Braves pulled up stakes and moved to Milwaukee. When they did, the Red Sox, under the ownership of Tom Yawkey, allied themselves with the Jimmy Fund.

That was the beginning of a long relationship between the Red Sox and the Jimmy Fund. The charity was made a part of every Red Sox radio broadcast, young patients received visits from generations of

Boston players and countless funds were raised through baseball clinics and celebrity golf tournaments. Red Sox greats from Ted Williams to Carl Yastrzemski to Jim Rice became a part of the Jimmy Fund. The close ties between the team and the charity were underscored when a Jimmy Fund billboard was placed atop the right-field grandstand at Fenway Park. On the billboard were the retired numbers of four Red Sox heroes—Bobby Doerr's number 1, Joe Cronin's number 4, Yastrzemski's number 8 and Williams's number 9.

Bob Stanley became initiated into the Jimmy Fund shortly after joining the Red Sox in 1977. Over the next thirteen seasons, he made many trips to the hospital to visit youngsters who were ill or in need of encouragement.

For Stanley, it was a way of putting baseball in perspective.

"A young kid would come up and be depressed or something about his hitting or fielding," said Stanley. "I would take him with me to the Jimmy Fund Clinic in Boston and say, 'Hey, you want to feel sorry for yourself because you're hitting .220? Look at these kids.' That kind of put a different outlook on a .220 batting average."

It was Stanley's willingness to help that prompted a telephone call one day from Mike Andrews, a former Red Sox second baseman who was in charge of fund-raising for the Jimmy Fund. There was a young boy at the hospital who was in need of help, explained Andrews. The boy had lost an eye to cancer and had been forced to wear an eye patch. Despondent over his condition, he had stopped talking, even to his parents, and when anyone came in the room he would hide in the restroom so he wouldn't be seen.

"Could you come visit the boy?" asked Andrews.

"Sure," said Stanley.

That was the way it always was when the Jimmy Fund called Stanley—never "Let me check my schedule"; just a simple "How soon do you need me there?"

Before leaving the house, Stanley grabbed a bat and ball and also one of his Red Sox jerseys, with his trademark number 46, to take to the boy. It was perhaps Stanley's favorite jersey, the one he wore in 1983, when he set the Boston record for saves with thirty-three.

Stanley went into the hospital room, and this time the boy didn't hide. The two of them talked for a long time, and Stanley signed the jersey before handing it over to his new friend.

Andrews, who was at the hospital that day, will never forget the impact the visit made on the sick and scared young boy.

"From then until his death, that boy never stopped talking," Andrews told *Paths of Progress* magazine. "His doctor couldn't believe it. 'No drug in the world could have done what that visit did,' he said. That jersey, with the number 46 on the back, became the most important thing in the boy's life."

The boy died a few months later. When he was buried, he was wearing Bob Stanley's Red Sox jersey with the number 46 on the back.

Later, when his own son was diagnosed with cancer, Stanley would spend a lot of time thinking about that little boy who passed away.

"He had the same kind of tumor, in the same area, as Kyle," said Stanley. "It kind of brought back a bad flashback, you know? They ended up burying the boy with my jersey."

Nineteen eighty-three was a good year for Boston's number 46. Bob Stanley saved thirty-three ball games for the Red Sox that year. He pitched in a career-best sixty-four games. He recorded a sparkling 2.85 earned-run average. He threw two shutout innings in the All-Star Game. When the season was over, he was voted Boston's Most Valuable Player for the second year in a row.

It was the pinnacle of Stanley's career. "The Steamer" was at his unflappable best back then.

As good as he was that year, Stanley will tell you today that it was not his best season.

"Not really. The year before was, when I broke the American League record for innings pitched for a relief pitcher. A hundred and sixty-eight and two-thirds innings. It's kind of a nice record to have. I pitched a lot of innings.

"I was in almost every game. I pitched ten innings in relief once. And had two days' rest and pitched five more. You don't see that anymore."

That was what gave Stanley the most pride. He was a workhorse pitcher. He pitched a lot of innings and he pitched a lot of games. Long relief, short relief, middle relief—it didn't matter to Stanley. He just wanted the ball.

"What I really wanted to do," he said, "was to be part of every game. And whatever it had to take, I did. I didn't like sitting around."

The key to his durability and his versatility as a pitcher was in his strong right arm. Other relievers limited their innings worked to keep their arms fresh. Starting pitchers took time between assignments to rest their arms. Other pitching arms broke down from overuse. Not Stanley's.

"I had a rubber arm," he said. "The good Lord gifted me with a rubber arm. And probably the secret of it all was I didn't throw too many breaking balls. Mostly, it was sinkers and change-ups. When you do that, you don't take as much out of the arm."

And his ability to throw a pitch that broke down so sharply, resulting in so many groundouts? How did that come about?

"God-given. God giveth and taketh away."

It hadn't taken long for Stanley to gain attention when he joined the Red Sox as a twenty-two-year-old rookie in 1977. He alternated between starting and relieving that year; then, the next season, pitching almost exclusively in relief, he won fifteen games and lost only two.

"They called me 'the Vulture,'" he said, "because I used to come in and swoop up a win. Every time I'd come in for Luis Tiant, I'd give up like a little bloop base hit that would tie it up, and then we would score like three or four runs and I would get the win. So, Luis always told [manager Don] Zimmer, 'If I see Bill Campbell [another Red Sox reliever] or Bob Stanley warming up, you're going to need more than yourself to take me out of the game.'"

That season ended with the famous playoff game between the Red Sox and Yankees for the American League East title. That game is best remembered for the home run that light-hitting shortstop Bucky Dent hit off Mike Torrez to give the Yankees the lead. But what is often overlooked is that the final run in that 5–4 New York victory came on a home run by Reggie Jackson off Stanley.

"I pitched nine innings on Saturday," said Stanley. "I started against Toronto, and I only had one day's rest before the playoff. But with the adrenaline flowing, I came into the game. I didn't have my good stuff at all. Everything was up.

"I think I gave up a hit to [catcher Thurman] Munson. Then Jackson hit a home run."

Stanley continued as Boston's most durable, and effective, pitcher over the next five seasons, culminating in his 1983 performance. He added a palmball, an off-speed pitch with an unpredictable break, to go with his sinkerball and change-up, and that made him even tougher to hit.

He also became one of the most popular and respected members of the ball club. And then Stanley signed the big contract, a lucrative six-year deal that would pay him more than a million dollars a season. That was when things started to go wrong.

He had his first losing record the next year. He began to suffer an assortment of minor injuries. The fans began booing him. After 1983, Stanley never had another outstanding season.

"It just seemed like everything that could go wrong went wrong," he remembered. "It seems like every time you sign for big money, things happen.

"I fell down the stairs and cut my hand open. I had no feeling in two fingers my last two years. Whatever could go wrong went wrong.

"And then the fans get on you. But I look at it this way—I didn't make a lot of money when I had the good records. So I said, 'To hell with it, I deserve what I get from years past.'"

Still, it wasn't easy to block out all the boos and catcalls at Fenway. Not when the fans were on him every game, all season long.

"I tried as hard as I could every single day, same as I did when I didn't make a lot of money," said Stanley. "But, yeah, it wasn't too much fun going to the ballpark. My family couldn't go because of all the harassment. So they never went anymore. My kids were young, and they didn't like to hear their father get booed. And I didn't like them to hear it, either.

"It was great on the road. When you did bad, they cheered."

When asked why baseball fans are so quick to turn on players, Stanley offered a surprisingly conciliatory response.

"Well, I can understand what they're doing. I'm out there making a million dollars a year. They're out working five days a week, eight to four, and they have to come pay money to watch this, and I'm out there stinking up the yard.

"I understand the way they come at you. They have short memories. They don't remember what you did for them before. There's an old saying, 'You're only as good as your last performance.'"

Adding to Stanley's problem with the fans was his perceived weight problem. He was listed as six-feet-four and 220 pounds, but his bulky build and stocky legs often gave him the appearance of being overweight. That was no problem when he was winning, but it became the focus of attention when he struggled through his difficult years.

"Every year I came in in good shape," he said. "I was always in good shape. A lot of times it didn't look like I was in shape, but I could run with anybody. It's just, as the guys used to say, I have a bad body. I never looked good in the uniform, and people said that I was overweight.

"In 1983, I weighed two hundred forty pounds and saved thirty-three games, and no one said a word. But when you have a bad year, they say you're too fat or overweight."

Then came the Fenway Park opener in 1986, when Stanley was booed off the mound and after the game found his son crying in the locker room. An angry Stanley vowed, "They can boo me now, but when I'm on the mound when we win the World Series, everyone will want to kiss my butt!"

Looking back, Stanley said: "I was just upset because that day they booed me, and my son came in—I think he was five years old—he came in and was crying. When I saw him crying, you get a little ticked off. That's when I said, 'Yeah, wait 'til I'm on the mound in the World Series.'"

Stanley paused before adding, "And I was there. I didn't lie."

Bob Stanley pitched in five games in the 1986 World Series, throwing six and one-third shutout innings. He got a save in Boston's victory in Game 2 with three shutout innings of relief. But all anyone remembers is the one batter he faced in that fateful tenth inning of Game 6.

He was in the bullpen that Saturday night when the Mets tied the score in the bottom of the eighth inning. The game went into extra innings, and Stanley was told to get ready, that he would pitch the tenth for the Red Sox.

"I was getting pumped up and getting ready to go," he remembered, "and then all of a sudden Henderson hits the home run. Then the phone rings, and they say, 'Schiraldi is going back out there.' So, I sat back down. I went from a high to a low. And then we scored another run."

The two-run Boston lead seemed safe when New York came to bat. But Stanley got up to loosen up again, just in case.

"I was always throwing, but when there were two outs, I stopped throwing and watched the game. And all of a sudden, boom, boom, boom, and then I started throwing again. I was ready."

The call finally came. And in an instant, Stanley was in the spotlight, facing Mookie Wilson with two outs, the tying run on third base and the winning run on first.

What followed was a prolonged showdown between pitcher and hitter.

"You have to give him a lot of credit," said Stanley. "He had a great at-bat. I made some great pitches on the outside corner, and he kept fouling them off and fouling them off. I never threw him a palmball because I faced him when we played the Mets in an exhibition game in Fenway and he roped one up the middle. I said, 'Oh, he must like that pitch.' So, I never threw him one.

"I just kept throwing him sinkers. I was always taught, way back when, if you're going to lose, you might as well lose with your best pitch."

Every pitch Stanley threw was to the outside part of the plate, except for the one pitch that became the source of so much controversy. That one exception was the pitch that came too far inside and got past catcher Rich Gedman, allowing Kevin Mitchell to score the tying run. It was ruled a wild pitch, but even that became a point of debate, as many insisted it was a passed ball, that Gedman should have handled it.

Stanley still can't say what happened on that unforgettable pitch.

"You know, to be honest with you, I'm not even sure. Things were going so crazy, and he kept fouling off pitches. Everyone says that it was a passed ball and not a wild pitch. It doesn't really matter—it was the same outcome. The Red Sox lost, and that's the way it goes. You can blame me, you can blame Geddy—in my mind, it doesn't really matter."

Stanley's wife, Joan, was among those who did blame Gedman. And she did so in an article published in the March 1987 issue of *Sport* magazine. That comment created some tension between him and Gedman, Stanley admitted, but he said the two of them worked out their differences.

"We just talked it over," he said. "There was a little hard feeling. That's just people talking from their heart. We got it ironed out."

As for the possibility that the wild pitch was in fact a spitball, which

Stanley had been rumored to throw throughout his career, he was adamant in his response.

"Nope. Nope."

Two more foul balls followed that pitch. Then came the ground ball that Wilson tapped down the first-base line, toward the ailing Buckner. That play also became the subject of much debate. Buckner missed the ball, allowing the winning run to score from second. Afterward he claimed Wilson would have made it to first base safely, anyway. He was too far from the bag to make the play and believed he, Stanley, would also have gotten there too late.

"No way," Stanley said firmly. "One thing about it: I might be big, but I can beat the best over there to first base.

"There's a picture of the ball going past Buckner, and I've already turned, going back toward our dugout. I stopped as soon as I saw the ball go through his legs."

A wild pitch, or maybe a passed ball. An error at first base. Two ill-fated pitches, and Bob Stanley and Bill Buckner, two veteran ballplayers with distinguished records, would take the brunt of the criticism for Boston's World Series loss.

Stanley was philosophical about it. "That's baseball," he shrugged.

"I look at it this way. They always go with the last thing that happens. Look at the box score. How many men did we leave on base? I think it was fourteen. We could have won that game with another hit here or there. It would have been broken wide open. It wouldn't really have gone down to that.

"But that's the way it is. Like Bill Buckner. Bill Buckner is a great player, and he's going to be remembered for that one play. I don't think that's fair."

There is one other thing people tend to forget, added Stanley.

"There's a lot of great players, a lot of Hall of Famers, who never even made it to the World Series. I wear my American League championship ring proud. No matter what happened, whatever the outcome was in the World Series, I still wear my ring proud, because I was there.

"A lot of people mention it to me. 'Well, 1986 . . . ,' they say. I tell them, 'Yeah, I was there. Where were YOU?'"

Bob Stanley pitched six and one-third scoreless innings and saved one game in the World Series, but is best remembered for his failure to preserve the Red Sox lead in Game 6: "A lot of people mention it to me. 'Well, 1986 . . . 'they say. I tell them, 'Yeah, I was there. Where were YOU?'"
Photo courtesy Boston Red Sox.

Bob Stanley announced his retirement from baseball in October 1989. After he did, a lot of friends and acquaintances encouraged him to stay in the game. "You can still pitch," they told him.

Stanley entertained the notion of returning to the field. Maybe one more season, one more chance to prove his worth as a pitcher, one more opportunity to help the Red Sox win that elusive World Series title.

Then his son became ill, and Stanley knew where he had to be.

"Even if I was still pitching, I still would have quit," he said. "Kyle needed me. He needed my wife. We all needed each other if we were going to do what had to be done."

The first step was chemotherapy and radiation treatment. There were long stays at the hospital. These were followed by long drives back and forth from the Stanleys' home in Wenham to Children's Hospital and the Jimmy Fund Clinic.

Kyle never complained, said Stanley. Instead, he was the source of strength the family needed.

"He kind of got us through it," said Stanley. "That, and a little faith. A LOT of faith. He was just a strong kid through it all.

"Not once did he ever complain. Not once did he ever say anything about the pain."

The needles caused the most discomfort. "Kyle didn't like needles," said his dad. "But who does?"

Sometimes, the doctors and nurses had trouble finding a vein to make the necessary insertion in Kyle's arm. Often, his mother put a heating pad on him for ten minutes prior to the needle's being used. She worked with him on deep-breathing techniques that she had relied on while giving birth.

Kyle's hair began to fall out because of the treatments. Stanley, whose own hair was thinning on top, remembers the day he pulled out the last patch from his son's head. Bob cried, but Kyle told him, "Don't worry, Dad. Mine is going to grow back. Yours isn't."

There were other side effects from the treatment. Kyle lost weight, dropping from sixty-five pounds to forty-six. He had always been a good ballplayer, but while playing Little League baseball that summer, he sometimes would start running and lose his balance and fall down.

"The chemotherapy treatment had taken all his coordination away from him," explained Stanley. "This particularly frustrated him."

That was the year Bob got Kyle into golf.

"They said he would lose his sight in his right eye because of the radiation," said Stanley. "He had the most radiation you could have around his right eye. They said he'd probably lose his eye.

"So, I wanted to get him in a sport that he could play with one eye. You know, it would be tough hitting a baseball with one eye. But it ended up that he didn't lose his eyesight."

After the year of treatments, the tumor had been reduced to 25 percent of its original size. The cancer appeared to be gone, but the doctors could not be certain until they removed the tumor. It was then that Kyle underwent his first surgery. It was an experimental procedure, "like a giant biopsy," explained Dr. Dan West of Children's Hospital. Doctors went under the top lip to the side of the nose, took out a small piece of the cheekbone, cut out the mass, replaced the

Bob Stanley(in white sports coat), accompanied by his wife, Joan and children Kyle, Kristin, and Kerry, is honored on Bob Stanley Night at Fenway Park in 1990: "When my son got cancer, [God] answered my prayer that way . . . Instead of being a hero, I got my son's health." *Photo by Steve Gilbert.*

bone and put the lip and nose back together. The operation took more than eight hours.

"It was a new operation," said Stanley. "They never did it before. They took his face off, and you wouldn't even know that they did it. They went in and cleaned out his sinus and took the rest of the tumor out. Everybody has, what, three sinus cavities? Now, Kyle has one."

The surgery was performed in January 1991. One year after the tumor had been detected, the Stanleys learned that the tissue was dead, that Kyle was free of cancer.

There would be another scare when doctors found a spot on Kyle's lung, and a second operation was performed to take that out.

"But it ended up to be a cluster of white blood cells," said Stanley. "It was nothing."

More than three years after the ordeal began, Kyle Stanley was healthy. He once again was the star player of his baseball team. He played golf with his dad.

He still went in for periodic checkups, but the long-term outlook was good.

"There's always a chance it will come back," said Stanley. "But right now, they say if you're clean for five years, usually you kick it. But he has to go back the rest of his life for checkups.

"Right now, he's on a six-month checkup. And the next one, if he's fine, he only goes once a year."

During his years playing for the Red Sox, Bob Stanley had an often rocky relationship with the fans of New England. They cheered him early in his career, then turned on him during the tough times. But when his son was in need of help, the response from the public was unanimous.

"The people around here were great," said Stanley. "They supported Kyle. You wouldn't believe the donations the Jimmy Fund got in Kyle's name. When you raise so much money, like through a golf tournament, you get your name on a plaque. You get your name on a stick plaque in the clinic.

"My son's name, because people donated so much money, is on one of those plaques."

He remembered the time he was on the mound in the sixth game of the World Series, and the thing he wanted most in life was to be the man who won the championship for the Red Sox. That had been his lifelong dream: to be a World Series hero.

He had learned so much since then.

"I don't care what people think about what happened to me in baseball," said Stanley. "Here I was on the mound praying to God that I'd be the hero. But God had something else in store for me.

"When my son got cancer, He answered my prayers that way. Instead of being a hero, I got my son's health. You can throw the 1986 World Series right out the window."

17

DAVE HENDERSON:

IT'S JUST A GAME

Reggie Jackson was the original "Mr. October." But Dave Henderson at least deserves the title "Mr. October II." Like Jackson, Henderson was at this best in baseball's postseason. His record bears that out.

In the five years from 1986 to 1990, Henderson played in four League Championship Series and four World Series. His postseason batting average of .298 is forty points higher than his regular-season average. He has a .324 batting average in World Series play. He hit two home runs in the 1986 World Series, one of them in the tenth inning of Game 6 to give the Red Sox the lead and put them on the verge of winning their first title in sixty-eight years. He hit two homers and a double and drove in four runs in a single game in the 1989 World Series.

Henderson hit three other home runs in League Championship Series play, and 197 in his career in the major leagues.

But no matter how many home runs he hits, whether they come in the seventh game of a World Series or the ninth inning of the All-Star Game or the final day of the regular season, Henderson will be remembered most for the one he struck on Sunday, October 12, 1986.

That was one of the most dramatic homers ever hit in baseball history. That was the home run that turned certain defeat into unexpected victory for the Boston Red Sox in the American League

Championship Series. That was the homer that kept the California Angels out of the World Series. That was the homer that turned around the AL playoffs. That was the home run that will never be forgotten by Red Sox or Angels fans.

And that was the homer that had a sad footnote to it. Angels reliever Donnie Moore served up the pitch that Henderson hit out of the ballpark with two strikes and two outs in the ninth inning. Three years later, Moore killed himself. Some people say that home run broke his spirit. Some people say that home run killed Moore.

And because he was the one who hit that memorable homer, Dave Henderson will always be linked to Donnie Moore.

The day Moore shot himself, Henderson was playing for the Oakland Athletics. He received word of Moore's death while he was in the clubhouse, where talk is usually confined to games that are played, not lives that are lost.

"We were playing a game," remembered Henderson, "and Don Baylor came over and told me, 'Donnie Moore just took his life.' And I said, 'Wow.' You know, what the hell is going on? You start to wonder what's going on, because me, I don't take baseball that seriously. You know, life or death.

"And then it starts to hit me when fifteen or twenty cameras showed up in the clubhouse during the game. That's when I knew it was not just another-guy-taking-his-life kind of thing. So I said, 'You know, he took his life and I heard the news. What else do you want me to say?'"

Baseball is a game played in bursts of activity. There are brief periods of action punctuated by frequent lulls. Fielders spend a lot of time standing around, waiting between pitches, between batters.

Dave Henderson liked to take advantage of these interludes to interact with the fans from his outfield position. He waved to them. He carried on running conversations. He entertained them.

"Yeah, you know, during pitching changes and things like that," he explained. "Pitching changes and managers talking to pitchers and things like that. I don't think you should have a stone face. There's only four or five things you need to go over in your mind to be ready when that hitter steps to the plate, to go one way or the other in situations and things like that. So, you go over that and you're ready to play.

"I'm a happy person, and I give all the credit to my mom for that. She's the same way. And smiling is just the way we go about things. But just because I smile, that doesn't mean I'm not serious. I'm serious a lot. I do a lot of thinking on the baseball field.

"But I take time out for a breather when it's appropriate. There's a lot of free time in baseball. And I take advantage of all the free time."

In Boston, Henderson played games with the fans in the center-field bleachers, conducting what he called a "game show," in which he was the host and they were the audience.

After he slumped with the Red Sox the year after his postseason heroics and was traded to San Francisco, about sixty of those Fenway Park ticket-holders signed a ball and presented it to him as a souvenir. Henderson keeps that ball at his home alongside his other prized possessions, his World Series baseballs.

His stay in San Francisco was brief. He helped the Giants win the National League West Division title in 1987 but was ineligible for the playoffs. He became a free agent after the season and signed with Oakland the next year.

There, Henderson became an integral part of the powerful Athletics team that won three consecutive league championships and one World Series title. He also endeared himself to the Oakland fans with his impromptu dances in the outfield, his exaggerated pantomimes and his waves to familiar faces in the crowd.

Henderson even had his own rooting sections in the Oakland Coliseum. "Hendu's Bad Boy Club" was located in the bleachers in right-center field; "Henduland" was situated in left-center. In the eighth inning of home games, his fans would throw Henderson a kiss, and each game he devised new ways to throw it back.

"I just don't take this baseball stuff that seriously." That was Henderson's motto.

Dave Henderson pointed a baseball bat at his visitor and called out to some nearby teammates, "This dude wants to write a book!"

It was the first week of spring training, and members of the Athletics had broken into four-man groups at Scottsdale Community College in Scottsdale, Arizona. Henderson's group had just arrived at its new workout "station," one of the four diamonds in the complex.

Dave Henderson is congratulated by third-base coach Rene Lachemann as Henderson circles the bases following his home run, which staved off defeat for the Red Sox in Game 5 of the AL Championship Series. In the background, a stunned Doug DeCinces sinks to his knees: "All of a sudden, everything there was just gone. You have everything, and to have it yanked away like that was difficult." *AP/Wide World Photo.*

It had been seven years since the Red Sox and Angels had met in that memorable series, but by chance two of Henderson's workout companions had also played in those games. Rich Gedman had been the catcher for Boston, and Gary Pettis had played center field for California. Now, all three men wore the green-and-gold uniform of the Athletics. The fourth member of their practice group was Kevin Seitzer, a former Royal and Brewer who was playing for his third team in three years. That was baseball. It seemed that no one stayed in one spot too long.

"With Pettis and me," continued Henderson.

"Both of you?" someone asked.

"Yeah. And we sayin', 'Wait a minute, man. Ain't you supposed to wait and write a book when you die or something?'"

Tony LaRussa, the Oakland manager, walked up in time to catch the end of the exchange.

"No, I'd wait to write a book when you DID something," said LaRussa.

His remark was greeted by loud laughs and hoots. Henderson's familiar high-pitched giggle could be heard above the others. "That's true." Henderson, still laughing, turned his attention to Gedman, who was looking through his equipment bag. "Hey, there's Geddy! He got hit in the head! He got hit in the ear-hole! He's the one who got hit in the head!"

There were more laughs, and some of the others joined in the teasing.

"He got hit in the ear-hole!" Henderson yelled again. "We got a lot of guys around here who was in that thing. Naw, we ain't writin' no book. We ain't writin' no books, man."

"What's it about?" asked LaRussa.

The 1986 playoffs, he was told.

"What about the '89 playoffs?" interrupted Henderson. Oakland had won that Series with a four-game sweep of Bay Area rival San Francisco. "We raked in that one."

The other players laughed on cue.

Pettis, a small, wiry player, spoke up for the first time. "He talkin' to losers."

"We raked in that one," repeated Henderson.

"You giving them any money for interviewing them?" asked LaRussa.

He was told there was no money involved, and the manager shook his head in mock seriousness. "Well, I guarantee you, you won't get much from them then."

The players laughed and slapped hands with one another.

"I see Geddy get hit in the ear-hole," Henderson yelled excitedly, "and I said, 'Move over, Geddy, let me in!'"

"Yeah," cut in Pettis, "you gonna try to run up there and say something about . . . "

His words were drowned out by more shouts and barbs.

When he could be heard again, Pettis was still needling Henderson. "Yeah, he almost stepped on Gedman trying to get in the box."

LaRussa grabbed a bat and moved toward the field. "We're going to practice some hit-and-runs here in a minute." He pointed the bat at two rookies standing nearby. "And these guys here, they're going to do it because they just want to make the club."

LaRussa then removed a wallet from the back pocket of his baseball pants and pulled out a five-dollar bill. "But Hendu, I gotta give him a five or he won't do anything."

"Hah, hah!" Henderson laughed good-naturedly. He looked back at Gedman. "If Geddy can hit-and-run as good as me, I will . . . No, he got the tape on!"

"Oh, you ain't gonna say it!" Pettis yelled.

"No, I ain't gonna challenge Gator. I ain't gonna challenge Gator this year." Henderson looked at one of the rookies, an outfielder named Scott Lydy. "But I don't know about . . . " He paused. "Lycie? Leezie? Lye-dee? Lettuce?"

"Here we go!" another player called out. "Here we go!"

Finally, LaRussa waved his hands to signal an end to the joking and bantering. "We got to go to work here!" he shouted.

"What are we waitin' on?" yelled Henderson.

"Geddy got hit in the ear-hole." Actually, the pitch hit him in the forearm, not the batting helmet, but it no longer mattered. Gedman got a free pass to first base, and the Red Sox were still alive in the 1986 playoffs.

But just barely. They trailed in the series, three games to one. There were two outs in the ninth inning. They were down by a run. Donnie Moore, California's best relief pitcher, entered the game, replacing Gary Lucas, who had thrown the pitch that struck Gedman.

The next batter was Dave Henderson. It was a fluke that he was even in the game, much less that he happened to come to bat in such a tense situation. Tony Armas, the regular center fielder, had hurt his ankle earlier in the afternoon and had to come out of the lineup. Henderson was pressed into duty, even though he also had a bad leg that day.

"My knee," he recalled. "It happened the night before against Doug Corbett, a sinkerball pitcher. I fouled a ball off my knee, and it was pretty swollen.

"I had very little chance of getting into that game anyway, even as a defensive replacement, because I couldn't run. But, you know, Armas went into the fence and hurt his leg, so I hobbled on out there."

Dave Henderson believes his home run that gave the Red Sox the lead in the tenth inning of Game 6 of the World Series was bigger than the one he hit off Donnie Moore: "The one in Game 5 in the playoffs was lucky, just a big guy swinging hard. But through the Series, the Mets . . . were pitching me like a real hitter." *Photo courtesy Boston Red Sox.*

He laughed quietly. "Yeah, it was hurt pretty good. I had surgery after the Series. But they kept it warm with hot packs and heat and things like that. I got by."

Henderson stood by the on-deck circle watching as Moore took his warm-up pitches. Hendu was well acquainted with the California reliever.

"He had been in the league two years. I hit a home run off of him before. But it was a tying home run and they ended up winning the game, so nobody cares about those kinds of things.

"He had a good fastball, and he had a great forkball. That was a time when the forkball was just coming on the scene and not a lot of guys had seen it, and he was getting everybody out."

Under the circumstances, everybody expected Henderson to be nervous. But he wasn't. To the contrary, he figured he had nothing to worry about. The way he saw it, Donnie Moore was the one who had pressure on him.

It was this same approach that Henderson would use to such great advantage in later years in solidifying his reputation as a "big-game player," one who rose to the occasion in the games that counted the most.

"The biggest key is realizing that there is no pressure at all," he explained, "because guys aren't supposed to hit the [Dennis] Eckersleys and the [Tom] Henkes and guys like that. So, when we strike out, we're supposed to. There's really not much pressure when you're supposed to make an out.

"And I guess I'm the only one who realizes that. So, I have a distinct advantage in that everybody else on the field is pressured, and I'm not. I'm the same old guy, and that makes me better."

Henderson smiled, revealing the trademark gap between his two front teeth. He added that his theory was especially true in situations such as the one he found himself in that Sunday afternoon, when there were two outs, his team was down a run and he could have made the last out of the season.

"That was even easier, because I was a backup player and defensive replacement for Tony Armas. I wasn't supposed to even get to hit that game. Guys that sit the bench and are defensive replacements, they're not expected to get hits. Their job is to go catch the ball in the seventh, eighth and ninth innings. So, that was even easier."

It didn't look easy when Henderson swung at and missed Moore's first pitch. It didn't look that easy when he barely fouled off a pitch with two strikes on him, and the California reserves were standing on the top step of the dugout, ready to run onto the field in celebration. It didn't seem that simple with more than sixty thousand fans screaming and cheering their heroes.

But Dave Henderson kept his poise.

"He threw me everything," he continued. "He was mixing them up. I fouled off about three pitches, and then he went with the forkball."

The forkball—the split-finger—was Moore's best pitch, but this one didn't fool Henderson. As soon as he hit the ball, he knew what had happened. He leaped in the air, did a little victory dance, and watched the ball sail over the fence for the biggest home run of the season.

"I was thinking we won. It was late in the game. When you hit a home run off relievers like that, usually it's a game-winner and you go home. Your stopper comes in and stops them, and everybody's happy."

It would take Boston two more innings to win that game, and again Henderson delivered the key blow, a sacrifice fly. But that ninth-inning home run was the hit that turned the season around and propelled the Red Sox to the World Series.

Henderson downplayed the significance of his deed. "When a manager sends a big guy for the last out of the inning, he's got a chance to hit a home run. You know, a slim chance, because I had a total of probably fifteen ABs [at-bats] in the last month. So, there was no way I was ready to hit off anybody. It was just a big guy swinging hard and happening to hit a ball out of the ballpark."

He is no longer asked that many questions about the home run, said Henderson. "Not as much as you would think, because I've hit so many others in the World Series and playoffs."

It isn't even the home run he remembers the most, he added. That honor goes to the homer he hit in the sixth game of the World Series, giving Boston the lead in the tenth inning against New York.

"People ask me about the biggest home run I ever hit, and that was it. Because, like I say, the one in Game 5 in the playoffs was lucky, just a big guy swinging hard. But through the Series, the Mets knew I was swinging the bat well and they were pitching me to my weaknesses and pitching me like a real hitter.

"And right before that at-bat in the tenth inning, Mel Stottlemyre— I started out with him in A ball and he knows everything about me, up and down—he went out and talked to the pitcher. And I still hit a home run. So, that's probably the biggest home run I've ever hit."

Perhaps if Boston had held the lead and won that game, and the World Series, that would be the home run people associate with Dave Henderson. But the Red Sox lost that game. They won Game 5 of the playoffs.

The home run against the Angels might have been a lucky blow, but it was more shocking in its suddenness and its effect. It brought the Red Sox back from elimination. It got them to the World Series.

And later, a despondent Donnie Moore killed himself. Some people trace his death to that home run. That home-run pitch killed Donnie Moore, it has been said.

Henderson said he barely knew the man, outside of his prowess on the baseball field.

"I've said hello to him and hi and things like that on the field, but that's about it."

But Henderson knew Moore well enough to dismiss the speculation that his home run was responsible for the pitcher's death.

"They can think what they want," he said. "The players know. We have a different world. We know a lot more things about what goes on on this field than you guys see. You guys see what we do, but you don't see what really goes on. So, it doesn't really matter."

And what if Moore had struck him out in that playoff game, Henderson was asked. Would he still have gone on to achieve all he had and enjoyed the same career?

"Oh, yeah," he answered. "I was supposed to strike out, right? So, I don't think it would have mattered." He smiled again. "Maybe I would have done a lot better if I'd struck out."

Henderson wasn't going to worry about it. Base hit or strikeout, win or lose, he was going to keep smiling. There was one thing about baseball he always remembered.

"This is a game," he said. "It's not life and death. This should be fun."

EPILOGUE

Late in the 1993 baseball season, Don Baylor found himself back in the visitors' dugout at Shea Stadium. The occasion was not a postseason game, just a late-season meeting between two teams going nowhere in the standings. And Baylor no longer was an active player. Instead, he was managing a big-league team, the expansion Colorado Rockies, who were in their inaugural season.

It was a Saturday and a heavy rain was falling on Shea Stadium, delaying that day's ballgame between the Rockies and the Mets. Baylor was sitting in one corner of the dugout, next to the runway back to the locker room. He looked out at the rain-soaked field and remembered another gloomy Saturday seven years earlier.

"Same spot, right here," Baylor said, indicating to Denver writer Bob Kravitz where he had been the night of Game 6 of the 1986 World Series, when Bill Buckner let the ground ball roll past him and the Red Sox missed their opportunity to win the elusive championship. "Me and Tom Seaver, right in this corner. We sat right here for outs one and two, and then we moved up toward that step, ready to run out onto the field and celebrate.

"I like sitting here. I like to torture myself."

Time had not erased the images of that postseason. Two years after their loss to the Mets in the World Series, the Red Sox won another American League East Division title and returned to the playoffs. This time, they were swept in four games by the Oakland A's. In 1990, the Red Sox won their third division title in five years. Again, they lost to the A's in four games in the American League Championships Series.

Hearts were still being broken in New England. Boston fans were still waiting. The years were still adding up since the Red Sox's last World Series title in 1918.

For their part, the Mets never established the dynasty many predicted following their 1986 World Series triumph. They finished second in the National League East Division three of the next four years. Their one first-place finish in that stretch came in 1988, when they posted a 100–60 won-lost record, the second-best mark in club history. But the Mets lost the National League Championship Series to the Los Angeles Dodgers in seven games, and L.A., not New York, celebrated a World Series victory that fall.

Following their second-place finish in 1990 and the departure of manager Davey Johnson, the Mets suffered an abrupt collapse. For the next three years, they would be a team of high-priced stars and losing records. In 1992, the Mets lost 103 games, only five fewer than their magnificent victory total of 1986.

The fall from grace was even swifter for the California Angels. One year after coming within one pitch of their first trip to the World Series, they finished last in the American League West Division. In the seven seasons following Donnie Moore's home-run pitch to Dave Henderson, the Angels managed a winning record only one time, in 1989.

The Houston Astros also failed to follow up on their 1986 success. They had a losing record the year after their epic playoff series against the Mets, and by 1991 had fallen to last in the National League West Division, losing ninety-seven games.

From those depths, the Astros rebuilt with young and exciting stars such as Jeff Bagwell and Craig Biggio, and by 1994 they were poised to make another run at the club's first-ever World Series appearance. Baseball had gone to a three-division alignment that year, and the Astros found themselves battling the Cincinnati Reds for first place in the National League Central Division. Houston was one-half game out of the lead when a players' strike shut down the 1994 season on August 12.

Baseball is like that. There is no end to the number of ways it can break your heart. It can be torture.

INDEX

Page numbers in italics refer to illustrations.